D1879950

WANDERINGS & WONDERINGS

WANDERINGS & WONDERINGS

INDIA, BURMA, KASHMIR, CEYLON, SINGAPORE, JAVA, SIAM, JAPAN, MANILA, FORMOSA, KOREA, CHINA, CAMBODIA, AUSTRALIA, NEW ZEALAND, ALASKA, THE STATES

BY

JOHN JAMES AUBERTIN

GYAN

© **Author**

All rights reserved. No part of this work may be reproduced, stored, adapted, or transmitted in any form or by any means, electronic, mechanical, photocopying, micro-filming, recording or otherwise, or translated in any language, without the prior written permission of the copyright owner and the publisher. The book is sold subject to the condition that it shall not, by way of trade or otherwise, be lent, resold, hired out, or otherwise circulated without the prior publisher's written consent in any form of binding or cover other than that in which it is published.

The views and opinions expressed in this book are author(s) own and the facts reported by them have been verified to the extent possible, and the publishers are not in any way liable for the same.

ISBN : 978-81-212-1551-0(HB)

First Published, 1892

Published, 2018

Published by

Gyan Publishing House
5, Ansari Road
Daryaganj, New Delhi-110002
Phone: 011-47034999, 9811692060
www.gyanbooks.com
E-mail: books@gyanbooks.com

Printed at: G. Print Process, Delhi.

FROM A PHOTOGRAPH BY ELLIOTT & FRY SWAN ELECTRIC ENGRAVING Cº

Yours truly,
J. J. Aubertin.

CONTENTS.

LIST OF ILLUSTRATIONS.

WANDERINGS AND WONDERINGS.

I.

DEAR DR. AND MRS. ALFRED BARTON, JOHN BEATON, AND CHARLES SEYMOUR GRENFELL,

These pages belong to you.

When I once more set foot in England, arriving in Liverpool on the 15th of September, 1891, by the White Star Company's steamer *Majestic*, after an absence of about three years' travelling—thus occupying about the same time as a certain other great man in the *Endeavour*, of 370 tons—one of my first recollections was, that when I left London on the morning of the 25th of October, 1888, you all came down to the Liverpool Street station to wave me off to the East with best wishes, and that I then promised to give you, on my return, my own account of my wanderings and wonderings.

It being almost impossible, nowadays, to go where others have not been, or have failed to write about, you asked for nothing pretending to an account of daring and original adventure, and certainly nothing in the shape of mere descriptions repeated from those of others; but simply an account of my own individual doings, and my own impressions and experiences of things and places, for whatever these might be worth.

To this style of letter I shall confine myself, and, in particular, I shall not dilate on Indian Government and taxation—such as "the reimposition of the patwari cess," for example—simply because I have seen the inside of Government House at Calcutta; nor shall I offer any pseudo-profound observations upon social life, simply because I have dined under the roof of a Rajah. As Silvio Pellico said of politics, "parlo d'altro."

Therefore I shall address this volume to you in the form of one long letter to the end. Thus I shall be sure of, at all events, four readers, and if any of the public, who have been indeed far from unfavourable towards me in my former volumes, are disposed, with your permission, to join the circle, I shall be only too gratified by their attention; and, in this view, shall endeavour to secure it.

In thus responding to my promise I must confess to some little self-satisfaction in hereby proving to you that I have not only returned, but have brought with me the capacity of accounting for my time. For although you accorded me your best wishes, yet I had reason to suspect that you were all besieged by certain grave doubts about the venture. Your minds misgave you that at my age, just six weeks short of striking seventy, the undertaking of a long journey, including India and Kashmir to begin with, was a very hazardous proceeding, the more so because, as usual, I was starting quite alone. However, I had no misgivings on that score myself, and here I am.

In point of fact, for those who have anything of the art and delight of travel in them, travelling at the present day presents no real difficulties (although in truth it must always present many inconveniences) unless you are disposed to penetrate where you apparently have no right to intrude; for the finger, and indeed the hand and arm sometimes, of England and Europe are to be found almost everywhere; or, at all events, often enough to allow of a respite, after any shorter or longer visit to the less frequented districts of any given country. So long ago even as 1773 Dr. Johnson expressed his annoyance at seeing a man come up with a complimentary Latin line, when he arrived with Boswell from his tour to the Hebrides, "I am really ashamed," said he, "of the congratulations which we receive. We are addressed as if we had made a voyage to Nova Zembla, and suffered five persecutions in Japan." Now, as regards Nova Zembla, perhaps a boast might still be made—I have not tried it—but as regards a visit to Japan, that now bears scarcely more importance as a journey than did a visit to the Hebrides in Dr. Johnson's day; while the persecutions you may perchance suffer in Japan are certainly not those he had in mind.

For my own part, therefore, I have no combinations of impossibilities to indulge in; I shall be rather showing you what you could do than what I did; and though, as I travelled alone, I shall often be obliged to use the egotistically sounding pronoun I, what else can a man do who travels alone? And if he seeks to avoid any stupid charge of egotism on this account, is he to sneak into the shuffling "one" in order to avoid a fool's arrow? I once saw (or perhaps have invented) a marginal note in pencil written against a certain "one thinks," and the note ran thus: "one, and only one, I should suppose; speak for yourself and say I, and hear that you are an ass." So I will run the risk of the "ego" accusation boldly. That same putting of the letter I for the first personal pronoun, by the way, I have found to be very amusing among foreigners. In no other language that I have known anything of does the like occur. In many the personal pronoun need not be expressed at all, the inflection of the verb suffices, and thus the writer in the first person escapes the silly charge. I daresay I may now and then be discursive, but you will not object to that in a familiar letter, for I must sometimes write to satisfy my own wandering thoughts. Any given scene or circumstance may start a sudden recollection; and it may be pleasing to me, at the moment, to wander up the stream of memory, and put on shore from time to time, and occupy the mind in rumination.

I start with confidence, for you will be my real critics, and your judgments will be benevolent. But I have had no reason hitherto to dread that of others. Almost all of those who have hitherto noticed me have done me justice; and how soon, even if it be in only a paragraph, does one see whether the writer is really of that peculiar and distinguished class called critics, or a mere cavilling coxcomb with no right whatever to occupy the chair. Now, if it be true of a poet that he must be born, so also is it of a critic. I have been more than once astonished at the flippant manner in which I have been told by one or the other that (after perhaps being called to hopeless starvation at the bar) "he has taken up literature," meaning criticism. I once much offended a youthful aspirant who informed me of this his resolution, by advising him to "put it down again." "Why?" quoth he. "Because," quoth I, "you are claiming to have a master mind." And such the real critic must have —a master and a versatile mind. A real criticism of any really good book is often more entertaining reading than the book itself; and is always a most excellent introduction to it. But any notice is perhaps better than none at all, for the phrase is not unknown, "There is such a saucy notice against that book, that I must buy it and read it for myself." I need not dwell on this subject, yet I cannot but recall one notice of my last book, "A Fight with Distances," which occurred in the pages of *Vanity Fair*, where I had twice been benevolently favoured. After reviewing (?) another author's book by saying that the only good part about it was the title, he came to mine, and speaking of himself "as *we* of the outer world" (the journal is professedly caricature), said that there was "nothing worth reading in it." Yet I had twenty-one other notices of it, and Mudie apologized to one customer of my acquaintance for the state of the copy.

In this case, therefore, it was a question of either one fool or many. When Gil Blas was bargaining for a coat the *fripier* showed him one and said "he had refused sixty ducats for it," "*ou je ne suis pas honnête homme*," whereon the reflection of Gil Blas simply was, "*L'alternative était convaincante*."

My half-mistrusted start, as you know, took place on the 25th of October, 1888, when I left the Liverpool Station to join the P. and O. Company's steamer *Ganges*, Captain Alderton, then sailing for Calcutta. And herein occurred for the first time what afterwards happened to me more than once in my life of travel. My first plan was upset, to my annoyance; but the result proved advantageous. For I had intended sailing for Bombay, and had bespoken my cabin, when a certain death occurred which prevented my departure. Nor could I obtain another cabin for Bombay to suit my time. Thus I was forced to Calcutta. How often these contrarieties occur in life, teasing us at first, and ending well at last. I could not have begun my Indian tour more successfully, as it happened, than by beginning at Calcutta; and, moreover, I was thus just in time to pay my respects, on the eve of his departure, to his Excellency, the Viceroy, Lord Dufferin, whom I had last visited in St. Petersburg. Thus it is one wanders over this small great world.

We formed a rather numerous list of passengers, and our captain was very pleasant. The accommodation was good, while, as regards the table, it struck me that with a less number of dishes the Company could give better dinners. Our usual passage, skirting "The Bay," was not particularly unpleasant, and permitted that well-known very difficult piece of navigation—the walking up and down decks, and meeting others. This time I passed Lisbon without touching there, which I had always done before in sailing to and fro between South America ; nor was I anxious to do so on this occasion, for a more rolling sea than that which tossed us all down that coast I never experienced; while as to the Mediterranean, we found that capricious female in one of her frowning and contentious moods. It was now we experienced one defect in our vessel, though possibly she is not singular in this : she could not carry her ports, as the phrase goes ; and therefore they were almost always closed, an inconvenience more unpleasantly felt in lower and warmer latitudes.

Who has landed at Naples in dark wet autumnal weather? Paris looks dismal enough in such disguise. I always compare her to a chicken in the rain. But poor lovely Naples, what shall be said of her? It was four o'clock in the afternoon of the 2nd of November before we touched, and of course all was dull and dark. Yet one or two young passengers, on their first visit of course, came on board again delighted. Naples has her reputation, and therefore she must command "enjoyment," and youth with novelty sees all with joy.

While I never saw Naples look so miserable, and scarcely had believed it so capable in this respect, I never saw the Straits of Messina look more lovely. The passage through must be almost the most smiling and glittering in the world; but to make the lovely picture quite complete, I think it should be approached from the south. I could not but recall a summer night's passage across from Messina to

Naples in May, 1883. The moon was full, and the water was a blue mirror. Everyone was on deck at midnight, and till early morning, male and female. Groups were gathered here and there, and guitars were playing to accompany soft voices. "Truly," I said to myself, "this Italy is the real home of the serenade and sonnet."

But who, with a stranger's eye, could at first believe that Etna is some 10,000 feet high? His angle, like that of most volcanoes, is so obtuse, stretching completely down into the sea, that the height of his crown is overladen with the vast circle of his base. In this respect how superior, as an object of beauty, is the Peak of Teneriffe, my ascent of which I have already recorded; he is a real Peak, with his 12,200 feet of height.

At ten p.m. of the same day we had steamed out of Naples in the dark for Port Said, and the next morning broke in glory over the azure waters, fair weather continuing till we came to Port Said on the hot quiet morning of the 7th of November; thus finding the very opposite in all respects as compared with our stay at Naples; for while beauty there lay hid in wet and dark, here the ugly was all bright. Coaling being now necessary, Dr. Reid, an army surgeon, and Mr. Thompson, a district judge in Madras Presidency, easily persuaded me to go ashore with them, where we indulged ourselves with some hot games at pyramids in that rather depressing station, and where certain melancholy efforts were being made for the diversion of idle strollers or dwellers; at 4.30 we sailed again for the Canal.

Port Said, however, must now be considered an interesting spot from its standing at the entrance to the Suez Canal, and for myself there gradually came over me, as we wandered listlessly about, remembrances of my visit to Egypt in 1879-80, with my late friend, Captain Sir Richard Burton. We passed through the canal in about twenty-four hours; its length is given as of a hundred English miles, or 160 kilometres, or so many five-eighths of a mile; but we were forced to wait from time to time in sidings. A striking ghostly night picture was thus presented to us when we met and had to give way to H.M. war-ship the *Audacious*, with all her crowded crew gazing on us, and reciprocating cheers. The effects of the intense electric lighting of the channel were indeed electrifying; all figures appeared to belong to another world, while all around seemed as if wrapped in another world's snow.

On Thursday, the 8th of November, at about half-past four p.m., we breasted Suez, but did not touch, merely lying-to for provision-boats. Here again I recalled 1879, when all was new to me in that direction of the world. From Friday morning, the 9th, till Tuesday, the 13th, we were in the Red Sea, but encountered no great suffering from the heat until we came to dry, hot, rocky Aden, after passing our little Perim Island, with its well-known tale of how the English Admiral dished the French by snapping possession of it. I must confess to having shirked going ashore at Aden. I had had plenty of experience of hot skies and rocks in the course of my life, and I had no great curiosity about the tanks as tanks, so I remained on board. It was here that Captain Angove, formerly commanding one of the Company's vessels, and now a visiting inspector, whose society was a help to me while it lasted, left the boat. I remember him for two special reasons, both anecdotal. It was he who, on an outward voyage, after several real captain's refusals, was at last downright over-captained by his passengers' unremitting entreaties to allow Blondin, then a passenger, to walk along the top-mast stays, from stem to stern. Blondin was successful, but declared the feat to have terribly tried him, as one might well imagine; and on arriving in Calcutta the captain was roundly taken to task by the Press for according his consent.

The other anecdote may be well laid to heart by too-confident talkers, as showing how you may be found out when you least expect it, even though you talk Hindoostani in London. It occurred in an omnibus to his friend Captain Symons, who told it to him as an excellent joke. A man and his wife got in and sat opposite to him, when the lady ventured a remark to her husband in Hindoostani, which I shall also give in the phrase furnished to me:—

"Dekho, Sahib ko kaisa bará nák hai," which, being interpreted, saith, "Look what a large nose that gentleman has."

Now, Captain Symons *had* a large nose, and he also had a not small wit. So, to the horror of the good lady, he immediately rose in his seat, and taking off his hat, politely replied in Hindoostani also: "Han, Sahib bahut bará nák hai," which again

Digitized by Google

being interpreted, saith, "Yes, madam, I have a very large nose."

Having Captain Angove's full permission to give the anecdote, I do not lose the chance of doing so.

We left on Thursday, the 13th of November, and on that day week, the 20th, behold, like a second Vasco da Gama, I caught my first sight of India, on the west coast towards Cape Comorin.

I cannot say the land at all corresponded in importance of appearance with the grandeur of the Empire. It must have presented exactly this same low, flat aspect to the renowned Portuguese navigator as he approached it from Africa, and made for Calicut, higher up on the Malabar coast, where he landed in May, 1498. But we were not going to Calicut, and therefore continued our course towards Ceylon. On the afternoon of the 20th we caught our first view of this island, which presents a far more elevated outline than Malabar, and among the heads there stood out prominently that of Adam's Peak, to which Camoens makes allusion in his tenth Canto.

At five o'clock we landed in Colombo, and Mr. Ford, of Hammersmith, one of the passengers, drove with me about seven miles out of town to the Grand Hotel, at Mount Lavinia, on the shore. Here we dined and slept, joining the steamer by railway in the morning, as we were under orders for sailing by ten, though we did not leave before one. Nothing could have afforded us a more lovely night scene than Mount Lavinia. The moon was full, and of a Cinhalese silver; the curving sands were white, and the sea of a lovely blue. The air was more than merely warm, and at eleven o'clock there were more than one dabbler within the water's fringes. All lay below the eye, for the hotel is built on a certain rocky height. In truth, as the story goes, this fine building was never intended for an hotel, and the style of the rooms (so to call them) that Mr. Ford and I slept in favour the tale. Our two compartments were arranged by a mere low perforated wooden screen being raised across a very large and lofty room; highly inconvenient, particularly as Mr. Ford was a very long while getting to bed, which joke he will remember. The story, then, is this: that Sir C. Barnes, when Governor, considered he was entitled to a marine villa, and commenced the building, which he named after Lady Barnes, in anticipation of the home Government's acquiescence. But after the long interval then occupied in sending home and receiving a reply, that reply came in the negative, and the building was sold, and degraded to its present uses.

On the 21st, then, we steamed out of Colombo—my real visit to the island being postponed for a later date—and made for Madras; in taking which course my ignorance was enlightened by finding that we were obliged to steer round the island of Ceylon to get there, as the direct course is blocked by the chain of rocks and small islands called Adam's Bridge, running between the coast of India and Ceylon. We reached Madras on the night of the 23rd, and the morning of the 24th showed us the low, desponding-looking shore in floods of rain. It seemed impossible not to pity those passengers whose destinations doomed them to disembark; and thus bestowing on them this cheap sentiment, we took our departure for Calcutta.

At about the age of nine I had first read of the Black Hole of Calcutta in 1756; and in 1888, at seventy, I was to first see Calcutta, but no real vestige of the Black Hole was to remain. How Europe has invaded Asia! The first incident of our passage from Madras was our being boarded by a Calcutta pilot. These pilots, as I shortly came to learn, are not merely the stalwart rough-and-ready officers that one is accustomed to meet in other ports; but they are men of education and position, and are in receipt of high pay; and well may it be so, for the Hugli river, through which muddy stream you approach Calcutta, is full of danger, especially near the "jal mári," or fatal water, corrupted into the "James and Mary." The most casual view of the map will suffice to show what the Hugli must be as a matter of navigation; but with the fresh comer novelty asserts her charm, even including the disagreeable. Observe Sagar Island on the right, with its light-houses, dense jungles, tigers everywhere, and snakes. These are not the Eastern grandeurs that Westerns come out to see. The whole of the Sunderbunds show nothing but the flat and marshy. Gradually steering onwards, you come to the deserted palace of the quondam King of Oude, looking as tawdry as many other highly-pictured eastern palaces and gardens do. Afterwards comes "Garden Reach" pleasantly spotted with comfortable-looking villas, the water being crowded with a small forest of masts, showing how vulgar Western commerce invades the East to make it comfortable. "Commerce is not everything," says some one. But what *is* Everything? Rather a vulgar robe than none at all, even in hot Calcutta. At last we are at the landing-place, having seen the city for some few miles down stream.

II.

It was on Wednesday, the 11th of November, that we arrived; luckily so early as half-past ten in the morning, for the noise and confusion among the natives on the quay were indeed noisy and confusing. One feature of this eastern crowd at once struck me as compared with others; the predominance of plain white loose clothing, with dark and black faces at the top. In the rush and push, I managed to get myself arrested by some officer from the Great Eastern Hotel, whither I had telegraphed from Colombo, and was carried off at once, without further hearing, in a flimsy, clattering cab or gáré. Behold me, therefore, safe at Calcutta to begin with.

On entering Calcutta I made my first acquaintance with it as it presented itself to me. I did not begin to think of all its statistical features, any more than one asks a person on first introduction as to age, pedigree, and capacities; and in this way my first impression was, after passing through certain other streets, that the Old Court House Street was a very fine one. Here I was shortly deposited at the entrance to the Great Eastern, mounting a handsome staircase to a long, handsome corridor, with a dark office on the right, where the baboo sat who was to assign me my room; and No. 46 was assigned to me on that same floor accordingly. This room lay on the left side of a long dark passage almost facing the staircase; and as I soon afterwards discovered that there are two Calcuttas, so, I may say, that I at once here discovered that there were two Great Easterns—that is to say, two very different aspects of the hotel. The passage and its rooms were not equal to the grand broad corridor. Continuing from this latter you enter a fine dining-room, a good reading-room and billiard-rooms, and in front is a fine, open balcony, looking full on the wide street, and almost commanding the lordly pile and grounds of Government House. Underneath, running the whole length, is an almost gigantic store, where you may purchase anything you do, or don't, want, from a sugar-plum to a blunderbuss, and where I at once, under sound advice, purchased a Shikar hat, to hunt the sun. As to my bedroom, though it was commodious, all was rickety, and suggested a valuation by pence. My windows looked out into a side street, and in the early morning I was very sensibly made aware of what frightful monkey jabberings the Bengalee workman can excel in. But the curiosity was exciting with which I opened the blinds to view the scene below. There they were in groups; some unloading cargo, and others loading rubbish-carts—a hateful sight—and while something more than usually offensive was being heaped on these, a watchful set of kites, or some kindred bird, swooped down in groups, and deftly seized the morsel as they flew past without settling.

For a new-comer, with a constitutional incapacity for tough meat, the feeding could not be very attractive; but the turbaned and naked-footed waiter (no servant must wear shoes in India), whom chance fixed me to, did his best among the number. The discharge of soda-water for the whisky was like that of irregular musketry, showing that the old pale ale days of my two late cousins twice removed, Hodgson and Drane, now really removed indeed, and of whom Bass is but a feeble imitation, had given place to hygienic considerations. Bectie is a good and constant fish at table, and if you order eggs for breakfast, you will find the Indian hens lay very small ones, and that the spoons you have to eat them with are very large.

A letter of introduction from General Scott Elliot to Mr. Hyde, a barrister of the High Court, led to a very pleasant visit, when I had the advantage of going over the whole building with him, and it was in partaking of his and Mrs. Hyde's hospitality a day or two afterwards that I became acquainted with the stately style of house and garden that forms the usual residence in the grand modern Calcutta, which is called the City of Palaces. Later on I dined with Mr. Louis Paul, on an introduction from his father, Mr. Kegan Paul, and was again struck with the same aspect of dwelling. Here it was what is called a "Chummery," where three or four "chum" together; but the apparent pomp is quite the same, and runs through all. It is a curious mode of life in India: natural, but curious to a new-comer. You never seem indoors. Doors nor windows are ever shut.

You really miss them, being all left open, but it is evident you could not bear them shut. Yet, when the nights are chilly, as they are apt to be in winter, you seem to want protection.

In the afternoon I found myself, by invitation, in Mr. Walker's balcony, overlooking the entrance to Government House, to see the arrival of Lord Dufferin, from the Sialda Station, on his return from visiting Decca. As an Indian procession it was novel and interesting. The body-guard was impressive; the white-dressed crowd was large, and as they dispersed across the park, or maidan, the effect was very striking. What the European eye misses in these multitudes is women.

On the next day I received a letter from the Viceroy's Private Secretary, in answer to cne from me, appointing 12.30 on Monday for my waiting upon his Excellency. In the meantime Mr. Paul had invited me to luncheon at the cricket-ground and to the races afterwards. Accordingly, on Saturday, the 1st of December, we went in Mr. Paul's dog-cart; and even as I had been astonished at cricket in hot South Africa, so was I astonished here at the zest and activity displayed in hot Calcutta in this truly English game. At this time of year, however, the ground is not so harsh and dry as I had seen it near Cape Town. The races followed, attended also by a numerous white crowd. It was what is called their First Extra Meeting. The Viceroy and Lady Dufferin were present, and the whole proceeding was a success. But a strange and, I should imagine, unique circumstance occurred with the chief race. Many false starts took place in the distance, until at last we saw two horses come right away. In total ignorance that they were not accompanied by the field, and that the start was again a false one, they came belting along and kept in view the whole way round, to discover their mistake at the end. These two horses turned out to be the two favourites, so that a mere outsider came in first. So much for the error. Now mark a curious result. One man only, by what is called the Totalizator System, I believe, had put his money by mere accident on that outsider, and by this happy chance thus became the astonished possessor of something between *70l.* and *100l.* In such hap-hazard manner do things happen for either good or bad.

On the Sunday I dined with Mr. Paul at his "Chummery," and felt as if I were at a lord's dwelling; and on the Monday I paid my private visit to his Excellency the Viceroy, having the honour, in response to a most friendly reception, of wishing his Excellency a happy voyage to England; when he kindly accepted a copy of my "Fight with Distances," which related something of his favourite Canada, and would serve to beguile an hour or two on his passage home.

Calcutta at this time of year, though always hot at noon, is particularly fresh at morning and evening. The climate, in fact, put me very much in mind of that of Rio in the winter, though Rio has hills about it. But the noons here are more trying. While waiting to see his Excellency, and holding a pleasant conversation with one of the aides-de-camp—Captain

Curling, if I mistake not—he asked the usual question, ' How do you like Calcutta ? " to which I replied in the above sense. " I hope," said he, very naturally, "you will not go home and say we have nothing to complain of." Perhaps they who suffer India all through the year are often vexed by such ridiculous remarks of inexperience made by those who come out at a chosen season only. But I relieved his mind, and then he told me that the very horses had dropped down dead in the streets during the last summer. Indeed, Mr. Hyde had already informed me that they had been obliged to shut up the Law Courts—ay, and, I believe, at the request of the Natives themselves ! Ere these terrible days arrive the Viceroy of the hour has safely started for the North ; and, alas ! for those whose duty still binds them to the South.

On my return to the hotel I was greatly pleased at finding on my table a card with the name of " James Ramsay." In this I recognized an old friend, who had worked as a district engineer on the Sao Paulo Railway in the now far-away country of Brazil ! It was more than twenty years since we had seen one another, and I now found him Engineer-in-Chief on the Western Bengal Railway. He happened to be in Calcutta, and had caught sight of my name; and you may imagine the novel sensation of such an unexpected meeting, after so many years, in so different a country, and in one so far away from where we had lived almost together before. So things turn out, and so people turn up ! We were not long in making up our minds that we would travel to

Darjeeling together, and see the great Kanchinjunga. But when? A few days did not then much signify to either of us. But the truth was that, while waiting for my interview at Government House, I had been dazzled by two most gorgeously-apparelled Rajahs, who went in before me; and as I heard that the Viceroy was to have a farewell garden party on Friday, the 7th December, I was most anxious to see (as I thought I should) a crowd of these astounders. We therefore agreed to delay our departure till the Saturday; that, indeed, being the day on which Lord Dufferin was himself to depart, and his successor, Lord Lansdowne, to arrive. Ramsay had the *entrée*, so I called on Lord William Beresford, who warmly engaged me to appear. When the day came, however, it was a dull afternoon, and an insipid mass of mere European costumes parasolled about the lawns. Few indeed were the gorgeous colours, except in the evening sky, which suddenly glowed with glory; but I had often seen that sort of sight; the Rajahs' suns had all "set" privately before; and the two that tempted me to stay showed but the last remaining glow.

One of my calls meanwhile was upon Sir Charles H. J. Crosthwaite, the Chief Commissioner for Burma, who happened to be in Calcutta at that moment; for Lord Dufferin had most strongly recommended me to pay a visit to that country, if only a short one, and to call upon Sir Charles. His Excellency made me a most friendly suggestion that I should come down with him on the 13th, which I was quite unable to do; and thus had to postpone

Burma for Darjeeling, for my friend could not stay. Saturday, the 8th December, witnessed a remarkable scene in all the preparations for the entry of the now present Viceroy, and the departure of the late. All the neighbouring quarters of the city were alive with life and colour; and amidst this mighty movement we two took our unperceived departure also.

III.

My friend's companionship proved of much importance. At the Sealdah Station he met an engineering friend, who introduced him to Mr. Prestage, the General Manager of the remarkable Darjeeling Railway—quite one of the sights of India—and this stood us in great stead, not only on the line itself, but also at Darjeeling and on our return. We left Calcutta at 4.30 p.m. (Calcutta time) by the Eastern Bengal Railway, and in about five hours and a half we were, after 120 miles' run, on the banks of the Ganges, and were to cross to Sárá Ghat by ferry.

"Why don't they bridge the river?" I innocently inquired of Mr. Prestage, to which his answer was: "So they will if you will guarantee them a certain line; but when your structure was ready the river would be elsewhere." Thus is it with these straggling and unruly streams. Of how far greater value our tractable silver Thames! The ferry-boat was a very good one, and the food they gave us very fair. We occupied about a quarter of an hour in crossing, and with a short walk joined the North Bengal Railway for 196 miles to Siliguri. Here Mr. Prestage secured us a sleeping-car to ourselves. This line, however, is constructed on the metre gauge only, and the travelling was very rough. Thus we passed through the night and again through the day over the flat hot plain; and as we went I could but wonder, thinking of the former times, what those who fled from Calcutta's summer must have then gone through on this same journey, and what must have been the heats of the city from which they felt forced to fly. The journeys must have been undertaken at night-time assuredly.

At length we came to Siliguri, having kept the great Kanchinjunga in distant view for several hours; and here we entered the domain of what they call the Steam Tram. It is a two-feet gauge railway of some fifty miles in length, and mounts to Darjeeling. It is at Sookna, the first station, about seven miles distant, that the tramway begins to ascend, and hence for the whole way the journey is most exciting. Not only is the wooded scenery, with its occasional vast forest precipices, continuously beautiful, but the railway itself, with its curves, and gradients, and circles, and switchbacks, is a perfect marvel; and every now and then, it may be confessed, is a rather alarming one. At Kurseong you obtain excellent refreshment, particularly in the bread—the best I tasted through all my three years—and while you repose, there lies a fine vast, outspreading view far below you of the main famous tea-gardens of Darjeeling. This gives you an altitude of 5000 feet, the highest point on the line being 7300 feet. It was dark when we arrived at the terminus on Sunday evening, the 9th of December, and here we were met by my friend Mr. Ford, who guided us to Mr. and Mrs. Roberts' comfortable "Woodlands Hotel," where everybody stays, and who very opportunely cautioned us (myself, at all events) to be careful of the first effects of the rarified air. This I certainly experienced at first in some slight degree, and was glad of an arm in making the last stiff climb on foot from the station to our hospitable Eyrie.

There is a certain advantage in arriving at a place like Darjeeling at night. You have no half-developed first view when you are tired, and you wait for the first grand scenic effect on the waking of the first fresh morning. Thus we went to bed and slept, with orders for early calling, to see the sunrise; and morning came, and before the sun-rise we were at our windows, and Kanchinjunga was before us. It is the very finest form of mountain, as seen from Darjeeling, that I ever beheld; and by-and-by the light increased, and gradually a growing brightness foretokened what was coming. The roses and the azures dawned and deepened, and presently the highest peak was glowing in live sun-shine. So came on the day to introduce us to more intimacy with, I should suppose, the finest, if not the very highest, mountain in the world.

On Monday, the 10th, we made a riding party, and visited the Observatory Hill, whence the view of the mountain appeared particularly fine, but I came to analyze the peculiarity of these views more minutely on my second and more prolonged visit, of which I shall speak later on. Let me at once remark, however, that his main form is pyramidal; that the colours of his massive rock become gradually lighter as they approach the top; and that the distance in a bee-line to his peak has been measured as of forty miles; thus corresponding with that of the main peaks of the Oberland Range, as seen from Berne, whereof let no man speak slightingly. We made a skirmishing inspection of the very picturesque surroundings to-day, and on the next, Tuesday, the 11th, we rode up to Tiger's Hill (as it is called), whence a sight is caught of just the peak of Mount Everest, or rather Gaurisankar, the really highest mountain in the world; but on this occasion nought thereof was visible, for the weather had changed, and in the place of a spotless sky our imaginative faculties were greeted with the very wildest and strangest possible broken masses of wandering and flying white mountain clouds. These rolled about among the enormous crags and gorges, never allowing anything to be clearly seen, and yet now and then opening to us glimpses of vast passing fields of intense sunshine. This was what we did not come to see; still it was impossible not to be charmed with seeing it, for the mountainous features of the country are so gigantic here that all effects are quite surpassing.

On the following day the weather had changed again, and all was bright; so I repeated this excursion, though I had to go alone. The panorama was spotless, and over the opposite brow appeared the three expected snowy tips or tops; and that is all one sees or guesses here of the great Mount Everest. Indeed, the largest to your right is certainly not he; his head is the middle one; this on my second visit to Darjeeling I verified in an excursion to Sundukphu.

Another advantage of our introduction to Mr. Prestage was his introduction of us to Mr. Lloyd, a Director, if not the Chairman, of the Darjeeling line ; for when I started for Calcutta on the Thursday morning, the latter took me down for a certain distance in an open trolly fixed to the train, and thence to the foot I joined Mr. Prestage in a separate trolly altogether. Thus I had the fullest possible opportunity of appreciating this astonishing fifty miles of railway ; the passage down which, however, was not quite so thrilling as my sixty-mile-an-hour descent in a trolly of the Santa Theresa railway near Rio, with the Minister of Marine. In descending, the vast tea plantations far below are opened out to the view in a very striking manner ; and the various aspects of Kanchinjunga from the ridges of the line, which we had missed in the dark on our journey up, completely engrossed one's astonishment and admiration. Mr. Lloyd informed me that these tea plantations—the cultivation not being new to me—were not more than twenty or thirty years old. The close of the border contests had left much waste lands to be redeemed, and tea was then hit upon for covering all slopes and valleys.

IV.

ON arriving in Calcutta my first thought was a visit to Burma (as had been recommended to me), with the intention of going up the Irrawaddy as far as Mandalay. It was the proper moment to do this, before entering on my Indian and Kashmir excursions; and accordingly I took my berth in the British Indian Company's steamer *Putiala*, which I was to join at Diamond Harbour on Thursday morning, the 20th of December. My native servant, I found, was to manage for himself, amongst a host of others, on the fore-deck, and I paid $10 for his passage. Not feeling quite certain about this arrangement, I was enlightened by the question, "What does he want more?" nor did he at all expect more. This settled plan gave me a week at Calcutta, and as I had a floating curiosity, and only a floating one, about Katmandoo, the capital of Nepaul, I obtained an introduction by Mr. Longley to an exile of the former royal family, then quietly living in Calcutta. This was General Kedar Nursing, or (as I have it) Kedarnursing Jung Behadon. He received me with great pleasure and pleasantness, and was not long in proving his familiarity with the English language by informing me that Katmandoo was "beastly dirty." With a little extra zest, perhaps, he strongly dissuaded me from undertaking the journey. All this was information, though I did not need deterring from any intention I did not entertain. He told me the journey would be very trying and fatiguing; that one must pass through a district of the most poisonous malaria; that when I got there I should be watched and controlled—indeed, that the English Resident was quite a prisoner—and that at that time of year the vast chain of mountains would assuredly be clouded. The Rajah, he said, was then only twelve years of age, and a mere Pagoda. He gave me his photograph, and wrote my name in Sanscrit, which, he said, was the real language of the country; but that the indigenous race who spoke it had been conquered and driven in by the Rajputanas when they fled thither from the tyrannies of the Mogul emperors. Our interview was so pleasant that, before finally leaving Calcutta, I paid him a second visit to say "good-bye." Singularly enough, a few days after my first visit, I had all his reports confirmed by Mr. Watson, a well-known dentist in Calcutta, to whom I had to appeal for a small timely service to prevent the necessity of a greater one by-and-by. He had been to Katmandoo, in aid of the teeth of the Commander-in-Chief — teeth, you see, can be troublesome in Nepaul—but he would not go again on any account. One reason for this was that, from some mere accidental oversight, he failed to salute his Excellency, whereupon that offended spirit (like all people of small birth) was highly indignant, and with indefensible ingratitude "showed his teeth," even against him from whom he had so recently received them. But the journey alone was enough; privations and fatigues were incurred throughout. Everything must be taken with you, and all is badly economized and cooked. Rough bearers, clumsy elephants—what elephant doesn't feel clumsy?—no howdah, and the animal's chain thrown over its back and against your own. All this would be nothing to a real explorer, but a professional man does not belong to that category, nor does every traveller. One anecdote which Mr. Watson told me I must not omit to add. I am not quite sure he saw the performance, but certainly he received it from a source that justified his repeating it. A group of common people were about to take their meal. They seized upon a goat and tied its four legs all together. They then flung it living on a huge bonfire, and when it had been well scorched and perhaps just heated through, they tore it open and devoured it. So much for Nepaul and Katmandoo! which I shall never see.

I had several drives with my friend round the grand maidan, or park, or meadow, a grand open stretch of grass, and after he left I employed the rest of my time in visiting the Botanical and Zoological Gardens and other scenes of the city. In the former, the grand sight is the most wonderful banyan tree in the world. The word "immense" is scarcely immense enough to give any idea of its almost fabulous extent, and when you have come away your memory misgives you as to what you have seen. I was surprised some years ago at the size of one at Alexandria. It is as a pea to the moon! For these Gardens you must cross the Hugli, and the sight from the middle of the bridge should not be omitted for its own self, even under the interruption of passing vessels. Life abounds and gives one life.

At the Zoological Gardens the object that chiefly struck me was the man-eating tiger. In general, I have been told, these man-eating tigers are the old mangy ones, that find their lord and master, man —the most defenceless of born animals in nature— their easiest prey, for they are unable to chase the fleeter animals. Thus, though man claims to have dominion given him over all things, many tigers are quite capable of teaching him another lesson, under mere natural conditions; and when this vaunted phrase was given forth, rifles and explosive balls had not been invented. In this case, however, the man-eater was no mangy tiger. He was a royal Bengal tiger of the most fearful size, elasticity, and power. I saw him at his best, and the effect was greater because he was in his own country. He was asleep inside, and I gave the attendant bakhshish to rouse him up. Forth he presently came, grand, alarming, and irate, and I felt quite willing to concede to him the empire.

I have already said there are two Calcuttas; they are the European, or the City of Palaces, and the native. My visit to the two above establishments took me notably through the midst of the latter. Nothing could be more picturesque, nor less palatial —nor less tempting for a dwelling. The contrast is extreme, and the impression lasting. Particularly note the moving, loose-robed crowds, among whom appear border men, called Pavendahs : also the small white oxen, labouring under their yoke, with the driver riding ; yet the eye is tranquil.

In making one more call at the Bengal Club I was fortunate in finding Sir Guilford Molesworth, though only on the eve of his and Lady Molesworth's final departure for England. But I mention the call because, in course of our conversation, he strongly urged me not to leave India without seeing the great Temple of Ramisseram ; and this I bore in mind and in course of time accomplished, but under singular circumstances, which will appear in their turn. The temple is on the Isle of Paumben, the largest of those forming the line of Adam's Bridge, as already mentioned, and is most difficult to attain. But I had with me a most valuable volume, the third of "Fergusson's Indian and Eastern Architecture," which had been recommended to me by Mr. Harwood, of Messrs. Bickers and Son, in Leicester Square. I know not what I should have done throughout India without this book. It was a never-failing companion and instructor, and when I looked out Ramisseram and read Fergusson's account of it, and saw his illustrations, it became with me a treasured resolution to follow, if at all possible, Sir Guilford Molesworth's advice.

V.

AT length, by the 7.25 train from Sealda Station on the morning of Thursday, the 20th of December (Madras time, which rules on Indian railways, as being the most central time), I left Calcutta to join the *Putiala* for Rangoon in Burma, which we call "Farther India," though there is no real India, after all. The line runs down to Diamond Point, or Harbour, about fifty miles distant. The scenery is flat, but the tropical trees and the various groups of robed and turbaned natives sprinkled among them gave early morning a very lively look to my own not yet surfeited eye. We boarded the launch and then boarded the steamer, and sailed forth upon a mirrored sea. Our next day, Friday, the 21st, was, as usual in the calendar, the shortest day, but strangely unlike our own. In this respect, though scarcely in any other, England fails to invade Asia out here. Our passage was a pleasant one both as to weather and companions, and among these I found an American Baptist missionary, Dr. Bunker, abroad. He is of twenty-two years' standing, and lives at Tongou, where his labours are chiefly among the Karens. These people, he informed me, are an indigenous mountain tribe, driven inland by the Burmese; but he finds them far more manly and straightforward than the latter.

They fought for England in the late war. He also gave me an account of a fearful Burmese snake, called the hemadryad; this reptile is six, twelve, or fifteen feet in length, and, unlike other snakes, will seek to attack, unprovoked. It is deadly poisonous, savage and aggressive, and pursues by leaps. By this description it would seem to outvie the Black Amba, of which I learned such fearful fame in Natal; and strong indeed must be Dr. Bunker's nerves and true his aim: for he told me that, being pursued by a large specimen of this tribe, he turned and shot it with a rifle. He might have been of some service in the Garden of Eden, surely. The snake appears to be well known in the country, and feared as much as known. Dr. Bunker is a very earnest missionary, and by all accounts has obtained great influence over the flocks he superintends and visits. He is an American Baptist, eager to defend his views; and, though a Baptist, considers that he agrees with the Churches in essentials. This is one of the points that greatly puzzle those who are preached to by entirely different, yet "Christian," missionaries.

On Saturday we sighted the Aguda Lighthouse; and on Sunday, the 23rd, after rounding the point which is veined with the very usual numerous mouths that characterize a huge river, the Irrawaddy (to which some add the name of the Bassein), we arrived at flat Rangoon, where I went to a curious-looking building, called "The British Burma Hotel;" and the establishment was as curious as the building. But independently of European intrusion, Rangoon would not have required an hotel at all. As time goes on our "civilization" will no doubt gradually improve the new necessities that it has created. The first feature of the town that presented itself to me was its broad, straight streets, lined with trees; and these breadths were plentifully adorned with many figures in variously-coloured costumes. What I soon noticed was that the Burmese are very fond of colour. Palm trees, tamarind trees, and mango trees mingled their various foliages. It would be difficult to describe the city farther, because there is nothing to describe.

Even more difficult it would be, but in quite another sense, to describe another feature, because it is quite indescribable: I mean the great Rangoon Pagoda, the most astonishing in the world, and called the Shoay Dagon, or Shoedagong, Pagoda. Before making my first visit to this wonder, however, I was tempted to walk round a lesser Pagoda, which was covered to the top by a most strangely interlaced scaffolding of bamboo, and this most strange construction I was positively informed had been reared in the incredibly short space of one day. There were several worshippers kneeling and prostrating themselves in prayer, and this before figures of Buddha; just as Christians worship before the crucifix or the figure of the Virgin. Indeed, it is difficult to understand how any believers who have pinned their faith to any once visible human being or beings can possibly abstain from visible and memorial representations of them, preservation of their relics, and a craving for their image in physical aid of their spiritual devotions.

General Spurgin had fortunately given me a letter of introduction to Colonel W. Cooke, then Assistant Commissary-General, whose residence was some short distance out of the town; and as my road thither lay by the great Pagoda, I naturally stopped for a first survey of it as I passed by. The whole mass of structure is most elaborate and confusing. In the first place, the Pagoda itself is claimed as having a height of 321 feet, and it springs from a vast square marble platform, which is itself approached by four sets of staircases, a set on each side; so that you mount considerably before arriving at the platform. When you get there you find this vast gilded Pagoda is surrounded by a number of smaller pagodas (said to be sixty-eight in all), something of the shape of their chief. Three only of these many, with the addition of a grotesque huge human face and figure, appear in Fergusson's engraving. Almost countless figures, large and small, surround the platform, among which is a huge recumbent one of Gautama, and at one end of this peopled platform is a monster bell, measuring eight feet diameter at the mouth, this being a great feature in Buddhism. The crowds of variegated worshippers in all corners were remarkable, and the permitted barking of dogs, who hate Europeans, and the loud cheerful conversations of human beings that surround the worshippers of the moment, make one wonder how devotion can be sustained. The outline of the great central Pagoda itself resembles that of a vast hand-bell, with a gilded framework, called a Hthee, at the top. The whole scene was enlivened by the moving crowds of costumed pilgrims, and one point of view especially attracted me: it was to stand at the top of the most frequented of the deep flights of steps, and watch the variegated groups passing up and down, and buying at the various votive stalls. This was my first visit, and in repeated returns the general effect increased; and all this mass of structure, with living and moving beings round it, like bees gathering honey, has grown into this vast reality in order to cover either some hairs or a tooth of Gautama, or Buddha, "The Enlightened." Verily, verily, how much alike all faiths are in many features! We are all idolaters; either of our own gods and our own saints, or—of one another.

It was now time to think of my letter of introduction and Colonel Clarke; but well known as he was, great was my difficulty in finding him. At last this discovery was accomplished, and he came in view, hard at work. On presenting my letter he surprised me by recognizing the name, and it turned out as an additional introduction that he and my nephew, Colonel Aubertin, had been at Cheltenham together. We were, therefore, friends at once, and he showed his friendship by unhesitatingly ordering me off; namely, ordering me to be off at once to Mandalay that same night, if I was really going there, or I should lose a week by calculation of the boats. I was, of course, wise enough to bow to this instant dismissal with thanks, the more so as I was pledged on my return to spend a few days with him in his tree-shaded dwelling before leaving again for Calcutta. Then came what was a real gift: a letter of introduction to Colonel Strover, the Commissioner at Mandalay. This new arrangement admitted of no delay, for I was to take the railway that night at 9.30 for some 190 miles to Prome, on the river; and here we were to join the steamer *Mandalay* for Mandalay.

At the hotel I found one of my fellow passengers from Calcutta, General Johnston, bound on the same voyage of discovery as myself; and we both started together, with our two servants; his being a Madrassee, of middle age, and by no means a pleasant individual. Our tickets being taken, we entered our car, as usual, but immediately received a kindly warning from an official: "Gentlemen, I must caution you to keep your door safely locked at night, for otherwise you are in danger of losing all your coats and luggage." A timely warning indeed, as we afterwards learned from many mouths of sufferers. One passenger on our return told me of several cases of this sort of robbery, including his own: "For," said he, "I lost every single thing I had with me while I was asleep." Nay, more, it was a well-authenticated fact that the Chief of Police, though attended by an escort, had on one occasion himself been the sufferer. It is easy to attribute these robberies to the Burmese; but those generally accredited with the trick are certain Madrassees, who come over to the country. The trick is to get upon the train, sometimes even under the train, and watch the opportunity of noting possible prey at any given station. Then, when the train is again in motion, they enter, throw everything helter-skelter out, hide themselves, and "disembark" at the next station, deliberately walking back and gradually picking up their spoil. It is not of the Burmese to do this.

For ourselves, we were on our guard, and arrived at Prome unrobbed, traversing our 161 miles uninterruptedly.

At about half-past six on the morning of Monday, the 24th December, we embarked on board the *Mandalay*, of the Irrawaddy Flotilla Company, whereof Captain Franz K. Timm was the sociable and able captain, and found ourselves on the ful, broad waterway of the Irrawaddy itself, for our 410 miles to Mandalay. This river course I shall detail, because I had been so much misled about it. We anchored at Mihnla for the night, and some of us walked up to the fort, where there had been fighting in the days of invasion; and when we had walked up we walked down again, not much wiser but very much more dusty than before. But it was "something to do!" and what a chance that is, very often—"to have something to do." We had passed Kama, with its pagodas, and had stared at them as we passed. The river throughout the day had shown itself vast in waters; and so many would say, "this splendid river;" but the banks were flat and quite monotonous. On one spot, however, by way of trade, an enormous mass of sawdust, more curious than beautiful, attracted my attention; this turned out to be some years' accumulation from the making of boxes for the dye called "Cutch." But the most curious and interesting object to me was on board, where a mother in the second class was waiting on her daughter travelling in the first. My attention was pointedly called to this fact, and the name of the young lady was then given me as a Miss Dumont. The explanation was startling enough. She herself was half-caste, having certain white blood in her veins, while her mother had none, being wholly Burmese. Therefore the daughter of mixed blood was waited on by the mother of pure. This strange circumstance somewhat serves to exemplify social relationship throughout Burma, and I soon came to know that in every case servants go down on their knees before their masters on receiving orders or delivering messages or food. This is so, as between themselves, and I presently observed this custom going on haughtily on board on the part of a master of the most ordinary type. I was told that Burmese servants are especially attached to European masters, and an instance of this was given me later by a young officer who was deploring having to leave his devoted servant behind.

Next day was Christmas Day, and throughout, the river was again vast—and this, though the water is always low at this time of year—but the banks were again monotonous. We passed the great Oil Station, Yeanang Young, with one solitary handsome group of trees; and here we witnessed a very picturesque landing and scattering abroad on the slopes of our costumed native passengers. The sunset colourings were gorgeous, as we anchored an hour short of the famous Paghan. And thus ended our Christmas Day passage. The day itself wound up with the usual fare, which need not be described, except as to one item : the neglected, insipid Papua. This fruit was despised, till there came a passenger on board from one of the stations, who, helping himself to a good slice, casually remarked it was good for the liver. On this, the two large melon-shaped fruits disappeared forthwith, and the following day saw the last of the fruit devoured.

On the morning of the 26th we rose early to have a good look from the river on famous Paghan: famous, that is, for its pagodas. They are so numerous, that there is a defiant proverb as to counting them : "Count the pagodas of Paghan." A passenger on board was enthusiastic as to an endless walk among them ; and possibly the novelty of such a meander may be exciting ; but it was quite evident to us all that the mass of them were dwarf ruins ; some few were more or less entire, but there were no evidences of fine structures. Pagodas, I may say, are to be seen everywhere up to Mandalay, and they are for the most part ugly. The day was again somewhat diversified by the embarking, and landing, and scattering of the natives, and in one case I was suddenly reminded of a water-colour by Turner.

On the 27th we passed what I called the eye of the river, viz. Sagain, one of the ancient capitals, with its various hills and pagodas ; and opposite to this, on the east or left bank of the river, stood Ava, also a former capital, and which now gives one of his titles to the Marquis of Dufferin and Ava. A little higher up we come abreast of Amarapura, which also was formerly the seat of Government; and another eight miles, completing our 410 miles in three days and a half from Prome, brought us at about noon to the dusty, steep, and ragged left bank, forming an unworthy landing-place for the present capital, Mandalay.

Now, on arriving at such a spot, and asking for the Commissioner, one would naturally suppose it to be an easy task to find him. Quite the contrary. If I had trouble in finding Colonel Clarke at Rangoon, it cost me many times as much to find Colonel Strover at Mandalay. Forth I started, with my man on the box, in a rattle-trap gárè (reminding me of Calcutta), in full assurance that it was "all right;" and after a long and tedious drive we came to the city walls, castellated, and with pagoda ornaments at intervals. We crossed the moat and entered; but, to my astonishment, I found no city at all! This remarkable fact was afterwards explained to me. Still we kept driving on to a large residence, which had been pointed out to me after interpreted inquiry. This was wrong: it was the residence of the Chief Commissioner, Sir Charles Crosthwaite, when there. Off again; and outside the walls on the opposite side. In this line I passed close to the late king's palace, with its pagoda, and afterwards came to some fine-looking barracks. When far outside we at last stopped at another house. This, I was told, must be the right one; so in I walked and proffered my letter. "From my brother," quoth the courteous gentleman. This took me aback, for I was evidently wrong again. "Oh!" he quickly added, "I see this is to the Commissioner, about two miles off." I then recounted my despair, and begged him "to guide my weary way." Very kindly he sent a man with me, and in about half an hour we arrived at the very residence of Colonel Strover. Here at last I found a haven, having travelled six miles instead of one, and was most pleasantly received and housed. Perhaps if you go there now, knowledge will have improved; but I do not forget what was.

The Commissioner was engaged that afternoon at the races as one of the judges—there are races everywhere and everywhen—and I spent my time among various pagodas, including the "Incomparable," "The Golden House," and the "countless pagodas." Here I wandered through a downright forest of them, and mounted a central structure to survey, from a bird's-eye view, the astonishing surroundings.

Early on the next morning, the 28th December, the Colonel drove me to see the Aracan Pagoda, where sits the great figure of Buddha, brought from Aracan. The figure was golden or gilded, and was flanked by two screens. I have said the Burmese are great colourists, and these two screens were indeed specimens of that art. Worshippers abounded, and so did their offerings of rice; but these, as they lay scattered for worship's sake, were licked up by the prowling dogs, who, as usual, now and then resented European costume. This pagoda is worth visiting indeed.

For the afternoon, Colonel Strover gave me a letter

to Captain Temple, at the Palace, also with its lofty pagoda, and which I had passed within the walls. He showed me the whole building, and strange indeed seemed the incongruity of a palace turned into Government offices. And now it was that Captain Temple explained to me the no-city phenomenon within the walls. The whole mass of inhabitants had been turned out, and made to carry their wooden structures with them. The Captain spoke of from fifty to sixty thousand inhabitants so dealt with, and thirty thousand more outside the walls; and all this had taken place without a single hitch; many bargaining with their neighbours for changing houses on agreed terms. Then came a highly interesting visit. This was to King Thebaw's Summer House, when I stood on the spot where he had signed his abdication, praying (as I was told) for so many weeks' or months' delay in his departure, and being answered by General Prendergast, "Not so many hours." There was yet one more mournful remnant of past power to be seen: the king's throne-room. Here, himself squatting in Eastern fashion, they who came before him approached in squatting movements to his feet, and spoke their prayer. But alas! the god is gone, like so many others.

On Saturday morning, the 29th December, I was to be on board again in time to sail at eleven, and the Colonel took me for an early previous drive to see other golden and glittering temples; the Queen's Golden Kyoung among the number, and the great solid gilded pagoda. These temples may be called tawdry and trifling, and probably would look so in our latitudes; but they have their special beauty in their native soil, standing out against their blue skies. The elaboration of their detail is astonishing. At length we came to the steamer, and I hailed our returning passengers, and so ended my visit to Mandalay, and to the pleasant entertainments of my generous host.

In our various drives I particularly noticed the Buddhist priests, young and old, dressed in yellow robes, and how they begged from house to house for their daily sustenance. Each has his district, and there is no invasion. Each carries a large bowl, the "Alms Bowl," and presents himself at the open entrance; open to the street. They never ask for anything, but simply stand and wait for perhaps two or three minutes. If no one comes to add to the contents they go away. Another feature to observe is the enormous quantity of tattooing of the almost naked legs and bodies. Even little children show it; and it is wonderful to think how the agony can be endured except upon the theory, applied to the Chinese, that the Burmese are very insensible to pain. This view indeed was confirmed to me on board by a Mr. S. C. Robertson, Assistant Superintendent of Telegraphs, who also spoke of their severities one towards another. While speaking of children, by the way, I noticed the large bracelets they carried, both here and in India, on their wrists and ankles; and was offensively confirmed in my suspicion that cases too often occur in both countries of murder and mutilation to obtain them. The oxen are driven as in Calcutta, with the yoke on the neck and the string through the nose, in apparent suffering, but the tranquil eye, here as there, disputes this impression. In size and form the Burmese animals are superior to those in Calcutta.

So down the wide, flat-shored river we went again, I being much struck by a single group of hills we had passed in the dark before; and we arrived at Prome at 5 p.m. on the 31st. General Johnston and I had at one time intended going farther up the river to Bhamo, but were threatened by the grounding of the steamer at this time of year, which verily came to pass. But there were only a few miles of picturesque shore to be seen, after all; and they who have travelled in flat countries know how molehills there are magnified into mountains. Major Clarke informed me that very much higher up stream, where he had gone with his forces, but where we could not then go, the scenery among the rocks was very fine.

It will be gathered from what I have written that the general aspect of the Irrawaddy, as a river, is tame; but I have no doubt that when the water is high you may be raised to get a fine extensive view of the country to the east, which would, of course, enliven the otherwise somewhat monotonous voyage; for Burmese views are by no means flat; what is flat are the general banks of the river.

On Tuesday, then, the 1st of January, 1889, at about six in the evening we arrived at Rangoon again, where I was met by a letter from Colonel Cooke, summoning me to his house. On this day all were enjoying a close holiday, and to me this summons was my holiday. In the evening the Colonel took me a delightful drive around "The Royal Lakes" and through the "Ladies' Mile," displaying views of the great pagoda. Then to the lively club. In the evening after dinner we lounged on the wide upper balcony under the trees, legs up, on those peculiar Indian chairs, to which I was always invited, but to which, in spite of prophecy, I could never get accustomed. A further drive out the next day displayed much large timber, especially the large-leafed teak tree; and, to my astonishment, an unlimited growth of pineapples under large plantations. It appears to be a common practice in the season, in morning drives, to get out and help oneself *ad libitum;* and the produce must indeed be inexhaustible. My last day, and my last long visit to the Shoay Dagon, was on Friday, the 4th of January. Major Cooke had joined us from Mandalay in the morning, and as my boat was to sail at 2.30 a.m. I bade my pleasant host and his brother farewell, and went on board in the evening, and on Tuesday, the 8th, I was in Calcutta again.

VI.

HAVING now returned to Calcutta, I was to prepare for my own intended "Voyage of Discovery" through India, and to the ever-vaunted vale of Kashmir; nor was I unwilling to be prompt in making arrangements for my departure, for I found the weather some ten degrees warmer than usual for the month of January, and, as I must confess, very depressing. Having availed myself, therefore, of the hospitality of Mr. and Mrs. Hyde in their very pleasant villa, and also of Mr. Gordon's, at the Bengal Club, who likewise had been a schoolfellow of my nephew—such is the world's easy intercourse at present—I made my way to Messrs. Thomas Cook and Son's office, No. 11, Old Court House Street, in order to arrange the usual railway through tickets, with which I had already travelled some thousands of miles in other countries, and found infinitely convenient passports in joining trains, without standing and crushing at the wicket for a ticket.

My first long journey was eventually to cease at Bombay; and, counted by the way I intended to go, I had to measure a distance of 1689 miles, the coupons, as usual, giving the liberty of stopping at the various places which I desired to visit, and my heavy baggage being sent on direct, independently. Therefore at 9 p.m. on the evening of Tuesday, the 15th of January, by Madras time, I left the Howrah station, E.I.R., in a good-sized car or carriage, where luckily I found only one other passenger, an officer; and in India officers are always pleasant.

The first object of my journey was the City of Benares, which I spell in the usual way, and will here remark that, as regards the spelling of various cities and places, I shall take my chance among all the promiscuous and contradictory authorities, spelling in any manner that at the moment happens to be in print before me, and I daresay spelling the same place differently and wrongly every time I write it. The first 470 miles took me to Moghal Sarai Junction at 14.45, or 2.45 p.m. on the 16th, and, starting thence at 3.35 p.m., another ten miles on the Oudh and Rohilkund railway brought me, at 4.25 p.m., to the "Sacred City of Siva or Shiva," where I rested at Clarke's Hotel; a habitation which was quite unknown to this God of Destruction, the Third in the Brahmin Trinity, though by some reputed as the First, or as comprehending all Three. It was at this first halting place that I realized the necessity of generally carrying with you through all India your whole bedding apparatus, even when visiting most of the hotels. Where there are none, and only dâk bungalows, this necessity is a necessity indeed. These Government post-houses are not expected to have any furniture whatever besides a table and a few chairs and sofas; all is very scantily provided. One's arrival there is generally followed by a loud cawing and cackling among the fowls, and I have described the reception in general to consist merely of a shrivelled old man and an impossible chicken. However, for India, the hotel, in this instance, afforded me very fair food, and bedstead enough to put my own things upon. Thus dinner and the night were accomplished.

Before seven on the following morning, the 17th January, my guide and I were moving to see Benares, the first aspect of which it seems to me should be sought from across the Ganges. The early horizontal rays of morning, striking the broad bosom of the stream, light up the wonderfully picturesque city, rising above the sloping banks on the opposite side, with its numerous broken ghats or high landing-steps, in an almost magical manner. The whole city lies upon the left bank or north side of the river, and the view is unintercepted. Then return and take one of the strangely made boats, or barges, and move quietly up and down stream for about a quarter of a mile, sitting on the outside top; and thus you will view all that goes on, on shore; bathing among the living, and burning among the dead. Sometimes these latter are cast into the Ganges, a style of disposal more popular with the obscene crocodile, and supposed to yield advantage to the soul.

The next movement was to visit the narrow and in many ways offensive streets and passages of the confined and unwashed city, and here the traveller's senses become bewildered with the crowded varieties that press round him. Among other objects must be mentioned a great Brahmin Bull, and among the Hindoo buildings the remarkable Golden Temple, dedicated to the God Siva. The

A POINT OF BENARES

symbol of Creation or Renovation under which this god of Destruction is worshipped appears everywhere, as if to point the view that—

> "In the boundless realm of unending change"

(as Shelley beautifully writes) there is really no such thing as death. Byron wrote a sentimental line—

> "Ah ! surely nothing dies but something mourns."

In the above view this might be paraphrased —

> "Ah ! surely nothing dies but something lives."

Hence, Siva the Destroyer is symbolized as Siva the Creator or Renovator, because in the "unending change" the dispersion of one contributes to the formation of the other. But you may remark for ever, and yet not paint Benares.

After becoming intoxicated with variety, if not yet overcome with fatigue, the last visit must be to the towering mosque of Aurungzebe, an awful intrusion, and in form a tyrannical one, upon the gloomy sanctity of Siva. But rival religions know nothing of consideration or forbearance, and always arrogate to themselves the truth, and this particular mosque is stated to have been the especial fruit of arrogance. When you have put on your shoes again, after visiting the Mosque, take courage, and take breath, and mount a minaret. The view will well reward you. Of its kind it must be unique: the river and the city close below you, and the country far around, form a scene to dwell on and to remember. There is something strange in Fergusson's remark, that after all "there is hardly any great city in Hindustan that can show so few evidences of antiquity as Benares," and that the Temple of Vishveshwar, which the Brahmins universally point out to you as their holiest and oldest, "was erected from the foundation in the last century to replace one that had been thrown down and desecrated by the bigot Aurungzebe. The oldest buildings indeed would appear to be the Moslem tombs and buildings, about the Bukarija Kund, and these only of the 15th century."

The Durgâ Temple lies outside, under splendid trees. It is said to be dedicated to the savage Siva's savage wife, under that name, which is intended to inspire that most essential element of all worship, terror; in some, diluted to awe. The leading feature here are the monkeys, which are too much made light of perhaps. Is not their presence connected with the worship of the monkey god? "Monkey," it is true, has been made to signify "Devil." But among all the numerous gods which the human brain has in course of æons invented we know that there appears "the monkey god."

I can quite understand that some few specialists could pass several days in viewing and reviewing all the curiosities that the city has to show. But it would be affectation on my part to pretend that I needed any further acquaintance with it than my one day's visit had afforded me, and which I felt sure would be quite sufficient for my future memories and uses. I therefore decided to leave on the following morning, looking with a careless eye on all shawls, while the glittering array of brass works that adorned a spacious saloon of the hotel were to my taste repellent rather than attractive.

But before leaving Benares, I sought and found a Brahmin Bábu, Ram Káli Chaudhuri, to whom I had brought a letter of introduction from the late Miss Constance Naden. He was a Brahmin priest of the first class, and wore the three threads over his left shoulder, having been so invested at nine years old. To this degree, he informed me, none can rise; but they must be invested in early life. It would be neither possible nor entertaining, if possible, to recount all our conversation, in which he spoke English exceedingly well. By my notes I see that the principal subject between us was the Congress question, of which he knew a great deal more than I did. But I refer to the conversation because I promised him that if I ever mentioned his name, I would make this declaration for him, and all his brethren: "That whatever might be the subject of their dissatisfaction or complaint, they were really loyal subjects of the Empress, and that nothing whatever could induce them to commit any act that might have the tendency to weaken a Government in whose capacity to protect and support them they felt such perfect confidence." He was highly delighted on my presenting him with a copy of my Translation of the Lusiads, and I afterwards received a remarkably well-written letter from him, which bore evidence of his having really studied our language with scholastic success.

Leaving Benares at 4.25 p.m. on the 17th, I

arrived at Lucknow at the ugly hour 2.16 a.m. on Friday, the 18th, and drove to Hill's Imperial Hotel, where I was again glad of my own covering. This hotel, I may mention, like almost every other throughout India, has its bedrooms built on a long ground floor row, with a corridor in front, and opening behind into a bath room, very commodiously arranged. After bed and bath and breakfast (as usual) I prepared to visit the ever-to-be-remembered scenes, so dark and so bright in history; dark in sufferings and carnage, and bright in almost unexampled endurance, valour, and victory.

The Residency is, of course, the one grand centre of attraction, and before visiting its now quiet ruins, standing on turf and adorned with thick flowering creepers, a great advantage is offered of inspecting, at the museum, a perfect model of it, carefully prepared by Captain Moore, as it stood with its surrounding houses before the siege. Then to the scene itself, in all its quietude and its engaging ruin, and do not by any means omit to mount its crags and survey the entire picture. The soldier might be here inclined rather to discuss, but the civilian rather to ponder. Explain things as the best qualified may try to do, the record seems to baffle the understanding. Remember that all this deadly strife and fearful suffering took place in summer, and note one small fact alone—"the greatest torment was the flies, which swarmed in incredible numbers. The ground was black with them, and the tables covered. The besieged could not sleep; they could scarcely eat for them." The Sikandara Bagh, which is given as of

120 yards square, and is surrounded by high solid walls, is also to be visited. Hither a large body of Sipahis retreated, expecting to escape at the other side. But there was no opening, and, being hotly pursued by the 93rd Highlanders and 4th Punjab Rifles, they were all massacred, some say to the number of 2000, and other accounts give 1643 as the number of corpses buried under one huge mound outside the gate.

Leaving Lucknow and its great Imámbárah, a visit to Cawnpore naturally followed, whither forty-five miles on the same line of railway took me by 4.30 on the afternoon of the 19th, and early on the 20th I was driven round by a pensioned English soldier to all the various spots of horror, including, of course, the Park, the Well, and the Enclosure, with its statue. Perhaps I was more impressed with the barren ghat, by the river side, whither the bewitched General Wheeler led his unarmed officers and men to be slaughtered, for there the ground remained as it had been at the time. So also the Sevada House, whither Major Viper and seventy officers and men had fled, also unarmed, simply to share a similar fate. It was much to have trod these scenes.

I was now on my way through Allahabad to Jubbulpore, on the river Nerbudda, to see the Marble Rocks, and a run of 120 miles between 11.21 a.m. and 5 p.m. brought me to the above city, where I lodged at Lawrie's hotel. The capital of the North-West Provinces, situated on the west bank of the Jumna, just before that river falls into the Ganges, is a finely built city, with wide, straight and well planted streets, stretching over a perfectly flat country, and containing many imposing buildings at a certain distance from one another, and involving the climbing of a great many steps for making calls on officials and professors. Its great curiosity is the Asoka Pillar, which ought to be stared at with all that feigned interest which the concealed ignorance and indifference of the general traveller may command for the occasion, and in the fine museum there is the skeleton of a ghariál, or long-snouted alligator. And there is, of course, a cemetery, containing the usual collection of hideous tombs. On toiling up several steps with a letter to Mr. Hugh Fraser, the registrar, from my connection, General Spurgin, I unfortunately found he was "on tour," as also was another gentleman up another forbidding staircase. But on mounting to the grand colonnade of the Muir College I was fortunate enough to disturb the Professor of Sanscrit in his occupations, by sending in a letter, also from the late Miss Constance Naden, as at Benares. This was Pandit Adityaram Bhattacharya, M.A., with whom, however, I could then have only just as many minutes in conversation as it would have taken me to salute him properly by his name. Afterwards, however, he paid me the favour of a long call, maintaining a most interesting conversation in good English, much on the same lines as my Pandit friend at Benares. Had I immediately afterwards conversed with a well-informed Indian authority I could better have repeated and understood various features of his discourse than I can now, which amounts to just nothing at all. But, not forgetting the repeated expressions of loyalty, I do remember that one leading form of protest and complaint was that they had to contribute a great deal of money without having any corresponding voice, by representation, or otherwise, in the conduct of public affairs.

The fine arsenal and fort I took for granted, but I certainly have an impression of being somewhat earnestly taken to jail, and let out again, after confessing that it appeared to me, so far as I was a judge of jails, to be remarkably clean and airy. My afternoon wound up with a visit to the imposing Mayo Memorial, the tower of which I mounted, some 150 feet high, with a finial atop, whence an extensive spreading view of the country round for miles may be enjoyed. A night of railroad was before me, and the penalty of an early dinner, in order to catch the 7.22 train for Jubbulpore, where I was to arrive, after travelling 229 miles by the E.I.R. at 5 a.m. on the following morning. This I did on Tuesday, the 22nd of January, settling at Clark's Hotel, in a quiet lean-to bed-room, looking out into a garden, the enjoyment of whose freshness and fragrance, however, I postponed for a few short hours of morning sleep. After breakfast, arrangements were easily made for the excursion to the river.

The distance is ten miles, and they gave me a tonga for Rs. 5, the regular charge. I did not feel at all sure as to what I was to see; for an Englishman and his wife, whom I chanced to meet at Allahabad, and who were most anxious to make the journey, but could not, had been told by another Englishman and his wife two different tales; he having expressed himself delighted, and she having declared she would not cross the road to see the rocks again. My own report, if I met my first-named travellers again, would be that, without saying it would have been worth their while to go and to return the number of miles it would have cost them, yet that no one with the slightest sense of beauty and refinement should pass this station without a visit. When I came to the river side, after walking down a steep descent, I found a boat and boatmen, and two good-looking young Brahmin priests with a friend, who, speaking a little English, asked me to allow them to come with me. To this I consented, but the men did not move, nor speak English to say why. Getting impatient the Brahmins asked for me "why?" and the answer was that one of the last party had disturbed the wasps, and they were afraid of returning so soon. Now there is no fiction about these wasps, who build their large black nests on the rocks, and on the slightest disturbance, either by the firing of a gun, or by the smell of fire, as of a mere cigar smoked near them, will attack and mortally attack intruders. But none of us seemed disinclined to try, and so we went.

We were soon among the marbles, and so singular an effect I have never before seen. The waters of the Nerbudda, sometimes furious, were lying like a mirror, and the marble rocks on both sides were reflected on them. The long vista was all marble, for there appeared to be a block at the end, and to this we rowed and turned. There is nothing grand in the scenery; perhaps none of the marble cliffs are much more than a hundred feet high. But the

MARBLE ROCKS : JUBBULPORE

fairy-like effect is charming. The colouring is most artistic. Strange to say I had been warned against being disappointed, because there would be what was called much discolouring. But in point of fact this added a charm. There was exquisite white below, where the waters more or less protected the surfaces; and then there were light roses, light and dark browns, and purples. The only slight disappointment I felt was that there was not enough of them. In going and returning you cannot make out your hour, and the men make a mere moving business of it. In our case, however, we had one additional chance. There had been a slight (and only a slight) disturbance of the wasps, for one man had insisted on mounting one of the rocks towards a high nest with a cigar in his mouth. No sooner, however, did the fumes arise than the alarm commenced, and the intruding smoker fled so quickly that he left his cap behind him. This cap he had given a rower something to recover; so we hove to at the spot, and the man mounted the crags, while we waited and gazed below. I kept everyone dawdling here and there besides, as well as I could, but all was over, nevertheless, too soon. I climbed to the road on returning in company with the Brahmins, who took the opportunity of hoping and ascertaining that I was not a missionary; and then broke forth in protestations against having their own revered religion interfered with. So ended my visit to the Marble Rocks.

I was now to complete my journey to Bombay—whither another 616 miles of railway still remained, by the G.I.R.R. But I did not intend travelling straight through, for I should pass by stations where I meditated a halt. The first was that of Pechora, for a visit to the Ajunta caves; and the second was that of Nandgaon for Ellora. As regards the first, however, my hopes were small, though I was resolved to make the trial. I had therefore written the station-master that I was coming by a certain train, and would take the advantage of a few minutes' talk with him on the subject. It was 6.10 in the morning that I left Jubbulpore, and between 10 and 11 at night that we came to Pechora, where I immediately got out and looked for the station-master, who was also looking for me. The hope was hopeless. Twelve hours each way in a bullock waggon over a vile road, and no one at hand to undertake the journey, nor any sort of refuge for the night; all this decided me to abandon the attempt. So on I went to Nandgaon for Ellora. From what I could gather the Ajunta excursion requires long preparation, and the real mode of undertaking it is to make up a party for a few days.

At Nandgaon we arrived at about half-past one in the cold morning of the 24th, and, having written to this station-master also, he was there to greet me when I left the train. Ellora was practicable, because there was a dâk bungalow near the station, and a Parsee postmaster to provide a tonga. But everyone was fast asleep: so when the train was gone, the master came with me to the post-office and knocked the Parsee up, who came cheerfully forth, showing no disposition to knock him down in return. He was a good, stout, manly fellow, evidently blessed with a good digestion—almost the whole secret of life being worth living—and at once acceded to my suggestions. These Parsees, as I came gradually to know, are the life and soul of the tonga business throughout India. Early mornings can be cold in India, and this one kept up that character. I was to get what rest I could in the barren bungalow close by, and to be up and out again at five. This task I managed to accomplish, and cheerfully resigning my hard sofa at that hour for some hot milk and coffee,

"Passed out in open air preventing day."

It is not necessary to go as far as Arungabad in order to visit Ellora, but the Parsee persuaded me to do so. It lies fifty-six miles from Nandgaon, and entails fourteen miles to and fro beyond the turning to Ellora. I passed the night at the bungalow, bare and uncomfortable enough, and learned that Mr. Caine, M.P., was in the next compartment, but I did not see him, and found a little whisky for my water, notwithstanding; while a shrivelled old man brought me in a screaming white young cock, to show me what I was to have for dinner. The only object worth attention in the town was the mosque built by Aurungzebe, in imitation of his father Shah Jehan's tomb, the celebrated Taje Mehal, of Agra. It was built (says Fergusson) in memory of his favourite daughter Rabia Dúranee; and he adds, that "it narrowly escapes vulgarity and bad taste." I must confess this remark quite chimes in with my impressions, later on imbibed at Agra, as to how much the building there owes of its fair fame to its material, and its careful structure. Here both were coarse, and afforded an unhappy introduction to Agra.

The morning of the 25th shone bright and beautiful, and I started with satisfaction for Ellora, my chief object being to realize the great monolithic Temple of Kylas. Fourteen miles back brought us to the turning, at first an open road, but afterwards picturesque. We crossed a stream at a descent, at the end, and came direct through shrubs to Kylas. But it was very difficult to make out what it was I first saw as I was approaching, for it certainly was not the temple. It turned out to be the dark, discoloured vertical face of the cut in the hill, where this had been dug out for the purpose of this wonderful monolith, which, with all its details, was to be formed out of the mass left in the middle. Fergusson gives 100 feet in height to this inner face, which fronts directly to the road you come by, and half that height to the outermost sides. The floor of this pit, with a flat entrance, is 150 feet wide and 270 feet in length. In the centre of this floor stands this elaborate temple, monolithic, carved out of a block of stone, interiorly and exteriorly, and flanked on its two sides and its inner end by these vertical cuttings, through all three of which runs a continuous dark pillared corridor.

I confess to have been profoundly impressed with this strange and imposing reality, and very little inclined afterwards to read how Fergusson dilutes the wonder of the structure by arguing that it is considerably easier, and less expensive, to excavate an elaborate temple out of a block, than to build one by separate pieces. This sounds like destroying faith by reason, or dispersing a miracle by proving sleight of hand. It is a luxury, sometimes, to be amazed, and I felt thus amazed by wandering to and fro, and in and out of Kylas. It is not a building; it is a great block of stone hammered and chiselled into an elaborate temple; and it rises out of and belongs to its own floor, standing in its own pit, and between its own precipices. And round and round the galleries in these I walked continually, contemplating the fane after wandering among its pilgrims in the interior. Fergusson's sketch gives some idea, and only some, of the reality, and in his pages you must find the details. I had but little time for the other caves, and did not much care to confuse my impressions, so that when I had mounted the hill side and looked down upon the structure and its elaborate roofing, and yet again had wandered through its interior, I came away with a memory, "unmixed with baser matter," of the solitude and solemnity of Kylas.

As I was determined to reach Bombay on the next day, I had to start very early for Nandgaon station to catch the 10.10 morning train, which a little extra bakhshish to the driver enabled me to do. The rough ponies in their rough harness travelled extremely well, though a great deal of time was lost at all the frequent changes, and I paid Rs. 50 for the whole excursion. Our train was late on arrival, in consequence, I believe, of various crowded ones to see a parachute descent. We passed the Thull or Tal Ghaut in full daylight, with which I was not so much impressed as I had expected to be; and, on arriving, I made my way to the best built hotel (at all events)—the "Esplanade."

VII.

WHEN McCulloch published his geographical dictionary in 1844, he wrote of Bombay that its best streets were scarcely equal to the suburbs of Calcutta or Madras. He could not have said the same thing to-day. Bombay is an imposing city, containing several fine large public buildings, principally constructed, as it seemed to me, in the mediæval, narrow arch window style; one much more adapted for that sky and climate than our London, where people are already far too fond of introducing it. The Esplanade Hotel itself is a fine building (I speak of the building) and close to it stands the Secretariat. You will not care to go through the list with me, but I will mention the enormous Law Courts, and the University Library with its lofty Clock Tower, 260 feet in height. Here also, as in Calcutta, there are two cities, European and Native: and an immediate drive from one to the other is the best of all modes of describing both to one's own satisfaction. It seems strange that all should be on an island, and a small one too—this being the capital of the Presidency.

Then, if you want, as of course all do, to see the Caves of Elephanta, you embark in a steam launch for another island, and a much smaller one, lying to the east in the bay. Come with me and see them at once. You must have already seen them illustrated, and will not need any very particular description of them. I might lightly describe our small party. There was an American preacher, and an English clergyman, who talked to him incessantly, and I am quite sure professionally ; and when we came to the caves talked nonsense about Athens and Greek architecture. Athens at Elephanta! Then there was an American of the softer sex, but of the harsher voice. She was not ill-natured, but very loud about equality—*à propos* to nothing. She was "as good as Queen Victoria : quite," and there was no stopping her, till I reminded her she had forgotten one question. "How's that?" "Do you think Queen Victoria is as good as yourself?" "Well, I daresay she is," was the reply, and a final one for the moment. Then said one of them to me : "We're an All Round party from the States, and that good woman has been a scourge all through." So much for travelling parties! The other two were an honest man and his wife, and he was connected with coal mining, and made much more sensible observations than the classical ecclesiastic. He was puzzled how the flat roof of a cave could stand so firm with such small support, and this circumstance is striking when the remark is made. For many of the pillars have been shot away, the Portuguese being accused of having religiously brought in cannon for that holy purpose. The delicate fluting of these pillars may be observed, as adding greatly to the general effect ; but the whole interior is not large. The island itself is very picturesque and well wooded, and you mount by a great many steps to the caves, whence you enjoy a very pleasing view of the harbour; and the excursion is a short and easy one.

I was very fortunate in having a letter of introduction from Mr. Thompson, of the *Pall Mall Gazette*, to the then Governor, Lord Reay, for this not only gave me the entrance to Government House, where I was received with all kindness, but, before I left Bombay, obtained for me several letters from Lady Reay that enabled me to visit the Kattiawar Peninsula, on my way north, which Fergusson's volume had made me very anxious to do, especially in regard to Palitana. No sooner had I had time to turn round in Bombay than I found a former Egyptian acquaintance, whom I had known in Alexandria, in the person of Judge Scott. Nor was I many hours before enjoying his hospitality, as also that of Mr. Forrest, of Messrs. Killick Lixon and Cie. Mr. Sedgwick entertained me at the Byculla Club, and, in particular, introduced me to the Library of the Bombay Branch of the Asiatic Society, which was a great resource for reading all the English papers. On Wednesday evening, the 30th of January, I had the honour of attending a very picturesque "At Home" at Government House. There was no lack of hospitality at Bombay. The only drawback to these entertainments was that I presently felt an unusual sensation in my throat, and, on consulting a chemist, was smilingly and heartlessly informed that I had "only got the Bombay throat;" and this, I found, was a penalty very generally paid by visitors, who would aspire to be entertained by friends in Bombay, living on Malabar Hill. Before I finally left I had certainly made up my mind that I did not like the climate.

I had yet another friend at hand, in the person of Mr. R. A. Willis, of Messrs. Faber and Cie., who, besides entertaining me at the Byculla Club, afforded me the opportunity of passing two interesting mornings—one very pleasant as well as interesting, the other, certainly interesting because most novel, but certainly scarcely pleasant.

I have already spoken of the Ajunta Caves and of my disappointment at not being able to visit them. Having mentioned this subject to him, he at once proposed to drive me to call upon Mr. Griffiths, the chief of the School of Art, with whom he made an appointment to receive us. On going there I was well repaid, for I think I must, in truth, have seen all Ajunta before me. The number and the variety, including colouring, of the principal features was really surprising. I scarcely felt I could wish to go with him on his next visit, and did not feel, from all he said, that I should have gained anything in going alone sufficient to repay me for an inordinate proportion of fatigue and a mere uninstructed stare. His reproductions were most remarkable; visibly so; and he possessed various most curious fabrics and vases into the bargain.

My second excursion with Mr. Willis was quite different. It was to the Parsee Towers of Silence. Mr. Willis had evidently considerable authority in our hotel, of apparently an official character, and the manager of the hotel was a Parsee—Cowasji, D.

Furdonji. On mentioning the subject, and my desire to behold the scene, our Parsee most courteously assented, and he was, of course, to be the guide under whose conduct we could be admitted to the garden. Accordingly, on the morning of the 2nd of February, we went, the Parsee offering me a small descriptive pamphlet, in English, followed by a long list of certificates of approval by those who had been visitors. The first three words of one of these I well remember: it was signed approvingly by Lord Randolph Churchill, and it began, "I permit myself, etc., etc." I kept the pamphlet till the end, but I then returned it for some one else. I had no right whatsoever to protest, nor indeed felt inclined to do so, but I could not "permit myself" to approve. The whole affair appeared so unpleasantly strange. I thought of the curse truly or fabulously pronounced on Jezebel, and then of the remarkable variety of sentiment of which the human brain must be productive. For here goes on a process in the name of affection and regard which ends in what was for her intended as the worst of insults, and a curse. For what is the mode of burial, so to call it? It is just what prevented her burial, which Jehu (if he was in fact contemporaneous) sent out to order. We had full licence of entrance all round the towers and garden, and that was enough. These Towers of Silence are, I believe, five in number. They are scarcely towers, for they are not more than fifteen feet in height, and from sixty to eighty in diameter; and they are built with great solidity, with an open hollow in the centre, occupied by many open stone receptacles. Round the edges of these towers sit silent and sulky-looking, high-shouldered, obscene vultures, still as the dead they wait for. But you are in a beautiful and well-kept garden of trees and flowers. Presently a funeral train appears, and a movement of hustling life begins among the nearest tower birds. They turn their filthy heads to see what is coming for them, and they are glad to greet the mourning group. The naked corpse is duly placed in one of the open stone receptacles. The bearers reappear with cloth and empty bier, and down swoop these birds from tower and tree, and behold a skeleton alone remains. Such are the Towers of Silence and such the mode of burial. Farewell, vultures—and roses.

There was nothing in the description of Poona that tempted me to go there, nor did I intend any excursions southward, considering all of interest I had to visit in the north before the heats invaded the plains. But I had made up my mind to see the cave at Karli, which Fergusson calls the finest of its class, and his illustration of which is most attractive. The proper station for this visit is Khandalla, about seventy-eight miles from Bombay, and not the next Lonauli, unless you mean to make a scampering return day of the journey, eating something at the refreshment room.

My fellow-passenger from England, Mr. Ford, was already there, to whom I telegraphed, and who met me at the station. The hotel was very comfortable, and the scenery remarkably picturesque. I slept, or meant to do so, in one of the small houses, but was awoke at about two o'clock in the morning by two arrivals in the opposite room, who appeared never intending to lie down in silence. At last I opened my door to expostulate, when, with a thousand apologies, they informed me that in fact they were not going to bed at all, but were re-costuming for a tiger-hunt—one of those animals having lately appeared on the neighbouring hills. The result was not satisfactory, for they returned without the tiger, having seen only the bright eye of a panther, lying inside a rock. But the effect on me was that I was kept talking to them until, when they had gone, it was time for me to think of going too—but not for a tiger. I was in the tonga by half-past five, with five miles along the Poona Road, lined with mango trees ; then we crossed a rough plain to the left for a good mile, whence I had to take foot for another good mile ; and then began the climb. Whatever the height was, it seemed to me something like 600 feet, and then you turn into certain recesses of the variously shaped mountain—the top being yet much higher—before you come in full view of the fine arched cave. Into this you look direct, with the slight interference of a screen and entrance. The interior consists of one entire arched nave, given as of 81 feet 3 inches in length to the dagoba, and of 25 feet 7 inches in breadth ; and it is flanked by fifteen handsome pillars on either side, with a narrow aisle behind them. The height is of 46 feet to the crown of the uniform arch, which is composed of curved beams. The light comes in copiously from the open front, and you see the whole interior at once. Great solemnity pervades the scene; and round the cold massive circular dagoba at the end there happened to be, while I was there, a living illustration of the dark superstition that is the spirit of these structures—of these, among so many others in all quarters of the globe—in that a solitary being was walking and kneeling by turns round and round, and counting his beads—for Buddhists have rosaries too—and muttering his special prayers, with all the attitudes of intense devotion and ardent expectation.

I hung about the place for some long time, and can even now somewhat vividly recall the tone of mind that it gave rise to. These dark Buddhists' temples impress one far more than do the mosques of Islam. And behold! my visit was on a Sunday. On the Monday I spent the whole day with pleasure at Khandalla, and on Tuesday, the 5th of February, returned by early train, with Mr. Ford, to Bombay. Hence, he and General Johnston scampered off to England at once, leaving me to begin and pursue my long course to the north.

On Thursday, the 7th of February, I had the honour of dining with a large party at Government House, where the whole scene with the turbaned waiters presented quite a brilliant Indian picture; and it was in a long evening conversation afterwards with Lady Reay that I obtained my valuable letters to Kattiawar, with much information on the subject. Nor shall I omit to say that her ladyship did me the honour to accept of me a copy of my translation of the "Lusiads." I was also fortified with several letters from Parsee B. M. Malabari; and by the 6.30 p.m.,

Madras time, on Saturday, the 9th of February, I started for my 310 miles to Ahmedabad, which Lady Reay had earnestly recommended me not to miss, by the Bombay, Baroda, and Central India Railway. I must not forget, by the way, that the day before Mr. Behrens, one of the tiger-hunters, suddenly appeared in perfect safety, and pledged me to dine with him at the Byculla. He had been out again and seen the tiger, and nearly got a shot at him ; but a companion spoiled the sport. That the tiger was really there was true ; for a few days afterwards the newspapers reported that it had been hunted and shot by a young officer.

VIII.

It was about eight o'clock on the next morning that I reached the station at Ahmedabad, where I made up my bed, feeding at the meals provided for the passengers; for this was a refreshment station. And after breakfast I drove into the beautiful old city. There was little indeed of Kylas or of Karli to be seen here, for all is Islam. The whole feeling was changed, just as might two languages mark two different peoples.

It is a most engaging old city, extremely picturesque in its old architecture; and in almost all the old houses you may remark quantities of beautiful wood and stone carving by way of ornament. Then note the noble triple gateway that spans the very broad main street, and all the costumed people scattered, marketing or otherwise, over the broad space. When I passed this spot at the setting of the sun, I bid the driver go very slowly that I might dwell on the living kaleidoscope. The structure I mention is imposing; the height of the arches is 25 feet, the centre gate 20 feet wide, and that of each side gate 17 feet wide; and the whole structure towers upwards in proportion. Of course there are all the well-known mosques and tombs to be visited, and the well. There is the famous specimen of stone window tracery in the desecrated mosque in the bhudder, or palace; there is the tomb of Shah Alam, and the Jumma Musjie, or Friday mosque, Friday being the Holy Day of Islam. This is indeed a beautiful building, with all its 260 pillars and its fifteen domes; but is connected in my mind with a great disappointment, seeing that Fergusson compares it with the temple near Sadri, which I had the greatest but ineffectual curiosity to see. At page 241 appears the illustration and his tantalizing description both of the building, with its "forest of columns" and "endless variety of prospective," and the "play of light and shade." But do what I could, and say what I could, no one could give me the slightest information of how I was to find "the remote valley piercing the western flank of the 'Aravulli,' being a spot evidently selected for its natural beauties," which Khumbo Rana of Oudeypore chose for rearing this charming structure. Only when I had reached Jeypur, still inquiring, did I by the merest chance find someone who could give me an inkling of the place; and acting on this I at length made the discovery, too late (and which I can only give to others inspired by the like curiosity with myself), that the station to stop at is Falna, on the Bombay and Baroda line, far away from where I was when at last I was informed. But there is no waiting-room, and only somewhat rough arrangements can be made for a sixteen mile ride to Sadri, whence a short excursion serves to show the temple. I invite nobody to go, but would have contrived to go myself.

It would not be permissible, however, to leave Ahmedabad without visiting the Temple of Thet

Huttising outside the Delhi gate. This is a Jain temple, and the Jains, or followers of Jina, a sort of dissenter from true Buddhism, are the most elaborate and picturesque of the architects in India. The elaboration of this temple is most extraordinary. Here, as elsewhere, the porch is truly beautiful, and indeed magnificent in its compound structure, full of perspective with its pillars, and leading to an inner porch with twenty-two pillars. The drawing in Fergusson gives an idea of the almost overladen building, but does not show the outer porch. I wandered all round the outside, and failed to see even a small blank about it anywhere, and of course the inside corresponds. Figures of Buddha are in the niches round the corridors, and in the middle is a large black one, before which my guide hummed a low, melancholy religious cadence. Into the cell, however, their "Holy of Holies," you are not admitted. There is a grand Buddha—no mere invisible supposed occupant: and all is dedicated to Dharmanath, the 15th Thirthanker, or (as I was told) Holy Pilgrim. But strange to say, a certain charm is wanting, from the mere fact that the building is not old, not yet quite half a century having elapsed since it was finished. Say what we will, we love the mystery of antiquity, and hate hard modern outline. Green parrots and doves were hovering round the roofing. So ended my visit to Ahmedabad, to which no passer-by should fail to pay his reverence.

Now came the time for my special divergence into the Kattiwar or Kattiawar Peninsula, for which I held passports from Lady Reay, and my anxiety to visit which had been awakened by Fergusson's illustrations and descriptions. The journey involved an extra distance of 230 miles to the utmost point, and the same back again, because I should be obliged to return to Ahmedabad in order to continue my main course northwards. But when one has started, with no tie on his time but the change into the hot from the cool season—a matter of mortal importance, by-the-way, in India—a few hundred miles more or less are not much thought of. And railways have, moreover, made such a difference within the space of so few years. I am old enough to remember our grand old coaching days: ten miles (or now and then a little more) an hour, including changes and meals; and in the cold weather, however warmly clad, the getting off without much knowledge of having either toes and fingers; compared with all which the comforts and rapidity of movement now have robbed almost all travelling of enterprise. I was lately carelessly looking through that ever-entertaining volume, "Sketches by Boz," and came upon the one entitled "Early Coaches." Look at the illustration by our immortal Cruickshank: it is a reality; and Dickens' pages are equally alive. The unfeeling indifference of the clerks and porters to the traveller's agony; they are as "cool and collected," he says, "as if nobody was going out of town, or as if a journey of *a hundred odd miles* were a mere nothing." We have almost come to think a journey of ten times that distance "a mere nothing;" and assuredly, with all the present facilities at command, at ten times told, we can scarcely hold ourselves so hardy as those of even sixty or seventy years ago. In the last century mere home travellers were almost explorers.

If you look at page 227 of Fergusson, you will find his illustration of Palitana; or rather of The Sacred Hill of Sutrunjya, near Palitana—that first word (rightly or wrongly spelt according to diverse authorities) signifying "The Conqueror of Enemies." This illustration is very striking, but gives no real representation of the scene itself. Indeed, no illustration could, for the configuration forbids it. I started from Ahmedabad at 8.10 a.m., and reached Bhaunagur by 5.12 p.m., where I was most pleasantly received with my letter by the Government officer, Mr. Proctor Sims and Mrs. Sims, and directed to the bungalow for a bed. On returning to dine and spend a pleasant evening there, I had the honour of an introduction to the Maharajah of Bhaunagur—a most genial gentleman—who was on a short visit of friendly ceremony at the moment of my arrival, and whom I had the advantage of seeing in all that glorious style of costume that I was so disappointed at not seeing at Lord Dufferin's final garden party. In coming to Bhaunagur, however, I found I had come too far for my ultimate journey; I should have left the train, on that one consideration, at Songad, the second station from Dhola Junction; but happy was I to be where I was.

My next letter was to Captain Ferris, the Assistant Political Agent, whose station was this same Songad; and in the morning of the 12th of February I breakfasted with Mr. and Mrs. Proctor Sims, and he drove me to the station. At Songad I found Captain Ferris, to whom Mr. Proctor Sims had already telegraphed, who took me home and introduced me to Mrs. Ferris; and after finishing his court, where I sat by his side, an entertained observer, furnished me with a carriage half way to Palitana, where I was met by that of the Takhore of the district. But I must not fail to mention that, at the moment of leaving my bungalow, there appeared two stalwart Eastern figures, with a huge tray of fruit and flowers as a present from his Excellency the Maharajah.

The evening found me at the Takhore's Guest House; a fine spacious dwelling, rather grandly built; and here I was fed and housed. Then there came the arrangements for my visit to the Sacred Hill the next morning, for which I found all was in readiness. Coffee and I were to be ready at half-past five, and so we were. A short drive took me to the foot of the hill, and there I met my bearers with a doli, or square open seat between two poles, four being the number to carry me, with a relay. We mounted some 1700 feet in all. And what a mount! Long winding lines of mounting pilgrims were making the ascent with us. The Sacred Hill is somewhat lonely on the plain, so that everything stood out intensely; males and females, grown people and children, all were going to kneel and pray, and to seek salvation from threatening vengeance, as in all religions, except perhaps the pure Buddhist, who "utterly rejects the belief in a personal god."

At last we are among the temples, the City of Temples; but really only the first of the Cities of Temples: and of Temples only. The mountains belong to the gods; the cities belong to the gods. No human habitations are allowed; none must cook food, possibly not eat, within the walls; none are dwellers save a few necessary priests, and the sacred pigeons; all else are pilgrims for the day. The temples are of all sizes, all dates, and in all styles of details. You walk through streets of them. Grain is offered, which dogs, of course, lick up. Prayers are said everywhere, and figures of Buddha appear everywhere. In short, to use an admirable phrase of Fergusson, you are surrounded (unless you are a mere tasteless scoffer) with "bewildering magnificence." But what I have written applies to the first city alone. Look down, with a bird's-eye view upon that vast group, a mere flight of steps below you. Those temples are built upon a neck that joins the two heads of the mountain. Revel in these, and then mount up to that twin crest to find just such another city of temples as the one you first wandered in. Such is a visit to Palitana Mountain with all its thousand structures (speaking indefinitely), which, according to Fergusson, date downward from the 11th century; and, for aught I know, are being added to at this present hour. All is Jain architecture, with whom the building of temples is a means of salvation; it is in itself "a prayer in stone," having reference to pilgrimage and not to congregations.

Perfectly satiated at last, I returned to bath and

breakfast, meeting as many coming up now as I had accompanied before. While at the table I was visited by a Mr. Dias, the Takhore's lawyer and manager, to notify that his Highness would receive me at three o'clock.

No interview could have been more cheerful and agreeable. His Highness spoke English remarkably well, and when at last I rose to go, he struck a small bell, at the sound of which there appeared a small group of servants carrying small salvers of special seed and sweetmeats, of which I was to "partake;" and finally his Highness took a small brush and sprinkled me over with an infinitesimal shower of an intensely fragrant water, the redolence of which threatened to last almost as long as does the memory of his good-fellowship and kindness. Afterwards I visited his stables, containing some 120 horses, some of a showy breed, and all stalled (as I found was usual throughout India) by being rope-hobbled on the hind fetlocks. At five o'clock I took my leave for Songad, returning as I had come; and having dined and spent a very pleasant evening with Captain and Mrs. Ferris, I passed a night of luxury in their luxurious tent.

But before I leave this recollection of their hospitality I must, if only for my own satisfaction, recount a small item of conversation. "Your name is Ferris," I said; "a neighbouring clergyman of my father's acquaintance was of the name of Ferrers, the Rector of Beddington, but I remember a somewhat stately lady of your own name who used to visit two venerable aunts of mine at Banstead: she came out of

Sussex." "That," said he, "was my grandmother, the widow of the Dean of Battle." And this in Gujerat!

I was now to prepare for Girnar Mountain, and by my notes I find that I left Songad station, on the 25th of February, at 2.29 by Dhola and Jetalsar Junctions for Junagadh, and covered these ninety-six miles by 9.30 p.m. I had telegraphed to the Dewar Sahib Haridas Viharidas, for whom I had a letter from Government House, but he was absent. I was, however, met at the station by Secretary Rajosali Chhaganlál Harilal Pandya, who conveyed me in a carriage to the bungalow of his Highness the Nawab Sahib of Junagadh, where I was his guest, including a welcome glass of champagne after my day's journey.

At 8.30 on the following morning, my friend and protector (who spoke excellent English) again appeared with a carriage to take me a drive round, the excursion to Girnar being fixed for the morrow. We first drove to some most extraordinary underground courts or halls, which had been discovered and dug out some twenty years before; the uses to which they were applied remaining a mystery. They are double-storied and lighted well from above, and have been carved out with care, the pillars and capitals being well worthy of attention in this respect. It is supposed they may have served for governmental purposes. This mystery overhanging them of course lends them a special charm, as mystery always does if there is any trace of imagination in the brain; because it gives rise to speculation, and speculation, whether fruitless in airy nothings, or ruinous at the gaming table, is always alluring. There was, however, very little room for speculation as to what I was next shown, the by far most enormous rhinoceros that I had ever seen. Next after this alarming, and almost impossible, animal, came the large unsightly boulder, incised all over, and irregularly so—the Asóka Stone, said to exhibit Edicts of Asóka, some 270 years B.C.; and then came a walk in the zoological gardens, where, among various engaging flowering shrubs and plants, showing that the more graceful pursuits and studies are cherished here, we came upon a centre enclosure of rock and water containing crocodiles. Boys were at hand, as usual, for a few coppers, with stones to disturb these basking reptiles, and make them move and show themselves. And nothing could be more frightful than to see their wide angry jaws, quite close by, as they opened their tongueless mouths and showed their frightful armoury of jagged teeth, as they dived into the water. "Did it ever strike you," said the Pandya, "to ask yourself, How could the Deity create such hideous things?" "But," said I, "they are not hideous to themselves, and there must be love even among crocodiles. Besides which, the Deity made house flies."

The next visit was the most curious of all; it was to a Vishna temple, called the Swami Nárâyan Temple. My friend belonged to this temple, so that we went in freely. Many were present, and a most curious proceeding was going forward. The gods were being fed. All we saw of this proceeding were two curtains drawn across two square recesses, each flanking the centre arrangements. But by-and-by these curtains were withdrawn suddenly, the tomtoms were loudly beaten, and lamps were flounced in the faces of two black squatting figures with bulging cheeks, indicative of good feeding indeed. Why laugh? or why pitifully sigh? Asia, in her different countries, has her own interpreted gods, and Europe has the same, and the question might not unreasonably be asked, Will either of these two quarters ever change the beliefs of the other? Is Europe more likely to change Asia than Asia to change Europe?

Afterwards the Pandya sent me two copies of a description, written by himself, of the mythological pictures in the dome of the temple, containing a succinct account of the prominent features of some of their Holy Incarnations, of which they have several.

The next day, Sunday, the 17th, was appointed for the Jain Temples on Girnar Mountain, these being the great object of my visit here; and we started in the carriage for the foot of the mountain, at half-past six in the morning. Less than an hour's drive brought us there. Here, again, I mounted a doli, and the Pandya kindly allowed his assistant, Ramji Bhimji, to attend me. We soon began to ascend, and an ascent indeed it was. The main group, some sixteen in number, are built some 600 feet below the highest peak of this most irregular and jagged mountain, but they are still some 3000 feet above the level of the sea. What might be the height of the plain, which is very far below, I do not know. It cannot be much. We were above two hours climbing to the chief temples. A long paved way conducts you at first, but afterwards you ascend by sharp zigzags of a craggy pathway (so to call it), consisting of steps cut in the rock. The doli often grazes the sides, in a manner that might serve to shake the nerves of certain travellers, particularly in the descent. Even beyond where you go there are temples built, where a long backbone leads to the highest crag. There one solitary structure stares against the sky. Here, indeed, you may well understand that the Jains did not build for congregational purposes. I was now and then reminded of my first climb up the Gemmi, in Switzerland, so long ago as 1846. Stupendous is the whole mass of the mountain compared with that at Palitana; but barren indeed in comparison is the grouping of the temples. In truth, there is no room here for those cities of shrines. But there is verily enough to see, and of quite a different character. In the great group there are carved and decorated cupolas, with the usual pendents. There is the Temple of the god Neminatha. The three temples, opening into one another, of the two brothers Tejpala and Vastupala; the palace of King Rachengár and Queen Ranek Devi, now converted into a temple. But you must not stop here in climbing, you must mount to a yet higher peak, say the height of Snowdon, to the temple of what was given me as of Anmbar. From this spot survey the various craggy peaks around you, and their dotted temples. You may, in fact, climb and crawl from one distant spot to the other, almost all day long. The view below of course is vast. It has been called "truly magnificent." The mountain and its peaks and crags, indeed, stand up, but stand alone, for the vast view beyond is as flat as a frying-pan, and about as brown. This is no magnificent view for me. In descending, after all is visited, you might perhaps feel timid, and should you incline to indulge in a little safe mental terror, mark out that harsh, hideous integral rock called Bherav, to your ascending left; for from this pilgrims of old cast themselves headlong down, in order to gain vast rewards in some other world. Going or coming, you will not find yourself the only pilgrim, though perhaps the only irreligious one among the number, as they themselves would be at Lourdes; the crags you would ever find sprinkled with them.

At noon I began my descent, and at the foot found the Pandya already there to meet me with the carriage. I was disappointed in not being presented to the Nawáb Sáhib Bahádurkhánjee, but he was in mourning and sent word to say he could not see me. Through the Pandya, however, he presented me with a book containing his portrait, and in the course of the afternoon, his Excellency, for many years Prime Minister, Báhavdinbhái, his Highness's maternal uncle, drove over to see me; a fine spangled, broad-headed, and cheerful countenanced man, who maintained a lively conversation of some quarter of an hour through his interpreter.

Thus ended my visit to Gujerat, to see Palitana and Girnár, both of which seem to stand before me once again while I am writing of them, and before 4 a.m. on the 18th I was getting ready for the 5.16 train to return to Ahmedadad.

Strangely different were two scenes I witnessed in the train, being transferred once or twice at the different junctions. On starting, I was confidentially called aside to have a caution given me. "There is a high-caste Brahmin in your carriage there: pray take care not to touch him, for if you do, he will have to wash seven times." When I got in, there sat my turbaned friend, legs carefully swaddled up along the bench on his side; so that I must have made an effort to touch even a corner of him; and he took no notice of my entrance whatsoever. Presently a harsh cry escaped his mouth, and brought a servant, whom he ordered like a dog to bring water; and this the other of course most humbly did. When I left him, quite intact, I had to mount another carriage, full of laughing and talking turbans and costumes; and one remarkably jovial-looking fellow was wearing a solid gold band round his neck. Scarcely had we moved on but scented tea was offered me, and an English-speaking companion told me I was expected to join in all, and that this was the Private Secretary to the Maharajah of Bhaunagar—whom I had met at Mr. Proctor Sims'. I kept pace with them as well as I could for as far as they travelled with me, and arrived at Ahmedabad at last, both musing and amused.

The rest of the day and the next I again spent at and about Ahmedabad, and prepared for my further progress north, Mount Abû being my next halting place; for here I was again to visit architecture by the Jains, before passing further into the regions of Islam, through Jeypur, to Agra and Delhi.

IX.

GREAT was my surprise and disappointment on starting, to find that hence all the way to Delhi the great main line from Bombay had changed at Ahmedabad into a narrow-metre gauge. It is impossible, of course, for a mere chance traveller to criticize this mal-arrangement, because it is impossible for him to know what tyrannical circumstances may have existed at the time of construction to force this terrible defect; but he is quite at liberty to express his infinite surprise and disappointment, and indeed personal disgust. However, at 8.30 p.m. on the 20th I entered my narrow jolting carriage, and having at about 3 p.m. accomplished our 115 miles, I found myself at the Abu Road Station. I had already telegraphed for horses, and found all ready; and a ride of about a mile along the flat brought me and my servant, with light luggage, to the bungalow. The food in this case was superior to an impossible chicken, and the keeper was not a shrivelled old man; but there was no bedstead whatever, and I spread my coverings upon a cane sofa. At early morning I mounted horse, and we rode some rather tedious distance, still along the flat, but now and then between trees, and always with the wooded mountain close before us. The moment we began to mount, the gorges became extremely picturesque, and forest surrounded us.

These solitudes as usual were illustrated by a number of large curly-tailed monkeys, who peered out of the branches, snatching close looks at us, and then scampering back into their hidings. It soon became quite evident that the temples I was about to visit had been built on a very romantic site indeed, and it was not till I had mounted 4000 feet through the very undulating forest, with its flowering trees, and covered a distance of some fourteen miles, that I reached the Rajputana Hotel. This hotel was kept by Sr. Costa of Goa, a Portuguese, of course, to whom and whose hotel I can offer my best acknowledgments, and with whom it was a certain pleasure to indulge in his language, as I used to do in days gone by. The scenery was rather brown, but charming: in the green season it must be more so, but curiously enough, and unhappily, the district is then malarious. The hotel is small, but comfortable, and mothers and wives of officers, with their children, come up to stay from time to time.

Very soon after my arrival two other travellers followed me, and we all three went together to visit the two temples. Outside they are nothing, but inside they are everything. Anything more beautiful—anything so beautiful, I could say—I have never seen. They are called the Delwarra Temples, and Fergusson says that the more modern of the two was built by the same two brothers, Tijpala and Vastupala, who built the Triple Temple which I had noticed at Girnar. All hail to them! The two interior courts are parallelograms—one measurement may serve for both in general description: 140 feet

INTERIOR OF DELWARA TEMPLE : MOUNT ABU

by 90. This is surrounded by a double peristyle. In the middle is the cell, and in front of this cell is a porch—a real Jain porch—which baffles all photographing and description in its cupolas and complicated perspective beauties. All is of the purest, and quite spotless white marble, brought from some great distance, and all is elaborately ornamented; indeed, to so minute an extent that you have almost to look again to believe it. Before recurring to the porch let me add that these double peristyles form porticoes to a range of cells, fifty-five in number, and in each of these is a figure of the Thirthanker, or Pilgrim Saint, to whom the temple is dedicated—Parswanatha. At the end of this court is an inner gallery, and in this gallery there are carved twelve perfect elephants in white marble and of nearly life-size.

To return to the porch: it is composed of forty-eight integral pillars, all most elaborately carved, and these support a dome and pendant, which must be seen, and seen often, to be at all comprehended. My companions were not less rapt than I. A drawing in Fergusson's volume exhibits only some faint show of the reality, and a photograph in my possession exhibits some little more. I had resolved to return and reinspect all this on the following day, of which my companions, however, had no intention. But when the to-morrow came, I really felt that the brain had not yet had time to digest all that I had seen the day before. I may seem to exaggerate when I say it required a longer interval than twenty-four hours between two repasts of such wonder and beauty, and to my great regret I had to come away without the satisfaction of a second visit, and to content myself with another chaff with the monkeys. Both in art and nature Mount Abu remains a leading memory amidst all I saw in my three years' wanderings; nor can I speak of nature without recalling a sunset visit to the little Nucki Jalas, or Pearl Lake, close by, a circular gem of blue water in a perfectly harmonious setting of surrounding mountains.

On the morning therefore of Friday, the 22nd of February, I rode down the mountain, witnessing some grand atmospheric effects in the early light; hailed by many monkeys, and longing to see just one tiger in the safe distance lounging through the forest: a rare occurrence here.

The mail train for Ajmir did not leave till the afternoon, and the run of 190 miles took me nearly eleven hours; so that it was not till after two in the morning that I found myself at Mrs. Rice's Rajputana Hotel. There I found actually tender cold roast beef, and beer, and bed. I came full of complaints of my night's journey; for though the Sojat Road Station had an asterisk as a refreshment-room, not even tea was ready, and on my asking for a biscuit I was offered a whole new tin for purchase. I saw there was a certain secret amusement mingled with Mrs. Rice's sympathy, which I next day learned was provoked by the fact that the stout individual by her side, her brother-in-law (as she afterwards told me), to whom I was complaining, was the very contractor for the station. Two features, I will here observe, struck me in this Indian railway travelling. The general tea and feeding stations are very poor, and in coming into stations, beside that the running is very moderate, no brakes are used, but the train is allowed to "slow" in. This may be economical, but it is very tantalizing. As to the non-eating and drinking, I daresay it has grown to be better, as was talked of when I was in India. But whether at stations or hotels, people seem to me to have become demoralized into swallowing tough meat without knowing it. One worthy gentleman, a traveller too, went so far as to say that he had met with refreshment rooms better than any at home. He must have been dreaming, surely, of some summer's picnic on the peaks of Kanchinjunga. One other striking feature that I noted all through my railway travelling was the multitudinous rush of native third-class passengers. One cannot but wonder what they all have to do here, indeed, among a race that easily lets time and life go by. On a fine night, too, you will find them lying asleep in scores outside the entrance, waiting for the very first morning train. Now, if railways have made them alert among themselves in all things, what a moralizer is the Indian locomotive! With us, he has surely made us restless, and when any given epidemic sweeps off such numbers of us, as has lately proved to be the case, is not this a result of nerves insensibly shaken by an almost perpetual rush and hurry through existence? The atoms of wrought iron, they say, are brought down to those of the cast metal by perpetual jarring. May not something of a similar character occur in the jarred human frame?

I remained in Ajmir till the 1st of March, visiting

more than once the Great Mosque and its majestic gateway, where "the Cufic and Togra inscriptions are interwoven with the more purely architectural decorations," the effect of this being singularly successful. As you stand in the court to gaze on it, however, you might feel well content that the large tree was out of the way. The mosque itself is a wonderfully well pillared mosque, and this again is due to the Jains, for it is one of their converted (or perverted) temples: in the language of the iconoclastic intruders the heathen or pagan (i.e. clownish) shrine was redeemed (that is, stolen) for the Faithful. In such cases the course pursued seems to be to destroy the centre cell and adapt the court of peristyle. But nothing I saw in India did I feel could for a moment compare with the interiors of the temples at Abu. Ajmir lies in a perfectly flat valley, surrounded by abrupt russet mountains; and there are several very pleasant drives in the immediate neighbourhood. You may go through the gardens to the lake, which I did twice. Here the view is charming, with a chateau in the centre of the farthest well-wooded shore. Again, the views on the Jeypur road are striking, with fine tamarind trees. Again, along the Pushgar road the scene is striking, and the Mayo College and grounds should be visited. I was detained at Ajmir waiting for information as to getting to Oudeypore, but what I received forced me to abandon that desire. So I left my pleasant hostess and hotel, inscribing these few lines in her Book of Visitors:—

This earthly shrine,
Though not divine,

May claim of travelling you'h and age.
An oft-repeated pilgrimage;
Where needs we all in common share
Are furnished in response to prayer;
The reason is not far to tell,—
An English hostess consecrates the Cell.

It required between six and seven hours on this narrow-gauge train to bring me over a distance of seventy-four miles to Jeypur, where I arrived at seven o'clock in the evening of the 1st of March, to find a bungalow under a plantation of trees, with good rooms but extremely bad food. To add to this disappointment—a great one to a traveller—I suffered want of rest from a constant barking and howling of Pariah dogs all night long. This is a frequent nuisance in India. Yet do not pay a man to drive them away, for this only means that he barks instead of the dogs.

But then came a real disappointment indeed. I found the Maharajah, with all his retinue, was absent, paying a visit to the Viceroy at Calcutta. And this really was a disappointment, for Mr. B. M. Malabari, my Parsee friend at Bombay, had given me a letter to his Highness's private secretary, and I had hoped for an interview, as at Palitana, and to be sprinkled with nectar at parting, by another Jove. As it was, I really did not care to get an order for going over a dreary empty palace, but wandered, moody, in the gardens, and saw and heard the tigers. These were grand animals truly; and it was the first time I really heard tigers roar, a very far finer voice than that of the lion, when he indulges in that vocal note of defiance, if so it is intended. With these tigers it was doubtless so, and fearful; for the attendant was provoking their fine open mouths all together. Rage among these noble beasts is real beauty; in certain other animals it cannot so be called.

The modern city of Jeypur I found remarkable for its flat, wide, and straight streets, and for the particularly native aspect of all the living objects that moved about in them, including elephants and camels. Two processions particularly attracted my attention. The one was that connected with infant marriage. The little bridegroom, I suppose about six or seven years old, in his open palanquin, gorgeously dressed, and correspondingly attended, was being carried to and fro into various streets on a visit (as I was informed) to relations and friends, notifying the event of his engagement, and as he thus had to make many turnings, I met with him more than once.

The other was most peculiar. It was a very long procession, including, if I remember rightly, camels, elephants, and horses, of a certain number, and in the middle there came a very curious-looking object: a sort of carriage completely covered over with a tent-shaped, tight sheet, tapering to the top, and resembling, on a large scale, those matted baskets in which nurserymen pack pots of flowers, or small sucklings, for the railway. "What on earth is that?" "It is the wife of the Maharajah, taking an airing." Thus was the imperious cloking up explained, for vulgar eyes were not to peer within. Whether the "airing" object was truthfully explained I know not; her Highness might have been on a visit only. At the same time my recollection carried me back to the system of quiet old ladies taking their "airing" many years ago (say at Brighton) in yellow chariots, with the windows well up, and the glasses well steamed; not for the pure and modest purpose of concealment, but in order to avoid the "air" which they had expressly come out to take.

The chief excursion from the flat modern capital is to Amber, the very hilly ancient one. And at early morning, on the 3rd of March, I started with one Phillips, a guide, to visit the abandoned seat of greatness, nor could I help noticing the very numerous flocks of the small Indian crow that continually accompanied us, in their apparently first morning flight, employed, like so many human beings are, in providing for the food of the day. As we approached Amber I noticed temples, or dwellings, one after another, on the left side of the road, all neglected—though still well planted by the hand of nature—melancholy examples, these, of desertion—all empty, all silent—their "own sad sepulchres." At length we came to a large gateway, and a large elephant reclining. Here you must begin the ascent, and it must be upon the elephant, and therefore on his Majesty I mounted. It was the first time I had ever ridden an elephant, and I shall not sigh if it be the last.

No greater contrast could be found between an old

and a new capital than appears between Amber and Jeypur. The flatness of the ground of the new city I have already mentioned : the old city is almost in a gorge : and observe, as a striking feature, the wall of this old city which you catch sight of at once—clambering the abrupt eminences and dipping into the abrupt hollows, in infant imitation of the great wall of China. The shattered palace is founded on a rock and seems to grow out of it, and the fort stands high above it. Below is a large lake, and in early morning the reflection on the water creates an imposing picture. Among the masses of former pride you may wander at leisure, and enjoy the various prospects that present themselves from various points of view, and after all this you may easily return by noon. I was not to escape, however, without an elephantine photograph, against which I much protested, and the fruits of which, probably unsuccessful on account of that indisposition on my part, I declined, on payment of a small outlay as previously agreed. But anyone may have his portrait taken on an elephant, if he likes to go as far as Amber and bespeak it.

My afternoon was spent at Jepyur in visiting the museum and the school of art and pottery ; and luckily not buying. And then came my afternoon's drive and amusement in joining the Natives in feeding the kites. This bird is sacred at Jeypur, and abounds in hundreds. The kites assemble on the house-tops about five o'clock in the afternoon, which is the general hour of their entertainment, as it is of hundreds in the city.

A small baked ball or pellet of something, the name of which I forget, is sold in very cheap abundance at a score of stores, and these the birds are very fond of. There is more diversion here than in feeding the pigeons of St. Mark's, and there is, moreover, religion in the fun. Indeed, any naturalist might be scientifically entertained by the sight. There are most diverting contests on the ground, exhibiting immense activity of wing and movement; there are contests, and more graceful contests in the air, before the well-thrown ball has time to come down; sometimes there are no contests, but a swooping pair of wings catch the moving atom without an instant's pause or deviation in so doing, and sail with it triumphantly away. The power and activity of the wing are, as I say, wonderfully displayed indeed, and I could not hold the entertainment as merely childish. If serious faces think it so, then there is Dryden's line to save us:—

"Men are but children of a larger growth."

A poet's truth, however, is too often sentimentally quoted and acknowledged with a sigh; but the individual application of it is never so much as thought of. Never care: if either of you go to Jeypur you will be found feeding the kites.

When I was leaving the bungalow the keeper was very anxious that I should report well of the food. The secret was that he held it of the Maharajah, who was understood to be very strict on the subject of the good treatment of guests. I was informed that this man made out his own bills to his landlord, and squeezed the travellers. Certain it is that in consequence of my most decided protests the food was suddenly and wonderfully changed, while the tariff remained the same. This was a plea by confession, and I was induced to enter "good" without marking the date, though two patient travellers had thanked me for the alteration of affairs.

I see by Murray's Guide of 1891 that there is now an "excellent" hotel, but I mention the state of affairs as I found it, because it very much exemplifies a feature in travelling through India. The whole mass of the inhabitants live in a totally different manner from Europeans; Americans of course included. You seem to move about in narrow tracks. You really have not the least affinity with your surroundings. Their ways and thoughts and entire modes of life are as different as their language or costume, and of affinity there can be none. You are always an outsider—not from mere counter feelings, but as belonging to totally different races, and coming from a totally different part of the globe. This sense of isolation—not by any means necessarily inimical—grows upon you at every step. Even though you know that you belong to the Ruling Power, you are—as all your conventionally known peoples are—"a stranger in the land," an absolutely incongruous atom, a winding rivulet running between banks, through a vast indifferent expanse. As travelling increases food and rest will of course gain ground, but as I found things then, I do not hesitate to say that travelling in India was often very trying.

X.

I WAS now to leave for Agra Fort, and the moment you see this name, your thoughts will spring to what we call—for shortness as usual—the Taj ; and, in response, perhaps I ought to make a wide search to see what so many others have written about it, and then try to write something yet more striking. But I am not going to do anything of the kind. I am quietly going to speak for myself.

I left Jeypur by the 7.27 p.m. mixed train, on Monday, the 4th of March, and we arrived at Agra Fort about 8 a.m. on the Tuesday, the distance being 145 miles. And as we rolled into the station I caught the first sight of the domes and minarets of the far-famed building, which from that point presented only a sort of confusion of milk-white excrescences. This appearance I called to mind afterwards. It was not the first object of my curiosity on leaving Lawrie's Hotel, for I had letters to two Pandits whom I wished to see at starting, and this led me towards the Fort, which I took the immediate opportunity of visiting, and descriptions of all the remarkable buildings in which are in every guide book. Here, of course, is the renowned white marble Moti Musjid, or Pearl Mosque, which occupies one end of a large oblong court, presenting its front in the shape of an open corridor of seven saracenic arches, in triple order. Through these it is very pleasing to wander. But I was impressed with a certain want of depth compared with the width, and though the symmetry of the building would not admit of a fourth inner row of seven, the centre row being constructed as central, the impression of shallowness seemed to be disappointing. While engaged in examining all the striking features in the Fort, I caught sight of a view of the Taj in the distance, which was not pleasing. The remarkable whiteness of the jumbled domes and minarets from that unfair distance was mixed up with the back of one of the red sandstone buildings that flank it on both sides, and of which I shall speak further on. The river Jumna rolled nobly below.

After the Fort I went at once to see the Taj. This word I found means crown, and the full title Taj Mahal can mean nothing else than Crown Palace. I was driven to the large, handsome red sandstone gate that forms the entrance to the garden, and, standing under it, I looked down the long walk with dark trees on either side, and beheld the delicate and exquisite building, now so familar grown in photographs and other representations. The effect of this picture is beyond dispute, and there can be nothing else that at all resembles it. In its ivory whiteness it scarcely even seems to have a perceptible outline. The mosque that I had seen at Aurungabad, too like it in a certain sense to leave a doubt in any ordinary observer's mind that it had been built in imitation, was yet not worthy of a second or third thought.

The afternoon in which I first saw the Taj was propitious, and fitted for the occasion, and the building, in all its toilet delicacy, looked (as I have hinted) as if it might have been made of ivory. It cannot be robbed of its undoubted peculiar attractiveness in these respects, but then these very features leave it quite naked of all the halo that surrounds old Indian tombs and temples in general. It is an adorned and draped-out beauty among the reverend aged: more for the showing of its own self than for awakening associations. After I had recovered from the first impression, two facts weighed much with me, in which I felt confirmed in after visits. In the first place, how necessary it is, in order to really see this building to perfection, to confine oneself to this one view of it from under the gateway; and secondly, how almost entirely it owes its extreme beauty to the very delicate material with which it is outwardly adorned, and to the very delicate manner in which that material has been put together. Had the Taj, as it stands, been composed of red sandstone, or even of white marble commonly put together, would it have attracted very special attention? And I think you have only to look at the engraving of the building, with all the hard outlines, in Fergusson's volume, to persuade yourself of this. Can anyone, looking at that engraving, call it an enchanting structure? The architectural formation is of the simplest. Fergusson himself correctly describes the form. It is "a square of 186 feet with the corners cut off to the extent of 33 feet 9 inches. It is surmounted by a large central dome and four campaniles," and that is the whole description needed to explain its form. It cannot compare in complicated details with other tombs, taking for example that of Akbar's Tomb, Secundra, close by. Nor is it left dependent only on its own intrinsic delicacy. "It would lose half its charm," writes Fergusson, "if it stood alone." But he does not quite define what he means. To my unauthoritative vision its beauty greatly depends on close contrasts. On walking down and looking round, I observed what made me feel quite convinced that the designer or designers had mainly intended to rely on texture, set off by contrast, for the general effect. There is a grouping on the spot. What is the meaning of these two flanking red sandstone structures, which intrude on you when you visit the spot itself? They are most evidently foils, in order to show off the exquisite delicacy of the now mausoleum to perfection. This object also seemed to me to be particularly carried out in the structure of the four handsome minarets that adorn the corners of the beautiful white marble platform, of eighteen feet in height, on which the Taj stands. For look attentively at the Taj. You have to do so attentively if you desire to detect the joinings; nay, there is even quite a toilet festooning run round the centre dome. Now, observe the minarets. Not only are the joinings visible, but to my own eye they are purposely and markedly emphasized, as in contrast. I found it impossible not to be struck with this antagonism, of which there is nothing in Fergusson's lines. Thus here, and altogether, it seemed to me that the main reliance of the architect was on material and refined workmanship. Of course proportion was held in view, and there is a certain indefinable sweetness in the whole form, as viewed from the gate, that may be attributable to this feature, as also the latent fact that the dome stands higher than the Kutub at Delhi. But what a pity it is, I could not help thinking, that the white marble trellis-work through which the subdued light is admitted to the interior is carved in squares. In the distance these bear the appearance of mere common casements.

Of the interior I have little to say: the light is of course subdued, as is the case in any other interior darkly lighted. The architecture cannot be remarkable from the form; the carvings and the jewels are mere adjuncts, and the echo is merely sharp and rapid because the space is confined. Yet here an American found them "float so deliciously" that he "heard them after they were silent." They who have been to Pisa know what vocal echoes are.

After a good walk round, admiring all the wonderful lacework detail on the surfaces, I mounted into one of the minarets. But if I were asked to commit myself to what I thought the exact spot on which to stand for the best view of the fantastically delicate structure, I should say, stand under the centre of the crown of the gateway, so as to make that a sort of framework, and so that the eye may just catch an almost insensible tinge of the red; then look down the dark avenue, again a foil, or artistic contrast, on the virgin white below. White, white, white—white it must be kept. As to the line of fountains and their ugly spouts, they are an ugly interruption.

There seems to be some little confusion about the

date of the building in reference to the death of Mumtaz-i-Mahl, for whose tomb the building is supposed to have been designed. But Fergusson and others treat it as originally intended, according to the custom of the Moghuls, for a "Bara Durri," or "Palace of Pleasure," during the life of the monarch, and for his tomb after death, so that it should thenceforth be sacred. Some suppose that after the designs were accepted, and the garden perhaps already marked out, the empress died, and that thereupon Shah Jehan consecrated it to her tomb at once, so that it was really never used, as would otherwise have been the case, as a "Bara Durri." What is certain is that when Muntaz-i-Mahl died she was no beautiful young woman, for she died in child-bed with her eighth offspring, in 1630. And read Dryden's drama. This sad catastrophe would appear to have crushed the first usual dedication of the building by interposing the last.

After this first inspection the next day I had a visit from my two Pandits. Pandit Peyaray Krishna came in the morning, and after a long and interesting conversation, very much in the tone of my friend at Benares, and after discussing many subjects on which I could not offer an opinion, he wound up with the more practical matter of recommending to me a most excellent coachman, with whom I agreed to go to Futtehpore Sikri, starting at seven o'clock the next morning. The afternoon I spent in visiting what might be called the very opposite of the Taj Mahal, and what I have already referred to—the complicated and elaborate red sandstone tomb of the mighty Akbar. It is impossible to wander over a structure of this magnitude and detail without some slight feeling of the ridiculous mingling with the marvellous, if it be admitted that such structures were meant only in the first place for retreat and recreation during life, but mainly for ever after to be consecrated to the funeral and repose of the departed founder. Life, as life, is entitled to its poor pleasures, unless there is a grievoüsly contradictory one elsewhere, equally proceeding from the same source, as interpreted by sour professors; but what can the mere dead want with such tombs as these? Is there not something ridiculous in the pyramids?

In the evening Pandit Jagan Nath favoured me with a call. Him I found far more restless and impatient than either of those with whom I had conversed. He lent me, for reading, an English pamphlet written by a lawyer in Madras, whose name I find I did not take, the literary style of which I cannot say I much admired, and the somewhat snarling dislike of Lord Dufferin which it evinced made me very much mistrust his motives. The Pandit spoke of himself, as I understood him, as being of the Congress Party, and I remember asking him what general combination and understanding could exist among them all, when they could not even sit down to their common food or modes of life together, but must all group themselves into separate knots, according to their castes. Of course he saw no difficulty in unity thus disunited, or united only for a while against something of supposed common grievance to them all, the disappearance of which might set them all wrangling one with another. But he was a very communicative man, and spoke sincerely of his discontent, and as he was suffering from want of proper spectacles, I immediately wrote to Mr. Adie to send him a pair, and these I trust he has received safely, and without erroneously suspecting any small latent allusion to his mental vision.

At six o'clock on the morning of the 7th of March the two-horse gárí came, and I had every reason to thank the Pandya for his recommendation. Starting at 7 a.m., I was driven splendidly both ways, with one change of horses, over the twenty-two miles. I entered the great abandoned city walls soon after nine o'clock, and, quite guiltless of any intention to insult the dead, I suddenly found myself in a large court, being landed at the Dâk Bungalow, which occupied nothing less than the Record Office of the mighty Moguls, and which I was about to defile by ordering an unbeliever's vulgar breakfast. If we are to indulge in mournful sentiment upon departed greatness,

> "And arts the splendid wrecks of former pride,"

how coarse all this present sort of proceeding seems.

The glory of Futtehpore Sikri, says Fergusson, is its mosque; and there is no difficulty in assenting to this. While breakfast was preparing, I went to view its great southern gateway. As it stands on rising ground and is approached by many steps, its vast height and volume seem something overpowering; but at the same time it is difficult to find any standing-place whence to obtain a really good view; and this defect a second gaze did not help me to remedy. This gateway certainly overpowers the mosque, but Mr. Keene says that it was built afterwards, not as belonging to the mosque, but as a triumphal arch. The mosque nevertheless is in itself difficult to surpass. But what a grand complicated mass of red sandstone buildings altogether is this Futtehpore Sikri. On returning from the mosque, and before sitting down, I wandered alone, fancying to lose myself among the long corridors and colonnades of the large group of buildings. And after breakfast again I wandered; and again I say, what an elaborate and varied mass of buildings it all is. How much forced labour was here employed, and how many lives sacrificed? Want of water caused its abandonment, and want of water had existed from the beginning. How strange, then, that this site should have been chosen. In a scene like this you are bewildered, and perhaps rather wish to be so. "Futtehpore Sikri," writes Fergusson, "is a romance in stone." If I should specially mark any one building it would be what is called The House of Birbal's Daughter, which seemed to me to combine, in a very singular manner, the cyclopean and the elegant. Once more then through those long red colonnades; and then back to Agra, passing many carts and waggons laden with red sandstone grindstones. It is, indeed, the material of the country.

As I was going to Gwalior on the following day, Pandit Jagan Nath very kindly called in the evening, and brought me a letter to his friend, the Chief Justice there, A. Srinivasa Row, B.A., which I found to be of infinite service, and at four o'clock on the afternoon of the 8th of March I left for Gwalior by the Itarsi line of the G.I.P., and arrived in four hours. But, before departing, I had spent the morning by the special invitation of the Pandit Peyaray Krishna; I had visited him, and gone over his new tan-yard with him. Here I was struck by his informing me that his fellow-religionists voted him an outsider, because, possessing the Janao, or Three Threads, he was going into trade. I may here remark that the tan-yard was close outside the precincts of the Taj Mahal; and that the same naked and confused look of the white domes and minarets that I have before remarked on, struck me here again.

On arriving at Gwalior I was driven to the large new and handsome bungalow built by the Maharajah for the convenience of travellers. But as it was totally unprotected by anything like a tree, all the upper rooms were ovens. Let anyone who telegraphs for a room, add "ground floor." Permission to see the Fort was readily given, and on the morning of the 9th of March I called on the Chief Justice, who received me with all courtesy, and ordered his carriage for me to drive round the town. This was a particularly interesting excursion, for the day was devoted as a religious holiday in honour of the God Shiva; and I scarcely think that one traveller out of a hundred ever saw him worshipped in the startling form I twice witnessed. To see the Fort I had again to mount an elephant, up and down, nor do I carry with me a memory of any very striking feature outside architectural curiosities, concerning which I am content to leave Mr. Fergusson uncontradicted. There are many things highly interesting to the artist which are "caviare to the general."

I regretted having been induced to visit the tomb of Mohammed Ghans, for it is in a most discoloured and neglected state, and did not arouse the slightest interest in me. Indeed, I think it is a great mistake to be making a point of gaping at everything. It spoils the eye and confuses the memory, and emanates from mere childish curiosity to see, and to be able to answer "Did you see?" It is sometimes a luxury to be able to say "No."

One curiosity this driver did incite in me: that of testing how bad horse, gárí, and driver could all be, and yet get on without falling all to pieces. It was worse than Calcutta, but it suited with the tomb.

On Sunday morning, March 10th, I took the early train to Agra, and on that evening I went to see the Taj by moonlight. The effect on the side was far greater than that on the front, for the angle of light did not fall propitiously upon the latter; and this, I suspect, has been the cause of mute disappointment in many cases. On the side the brightness was almost intense, and with the foil of the red sandstone structure, as I stood in its eye-protecting shadow, the Taj seemed almost like frosted silver.

XI.

At half-past ten on the night of the 11th I started for Delhi, and was uncomfortably delayed for more than an hour at the Tundla Station, about fifteen miles on the road. At last the train arrived, and being almost dead tired, I made for my first-class carriage, in all such of which I had hitherto managed to find myself alone, or nearly so. But in this case there was but one such carriage, and I found three in it already. Still they might have been three small or moderates, but they were three enormous ecclesiastics. Being French, I soon found out that the oldest was a bishop, and the two were of course priests. We were all very polite to one another, though we were rather crowded, which therefore made our politeness doubly laudable; and while refreshments were going on between them, though of something not exactly savoury, I lay along my seat undisturbed. But, when their own lying down came to pass, I confess my terrors were awakened. These carriages contain four beds at need. The two seats run sidewise and are adjustable; but in case of need (as in this case), two more above them can be let down on chains, thus making room for four; and that is the style throughout the railways. The bishop was the first a-bed, opposite to me; and, in spite of my secret prayer, by far the largest and heaviest of the two other divines cast his eyes upon the berth suspended above me. Allowing for the exaggeration which panic always paints for itself, I am still quite sure that the chains groaned and the bed trembled, while my own heart beat. These sounds, however, soon subsided into long-noted snoring, and somewhat before we arrived at Delhi the carriage was safely delivered of the three. Happy was I when the creakings of the descent subsided. As the sword of Damocles never fell, so was I not crushed by divinity.

Arriving safe at early morning, I was driven to the Northbrook Hotel, which I at once declined to patronize, and sought shelter in "The Grand," well situated, and very fairly conducted. But what strikes me in all these Indian cities, as regards the European quarters (so to call them), is the distance that lies between the various buildings—the native quarters being all so crowded. Every shop, for example, occupies a separate house, and between the tailor and the draper there is a long drive. Though I mention this here, I do not know that Delhi thus struck me more than other places; for the observation is of general application.

The historical associations with Delhi are indeed fearful. Carry your memory back to the days of Nadir Shah, and then bring it back quickly to 1857. Speaking of this latter date, surely we may say it needs not fields of hundreds of thousands to make a war of giants. My first visit was to the Ridge, where all is quiet now. But the Mutiny Memorial is there, mute but speaking. Read as much of its inscriptions as you please, and ascend it for the view, and fancy all that was going on while we were at home in quiet. From the middle of May till the middle of September the storm and tempest of siege and assault were raging, and mutinous Delhi at last succumbed to British valour. The scene is very striking from the Ridge, and the drive occupies a very pleasant afternoon.

The next day I devoted to visiting that strange towering individuality called the Kutb or Kutab (both of which appeared to be corruptions) Minar—which word is, of course, the large of Minaret. A more extraordinary structure than this, or so extraordinary a one as this, it would be difficult to conceive of. If it is not a physical incorporation of the spirit of pride, what is it? And a yet larger one, for the mere purpose of out-topping it, was begun, but the builder was not able to finish. I could not divest myself, while gazing on it, of something of the sentiment of the ridiculous. This much said, the structure must be appreciated. It stands 238 or 242 feet high, and tapers from a diameter of some forty-seven or forty-eight feet at its base, to scarcely nine feet at the top, and it consists of five storeys. According to Fergusson it was even once some twenty feet higher. Each storey is ornamented with a balcony that protrudes very handsomely. The depth and outlines of the moulding show how well the builders understood the effects of light and shade and of variety, and, in its own character, this Minar is held to stand alone in our small world.

The Iron Pillar, dilated on by Fergusson, must not be overlooked, nor is very likely to be so; nor indeed, is the Mosque—an evident converted Jain temple. Mark also the large arch, reminding one of Ajmir. Various tombs are visited on the way back, some worth seeing and some not, but all somewhat causing confusion of memory and impression.

The whole of the next day I devoted to the Fort and the Jumma (Friday) Musjid. With this latter I was not so much impressed as I was with others. But as regards the Palace in the Fort, as it was originally built by the renowned Shah Jahan, it is difficult to understand that everything you now see belonged once to that Unity. There is now a total want of connection, and instead of finding yourself passing through and through corridors and courts from one great feature to another, all this effect has been destroyed, and you pass to mere separate structures. In his volume there is an admirable general plan of what Fergusson calls "perhaps the most magnificent palace in the world," among the features of which figures the fantastic Moti Musjid, very small in proportion to the other arrangements, but probably intended (as in more modern instances) for exclusive Royal worship. But among all the buildings that which most drew my attention, and most rests on my memory, was the Diwan-i-Khas, or Private Hall of Audience. This Diwan-i-Khas is erected on its own marble base, some eight feet high, and consists of a large oblong assembly room, all in white marble, and formerly intensely adorned; and instead of being walled in, it is marked out by a double row of integral peculiar-shaped pillars, verging into arches on the roof, so that as you stand in the centre you look through and through a wonderful perspective of pillars on all sides.

With this much said, I leave you, if you go there, to wander about as you will, and meanwhile to accompany me to see the Golden Temple at Amritsar. But there is a distance of 316 miles, and starting at noon on Friday, the 15th of March, I arrived at seven the next morning, having in the daytime passed through vast streets of the most beautifully growing wheat. Will it tempt you to make the journey if I tell you that strawberries were offered at the Delhi Station?

XII.

WHAT you have to visit at Amritsar is the Golden Temple, and what I was most fortunate in hitting off, by pure accident, was the celebration of the Feast called "Holi." This golden temple stands in the midst of a large pool or tank (as it is called) of pure water, carefully edged with stone, and called the Pool of Immortality; such, indeed, according to Murray (1891), is the meaning of the word Amritsar. It stands on its own platform, sixty-five feet square, and is approached by a long marble causeway, following the level of the water, and constructed of white marble. The structure inside and out is overwhelming with golden eccentricity and variegated decoration. And to all this was added moving crowds of worshippers, on whom I looked down from above. They were all crowding, moving, praying and talking together, like a great living nosegay of various flowers in a golden vase; for in addition to their own costumes they were painted in careless chance splashes of red ochre. In this holiday, with a motive which I leave others to explain, the excitement consists in squirting all this coloured liquid over one another, motion adding to the undoubted effect. The outside scene for the moment was enchanting; and nothing would have marred the effect, had it not been for the grossly vulgar and ugly high Clock Tower, of barbarous English design. Do either of you remember old King's Cross, long and long since removed? The monster at Amritsar is just as much uglier as it is larger. As to purchases at Amritsar, you may buy shawls, and chudders, silk fabrics, and carvings, and fancy you have made great bargains; and when you bring them home and find you don't want them, and have them valued by disdainful tradesmen, you are certain to find about as many shillings put upon them as they cost you pounds.

Still through smiling spreads of wheat, of strong and even growth, I undertook my two hours more to Lahore, and found myself in the capital of the Punjab, or Panjab, at Nedou's Panjab Hotel, thus yet more nearly approaching my looked-for entrance into Kashmir. Delhi is, of course, in the Panjab also, and for my own satisfaction, if not for yours, I will write down the names of the five Rivers—Panjab—that give this name. The Indus has often been mentioned as one, but it is not so. Here they are: The Ravi (or Bavi), the Dias, the Jhelum, that flows through the Vale of Kashmir, the Chenab and the Sutlej.

At Lahore, amidst all the buildings that are worth a visit, I again witnessed the extremely picturesque effects of the festival of the "Holi," which were yet more striking than at Amritsar. For the crowds in the narrow streets were far more densely packed, and all were in constant voice and movement. Add to this, as my carriage perforce moved very quietly along, there was ample opportunity for appreciating the incessant appearances of delicate carvings, and bal-

GOLDEN TEMPLE : AMRITSAR

conies, bay windows, and indeed whole houses themselves, of the quaintest and most picturesque descriptions. Bazaars and bazaars abounded; with oxen, goats, and buffaloes interspersed, and vocal sounds of every sort and kind.

Here I learnt that the Bays, my nephew's former regiment, were at Sealcote, and that his friend, Colonel Lister Kaye, who had succeeded to command, was there. I was to pay him a visit, and this made a divergence necessary from the line to Peshawur at the Wazirabad Junction, a distance of sixty-two miles. A morning train took me there on the 20th, where I found a letter from Adjutant Captain Dewar and Colonel Kaye's dog-cart, and was driven to the Colonel's quarters, he being absent for a day or two. Meanwhile I was hospitably received by Major Sadlier, my acquaintance with whom afterwards stood me in excellent stead. I stayed from the 20th till the morning of the 25th, starting with Colonel Kaye, who went straight into Kashmir for the far mountains beyond, on his real sporting excursion during his three months' leave. For myself, I was to visit Rawl Pindi, staying with Captain Heyland, R.A., and his wife, my goddaughter of far-away Brazil; and thence to go on to Murree for Kashmir, with a divergence, however, to Peshawur.

In this journey I experienced my least pleasant experience. For, leaving Wazirabad Junction between one and two p.m. on Monday, the 25th of March, I arrived at Rawl Pindi at 11.30 at night, in a pitiless downpouring of rain, and there I found a messenger from Rowbury's Hotel, whither I had telegraphed, informing me there was no room. The "Imperial" was suggested to me, but there was no gárí to take me there. It would have been too wet for even a duck to attempt to walk. At last a kind fellow-passenger, who was detained by luggage, lent me his gárí to go and to return it in a quarter of an hour. In less than that time, not only did the gárí return, but I returned with it; for so abject an apology for a resting-place I had never till then beheld. I never thought of the place again, and the house might have been full; but you are liable to such things in India. When once more at the station I changed my front, decided to sleep in the waiting-room, as best I could, and to start for Peshawur by the first train in the morning; thus postponing my Rawl Pindi visit till my return for Murree. Accordingly, at 8.30 a.m. on the 26th, I left for Peshawur, and drove to the Dâk Bungalow, though I had a letter to the Commissioner, Colonel Ommanney, from my friend Colonel Busk in England. Fortunately for me—fortunately this time—the Dâk Bungalow was full, so that I had no option but to drive to the Colonel's, on whom I had not chosen to force myself in the first instance. A more pleasant house and garden, and a more pleasant reception to correspond, I never met with. No sooner was my letter opened, than the question was put, "Where are your things?" They were on the gárí, of course; but in a very short space of time they were in a glorious airy bedroom, and so was I, with servant well housed into the bargain; nor did much time elapse before I found that in former days I had known, among old friends, the colonel's great-uncle, Admiral Sir John Ommanney.

The open hospitality in India many years ago is abundantly historical. Visits from Europe were not so numerous as now, and, moreover, strangers do not now by any means stand in so much need of assistance. The response is to-day made to letters of introduction, which in the olden time were not necessary. But with this condition, I found in more cases than one (which will appear in turn) the most benignant welcome. And this subject calls to mind a conversation which I held with a retired colonel in the Indian army, whom I met so long ago as July, 1888, just three months before I left England, at the house of my esteemed friends, the Rev. E. A. and Mrs. Pitcairn Campbell, of Vicar's Cross, near Chester. The very interesting anecdote he told me, while we were naturally conversing about my then coming journey, he has lately confirmed by letter, with his full authority to make use of the particulars, which are really most amusing. Even this anecdote, however, is not older than 1850.

In that year, Colonel MacDougald, as a young ensign, was travelling from Hansee, near Delhi, to Segowlee—both railway stations now—on the borders of Nepaul, to join the 10th Regiment Irregular Cavalry, as Adjutant. On the 18th of April, 1850, he took the steamer *Mirzapore* at Benares, intending to drop down the Ganges as far as Dinapore. But as the steamer made only twenty-five miles in four days—mark the difference of now-a-days—he induced the captain to put him on shore at

Syndpore, where he hired an ekka, and in that terrible vehicle he underwent a wearisome, happily not mortal, journey of absolutely thirty miles. What is an ekka? I saw several, and most fortunately, sight was the only sense that was affected by this cramped-up instrument of torture. The colonel shall describe the vehicle himself. "An ekka is a light two-wheeled vehicle, drawn by a pony, without springs, inflicting terrible punishment on a traveller if he has to ride any distance. The legs of the unfortunate occupant hang over the side without support to the feet, and there is none whatever to the back. The wheels being small, you are close to the ground, and the dust is intolerable. The punishment of that drive I shall never forget; and having been kept awake for four nights previously by the largest mosquitoes I have ever experienced, I was by no means in ordinary good trim for a long journey of any kind."

The young ensign, however, survived this agony—but only try to imagine what Indian travelling then so lately was. On reaching Ghazeepore at three o'clock in the morning, the driver made for the first bungalow in the station, which proved to be that of a Mr. Shaw. Notwithstanding the early hour, the servants were roused, refreshments offered, a bed made up, and a comfortable bath prepared; and at the breakfast table the host and hostess first became acquainted with their guest. Great kindness was shown to him during the day, and after a comfortable dinner he started with twelve palankeen bearers for Buxar—now also a railway station, and also a refreshment room—a distance of twenty miles, Mrs. Shaw kindly lending her palankeen.

Next comes the final scene of the exhibition of Indian travelling; and it contains so amusing an incident, that the colonel shall again tell it in his own words :—

"Early in the morning Rarunkadhee was reached. Nothing, however, would induce the palankeen bearers to cross the River Ganges to the rest-house—Dâk Bungalow—at Buxar, where I had intended to pass the heat of the day. Neither threats nor promises were of any avail, the bearers insisting that they had always taken parties to Major Sherer's house, and thither and to no other place would they go. In vain I expostulated that I did not know Major Sherer (then superintendent of the Government studs), and that I would prefer the public rest-house. But no: the bearers argued that I should be well received by the Major Sahib, and that he would be dreadfully offended with them if they took their travellers elsewhere. So, lifting up the palankeen on their shoulders, they entered the grounds, making as much noise as they could to attract attention, as only palankeen-bearers know how to disturb a household, and carried me up to the front door of the house. Out came the servants, regretting that their master and mistress had just started for a drive—the regular hour in India—but assuring me that a bed-room was prepared, and a water-carrier ready with his mussuk to give me a fresh bath, and that tea also was forthcoming. I had hardly finished my toilet and entered the drawing-room when up drove the carriage. And here comes the curious incident. The major and his wife, seeing a palankeen and the bearers taking their rest under the trees, made up their minds that their own young son, Joe, whom they were expecting and had not seen for many years, had really arrived; and, rushing into the drawing-room, Mrs. Sherer gave me off-hand a most warm-hearted embrace, at which Major Sherer, delighting in the joke, laughed most heartily, when a few minutes had served to dispel the illusion. This kind host and hostess never forgot their guest during the remainder of General Sherer's distinguished services; and I and the son have up to this time entertained the most friendly relations with each other. I was pressed to stay to meet their son, but I had to join my regiment; and thus, loaded with all sorts of good things for a journey, I left this hospitable family. Strange to relate," continues the colonel in his letter to me, "about fifteen years afterwards I lived in this very same house, and enjoyed the appointment which Major Sherer had so long occupied."

Connected with the hospitality I experienced in India, this anecdote, independently of its intrinsic interest, has appeared to me to be worthy of recalling and recording. With Major Ommanney, whose life was enlivened by the presence of his two musical and cheerful daughters, I passed five full days most pleasantly, and with one great advantage, namely, that of visiting the historically famous Khyber Pass, under the authority of Colonel Warburton, who was in command of it.

XIII.

It was on a fine fresh morning on the 27th of March that Colonel Ommanney drove me into Peshawur—an extremely picturesque old city, but far more fitted for a visit than a stay. The grand bird's-eye view of all is from the top of the gateway, belonging (if my recollection serves me rightly) to the old palace. The surrounding scene, with wild mountains in the prospect, is remarkably striking—the city lying below—and in the far distance to the west were pointed out to me those prominent hills, looking quite clear, that form the entrance to the darkly famous Pass which I was anxious to enter. One great feature in the city are the bazaars, and the remarkable variety of the attending crowds coming in from all regions, with Afghans about everywhere. As to the city itself, it must be confessed that it does not enjoy a very exalted general character. It is one that ought assuredly to be visited and realized by any traveller endowed with enterprise enough to seek variety and strangeness, and desirous of witnessing what those parts of the earth (not exactly belonging to Islington) have to show. And this may well be done so as to leave a strong and lasting impression, without counting all the ugly corners that abound within its precincts.

Colonel Warburton came to luncheon on the 28th,

and then it was that a visit to the Khyber Pass, as far as Fort Ali Musjid, was arranged. It was more than the mere satisfaction of curiosity that influenced me in my desire to see even that much of a scene that would surely bring back vividly my recollections of 1842. Not so many now living can clearly recall the effect of the long account of carnage and disaster that shocked all England at that momentous period. It was in the beginning of 1842 that despatches from India made us all aware of the horrors of the Afghan war, and the retreat from Cabul. I had then not completed twenty-three years of age, and was staying with my eldest brother at Alresford, then a curate of the late Lord Guilford. He was engaged to be married in the following October to Miss Dunn, the half-sister of Captain Hopkins, who had accompanied Dr. Brydon in the flight to Jellalabad, and who was massacred within ten miles of that city, Dr. Brydon alone escaping of the small company that had found their way almost to the walls of safety. And what has most particularly barbed this story in my memory is that the news was brought to the mother, then Mrs. Dunn, at Alresford, with all the peculiar anguish clinging to the fact that with but a few more miles of riding her son would have been safe. He was only just near enough to safety for safety to laugh at him. I have of late been looking back to the files of the *Times*, with the aid of "Palmer's Index," to find the letter which I have always so well remembered, and which appears in that journal under date of April 7th, 1842; I mean the letter that Dr. Brydon wrote his brother "Tom" after his safe arrival at Jellalabad. Nor was it possible for me to forbear wandering through all the neighbouring dates and columns of that period, so that I seemed at last to live again in the days of "Disastrous Intelligence." Out of 4500 fighting-men and 12,000 camp-followers who left the cantonments, leaving behind them their provisions, guns and ammunition—all under arrangements blindly made by General Elphinstone with Akbar Khan, after his treacherous assassination of the British envoy, Sir William MacNaghten, at a conference—those who by mere accident survived might be numbered by a few score.

Dr. Brydon recounts that their party of seven officers and five European soldiers reached to a distance of thirty miles from Jellalabad, Captain Hopkins being one of the seven. They were attacked, and three of the officers and all the soldiers were killed, Lieutenant Bird falling by his side. Captains Bellow, Collyer, Hopkins, and a fourth reached to sixteen miles of Jellalabad, but these first-named three being well mounted had ridden on alone. The fourth gave in and was slain. Dr. Brydon continued slowly, and at last met a party of six of the enemy, one of whom wildly rode at him and, wounding him, galloped by. The three who had ridden forward he never saw again; but this party of six were leading a horse, and, for reasons which I forget now, this horse was recognized at the time as having been Captain Hopkins's.

At six o'clock on the morning of the 29th of March, armed with a permission, I started in a two-horse wagonette for the entrance to the Pass at

Jumrud Fort, a fort belonging to us and lying at a distance of ten miles. The weather was fine and fresh, and I had furnished myself well, as I thought, with wraps at starting. "You must take more," said Colonel Ommanney, who was at hand to see me off. "Oh! these are quite enough," quoth I. "No such thing, I assure you," he replied; and well was it for me that he was there to say "No." It is quite a mistake to suppose that all India is always hot. The latitude of Peshawur is about 34 degrees, barely that of Cyprus; but Peshawur can be very cold as well as very hot. I was well satisfied to be well clothed in my drive, and, attended by one mounted guard, I arrived safely at Jumrud Fort. Here I delivered up my pass, and my mounted guard left me. But he was at once succeeded by two, who rode forth from the Fort to attend me; and thus I entered. Another ten miles brought me to Ali Musjid, the intended limit of my excursion. This indeed, as I was authoritatively told, is the most striking feature in the Pass. The scene is very mountainous and wild, and the road rises and falls from time to time very picturesquely. But it is not a bold, hard, rocky Pass; on the contrary, the formation is shaly and slatey. Fort Ali Musjid is a sort of double fort, and is built on a huge middle ragged eminence, on each side of which there is one still higher, and quite as ragged. The Pass here is naturally very narrow, and the whole view afforded ample facility for comprehending all those arduous sufferings that have stamped it with an ugly immortality. In that Fort, now desolate and silent and indifferent, I was to breakfast. Half an hour's hard climb took me to the warderless gateway, and my coachman quietly carried up and laid out for me my undisturbed repast. But I was not alone, for within there were a number of rough tenants, and these at once came round me and watched me as a Feringhee, or foreigner. There they stood while I ate, and when I had satisfied my appetite they appeared to have satisfied their curiosity, leaving me and my coachman and the basket to depart in peace. It would not have been so in 1842.

On coming down I was somewhat surprised to see an escort of Afghan Cavalry, and, while wondering, was saluted with an English "Good morning." This I found afterwards was an Englishman, representing a well-known firm in Calcutta (the name of which I ought to have taken) engaged in rather large contracts with the Amir, and this partner was in the habit of making the long journey, to and fro, as far as Cabul—190 miles from Peshawur—under special escort. These journeys, I was told, are permitted by our Government under the express understanding that there is no responsibility for personal safety. I was by no means sorry to sit and talk with him for a certain period, for it enabled me to dwell upon the strange scene around me, and to imbibe a certain inspiration from the reality.

In my morning journey I had been delighted with the beautiful effects of the early sunshine on the distant snow mountains to the north, with the purples on Tartarra and his indented ranges. On my return my curiosity was correspondingly awakened by the crowds of life I met coming in. It was just the time of year for the return to Cabul, and hundreds of turbaned, swarthy Afghans, attending their hundreds of laden, hairy camels, for some time intercepted, and happily in no hostile mood as of yore, my retreat from the Khyber Pass.

My next day's occupation was of a very different character. I went with Colonel Ommanney to a distribution of prizes among native students in the Public Gardens, a most satisfactory exhibition, all countenances exhibiting the becoming sunshine of the occasion. But no one ought to leave Peshawur without speaking of the vast spread of stuccoed lawn-tennis grounds: the nurseries, these perhaps in England, of female voters, by their developing power. If Peshawur of to-day is celebrated for anything innocent, it is so for its lawn-tennis grounds, and if Colonel Ommanney is celebrated for anything outside his official duties, it is for his warlike pursuit of tennis—but not of lawn. Cold as I found the morning on my visit to the Pass, Peshawur soon gets hot, and people who can do so, get away. Yet there are mountains all round, more or less distant certainly, but still all round; and one particular feature of the scenery results from this: look which way you will there are mountains at the end of every flat line.

XIV.

FROM my pleasant divergence to Peshawur I returned to Rawl Pindi on Sunday, the 31st of March, and here my second attempt was far more successful than my first. I found myself very comfortably housed at Powell's Hotel, and in full communication with my friends, Captain and Mrs. Heyland. At Rawl Pindi I spent a few pleasant days, but the weather was rainy, and the changes in the thermometer frequent and important. Mrs. Oliphant, with whose husband in the Army Veterinary Corps I found I had made chance acquaintance in travelling, and who shortly afterwards appeared, drove me to witness the distribution of prizes at the Horse Show, by Sir Thomas Baker, Commissioner of the Division, where I afterwards saw the singular exercise of what is called tent-pegging. The horseman gallops by and is to wrench up the peg with his lance as he passes. This attempt the native lancers accompanied with a wild, warlike and somewhat alarming cry, but the peg very often remained wholly indifferent to the alarum and attack. The company was large and gay.

I would mention that it was here Lieut.-Colonel Oliphant called my attention to two photographs of two very ancient and rather imperfect figures, but exceedingly Grecian in their appearance, which I at once bought, but which I regret to find are not admit of reproduction. He informed me that there are several of the same character in the Mess Room of the Queen's Own Regiment of Guides at Hoti Murdán. They were brought (as I understood) from the Swats' country after the Black Mountain War, and not far from the Indus. Whence they derive their Grecian aspect may be a question of much curiosity.

My chief matter of business at Rawl Pindi was to arrange my journey to Murree, and thence onwards to Kashmir; and again the Parsee was the coach proprietor, Mr. Dhanjiboy. With him I engaged a two-horse tonga to take me as far as Gharri. This is the fifth station beyond Murree, the distance being forty miles to Murree and sixty-two more to Gharri. Hattian, twelve miles more, was the usual limit, but some bridge had given way, and from Gharri ponies were to be obtained for Baramula, fifty miles farther —this being the foot station of the Vale. I speak as I found, because I am writing my own record, but all this is altered now under the new road system.

Now, as a general rule, I could have gone on from Murree on the day following my arrival, six hours serving to take me thither from Rawl Pindi. But I was detained there longer than I had intended, passing through one of those phases of life that vex with present annoyance, but result in subsequent advantage. "How very wrong to be vexed," says the would-be moralist, not being himself vexed at the moment, but just as liable to that frailty as those whom he would lecture. If we knew that good was coming we might not be vexed, but then sometimes the present seeming advantage is followed by the opposite, and in that case foreknowledge would check satisfaction. In fact, doing right and doing wrong are just as contradictory in their results as the happening right and happening wrong. This sort of confusion of consequences, measured by our expectations and desires, happened to be vexing my philosophy at that moment, so I composed a parody, which I shall detain you by printing here. I daresay you all remember, or will easily recall, the paradox of the "Rules of the Road," as propounded by a learned judge some years ago :—

> The Rules of the Road are a paradox quite;
> For, as you are driving along,
> If you go to the left, you are sure to go right,
> If you go to the right, you go wrong.

Then comes my parody :—

> The Rules of this Life are a paradox quite;
> To their course contradictions belong;
> For if you do wrong, you too often prove right,
> Doing right, you are left in the wrong.

But if the occasion of all these reflections was not great to any besides myself, the man that occasioned them was assuredly so. For in point of fact my departure from Murree was fidgeted from one day to another because Sir Frederick, now Lord, Roberts, the Commander-in-Chief of the Indian Army, was going into Kashmir just at the moment that I had settled to do the same thing myself. However, on the morning of Saturday, April 6th, I left Powell's comfortable hotel at Rawl Pindi in my tonga, taking with me in the back seat my travelling servant, "Mogul John" (of whom hereafter), and my cook for Kashmir, Bana. It was only half a good-bye to Captain and Mrs Heyland, for he had his leave and they were to follow.

My tonga-start from Rawl Pindi was the admiration of more than one beholder, and I must confess to their laughter and my own distrustful astonishment. But I had faith in Zoroaster, and away we got at last, after having described certain wheel figures on the hotel drive which could not have claimed a problem in Euclid for any Q.E.D. Now, if that one start was astonishing, what were some of the others among all the very rawest of ponies that were from time to time put to? The fights, and the breakings loose, and the bringings back again, and makings to go, beggar all description. But the thing was repeatedly done, and admirably done indeed. I never had seen the maxim so well applied, "Never let a horse get the better of you,—if you can help it."

Murree lies 7000 feet above Rawl Pindi, and the road very soon becomes picturesque. There is a good deal of up and down among round hills decked with stunted green, and there are cultivated valleys. By-and-by the necessary ascent begins and the views enlarge, all culminating at the last change in a vast range of folding hills and valleys. To Murree we came at last, and quite in good time, but there was still another mount to Powell's Hotel, called, I believe, "Viewfort." Whether it is the best hotel I know not, because I lived in no other, but I can say that it was very good, and that Mr. Powell was very cheerful and obliging, while, as to position, having seen the other leading one, I have no hesitation in saying that the position of Powell's is incomparably the best. Nothing could well be more striking than the enormous expanse of mountainous ranges and undulating valleys, all interspersed in untraceable confusion, that lie far below you, extending to the far-distant snowy ranges that border Kashmir. Much terraced cultivation of bright green corn in broad lines and patches, amid the general brown of the month of April, help to soften the scene, and remind one that busy life yet claims a dwelling among the comparative solitudes. But it was time to go in and get oneself comfortable, and I found my cheerful landlord just the man to make me so. Not many at that moment were there, and he gave me a chosen corner room in his outside row, which commanded all the majestic prospects.

The first fruit, not a very large one perhaps, of my being detained by Sir Frederick Roberts (that was his title then, and so I shall speak of him) was that I saw him. People say they can believe without seeing, but they always like to see nevertheless, and while we are flesh and blood—and who can prove what else we are?—we are always striving after the visible and tangible. Well, I saw Sir Frederick Roberts. On Sunday morning I was standing at the end of the veranda with Captain McRae, when there rode into the courtyard one or two horsemen and one or two ladies; and the eldest of the party jogged up towards us. "Who's this," I said, "like a lightweight at covert side?" That was his appearance: nothing like stiff soldier parade seat: and I daresay he won't be angry if he sees this. My companion of the moment had just time to say, "That *is* Sir Frederick," when he hailed us with "Good morning," and asked for Sir Thomas Baker. "I will go and find him," said the captain. "Thanks, I am going on to Kashmir and wished to bid him good-bye." The very first observation Sir Frederick made to me was, "You have a very fine view here indeed," to which I responded, and, after a few casual remarks between us, Sir Thomas was found, and I saw no more of Sir Frederick till on a memorable occasion not long forward in the future. But I had now realized the man whose name only I had known, and having judged by a photograph that he was a large, swarthy officer, I now knew he was nothing of the kind. How many of our unseens remain only creatures of the brain to the end, and even when seen, how much it still costs to get rid of the figured unseen.

From this profound reflection I passed to my inevitable preparations for Kashmir in procuring all necessary household or tent utensils, and a pair of long wicker baskets, covered with leather, called kiltas, in which to carry them. But to the contents were to be added certain tins of provender. Among these, one grand item should always be remembered, Paysandu tongues—there is nothing like them. They come from the Republic of Uruguay, and are by far the finest specimens of preserved tongue, or preserved anything, I have met with anywhere. A very nice pony was offered me for Rs. 40, but I was too far from the riding point to take him, and it was well for me I declined him.

Murree, though 7000 feet above the sea level, is not considered a remarkably healthy place; indeed there had been a very severe course of cholera there in 1888. And in looking over the grand view I have spoken of, I could not avoid a misgiving that it must be sometimes invaded, when the wind sets that way, by miasma from the not too distant flats. The weather also is apt to be very unsettled at times; and so I found it while there, though I secured a pleasant ride or two to Pinnacle Hill and other spots. The scope for excursions is, however, limited.

It was in fact bad weather that prevented my leaving before Saturday, the 13th of April; for in the night of the 9th we had a very heavy thunderstorm, accompanied with that grim and ghostly phenomenon, a high wind in the dark. Nay more, there was snow; ay, and a small shock of earthquake into the bargain was felt by all of us in the course of the night. The next two days were but little better, and bad reports of the roads came in, large landslips being announced. However, on Saturday, the 13th, as I have said, I came away in my tonga, notwithstanding all misgivings, and reached the station of Domel for the night. The road descends rapidly from Murree towards the River Jhelum, which flows through the Vale of Kashmir and falls into the Indus. Almost immediately after leaving Murree the scenery becomes charming. The road descends through a steep, hanging mass of wood on the hills and mountain sides, and shows the distant snow ranges through the forest trees on the left. Then it mounts and falls, and turns to and fro, and round among the valleys, gorges and vast ridges which are seen from Powell's Hotel, until descending within a few miles short of Kohála, the Kashmir Jhelum is first caught sight of. When you have passed Kohála this river is followed up the whole way in a gorge to Baramula, and is always a rushing noisy stream. But at Baramula, where the traveller finds himself at the foot of the Vale proper, the river has suddenly become a sluggish stream.

Perhaps the chief eye of this day's journey is to be seen shortly after leaving Daywal, ten miles from Murree. But on approaching Domel, about the hour of sunset, I was particularly struck by a fine white mountain in the distance, the name of which was given me as Karnar. I arrived at about seven in the evening, and had found to my cost in this journey that the report of a large landslip was not untrue. A long, trying walk to meet another tonga was the result, but here also struck in a happy small incident; for at Dulai, on the way, a few minutes' conversation with a quite unknown gentleman turned out to be of infinite service to me long afterwards in Kashmir. As to the changes and startings of the horses, these were as before. One instance, however, shone out supreme, where the animal twice kicked itself right out, and was twice brought back. At Kohála British territory ends.

My next day, Sunday, April 4th, took me some fifteen miles perhaps, to Gharri, and here my tonga contract ended, and I was to depend on pony and coolies for baggage. I had brought my two servants with me, and had engaged a chustas, or water-carrier, Camala by name, at Murree, and he had taken charge of my luggage, which he now brought in. But now arose the next inconvenience from the visit of the Commander-in-Chief. He and his retinue, like a marching army, had swept the country of every coolie and every pony, and I and others were completely stranded. The Heylands had come in in the evening, and I found them comfortably tented out with their two sturdy boys, quite children; but they had made their own private arrangements, and could get on with their own people, which they did. All next day I had to wait, with a prospect of the next and perhaps the next.

But while in this predicament there arose one alleviation as regards monotony. I was not alone in trouble, and I presently made the acquaintance of a very pleasant lady, who was likewise, though more patiently than I, waiting for her release. In opening conversation I observed, among other things, that according both to Lavater and Gall, she had a large organ of language, as betokened by the lower eyelid; and pursuing our intercourse farther, I soon discovered that she had travelled a good deal. This led to reciprocal recollections and an interchange of experiences and impressions, until I said, "I went also to the Hawaiian Islands, and I had Miss Bird's book with me." Whereupon forthwith there came the short reply, "I am Miss Bird." Thus, then, so far I was rewarded for delay. What next?

"Why e'en in that was heaven ordinant."

"Hallo! are you here?" said somebody who had seen me at Sealcote. "Yes," I replied, "and likely to remain here." "Why," quoth he, "Major Sadlier is to be here to-night, on his way to Baramula." So far, so good; but what then? With evening came the major and his friend, Captain Armstrong, of the Fusiliers; and recognizing me with a hearty greeting, and hearing why I was still here, "Oh," said he, "come on with us to-morrow; I have all my four polo ponies with me, and you can take one of them." Thus was I, after all, more than compensated for the delay; and in the morning we cheerfully journeyed on together, I delighting in my pleasant mount and —in my English saddle. Thanks, therefore, to Sir Frederick Roberts for having detained me till Major Sadlier came.

It was at Uri, two stations short of Baramula, that I saw the last of Mrs. Bishop (Miss Bird), and, bidding me a very gracious good-bye, with a hope of meeting again, she added, to my amusement, "And, do you know, I have been quietly laughing all the while, for you are wearing my hat. Now do tell me where you got it." "Bless my heart," I said, "this hat was given me by my own servant, to whom (as he told me) it had been given by somebody else's servant." "Well, I'm delighted to hear that, for I charged my man with having sold it. I gave it away because it made my head ache; and I am delighted to find it so well disposed of at last." The anecdote is trite, but happening between a distinguished and an undistinguished traveller, and with a hope of meeting again, I choose to record it as an incident by the way. I must record, also, that in a very few days I found my own head was just so far entitled to affinity with Miss Bird's, that the hat, which was one of those great ventilated saucepans, made mine ache likewise; and as it had been given to me, so gave I it away to somebody else, who did not wear a turban. If ever I have the hoped-for pleasure of meeting Miss Bird again, the hat is quite sure to be revived in our conversations.

Throughout the journey to Baramula the class of scenery continues much the same. The mountains are nearly all round-headed, though vast. Some appear to be high enough to carry snow through the year. All the rest are green, and show cultivated terraces. Now, however, that the carriage-road is made, the length and the rugged fatigue of the ride are matters of the past; but our own enforced deviations were not a little trying. The mountains are always there, and the rushing river is always there; there is a sameness of variety, and a variety of sameness.

XV.

PASSING through Hattian, Chicoli, Uri, and Rampore, on Friday, the 19th, we made an early push to Baramula. My companions, taking a turn to the right without my observing them, passed over into the Vale by what is called the Baramula Pass. This road I took on leaving the Vale, and will speak of it then. But in going in I was directed by the new road, which takes you round by a level entrance. And here, I must confess, was my first disappointment; for I beheld a very wide, flat valley, with no feature that very particularly struck me. My companions arrived by their road almost at the same moment as myself, and there we met the agent of Bahar Shah, of Srinagar, to whom, by the good advice of Colonel Lister Kaye, I had already telegraphed, and who proved of excellent service to me throughout my visit to the Vale. In short, this is the real house to rely upon. My companions at this point arranged their own two boats, and I took possession of my two, already prepared for me. These were to be the dwellings of myself and servants throughout Kashmir, excepting when I was in tent, and the names of the owners were given me as Rahmana and Arfa. I had full reason to be satisfied with them throughout.

These boats are rather rough; they are long, and

of course flat bottomed; the prow is left open for working, and the stern is reserved for the rowers' and towers' uses. The larger third, in the middle, is partitioned off, and furnished according to your own taste, for your own sitting-room, dining-room, and bedroom; and from time to time you can of course walk out and sit in the prow. You are covered in with double matting, which is fairly comfortable, but requires a good deal of tying and tucking in when the wind blows. Your second boat is reserved especially for your stores and cooking apparatus, and for other general uses, including the people who work it, and your own crew also. On the first day all our four boats anchored for the night above a famous fishing spot called Sopur, but, being no fisherman myself, I need not pause on that particular fact. At very early morning my companions went on, my own men starting much later.

Now I have told you what were my first impressions of Baramula, and my entrance into the Vale. What were they of my six hours' journey up to Sopur? In the first place, my enthusiasm was not greatly exaggerated by finding that we were to be towed up the river; and thus it was all the way to Sopur, to begin with. The banks of the Jhelum were as flat and barren as those of a common canal; and this is a feature that belongs to a wide and totally flat valley. In its main characteristics thus far, to begin with, I found it much wider and much flatter than my too-well-tutored expectations had led me to anticipate. There was a continuous show of middle-distance mountains, and farther off of snow mountains; but these were in the decided distance, and then came the thawing information of one of my boatmen, "Snow disappears on many in summer." Such are not thoroughbred snow mountains. This distance that I speak of prevents these mountains from appearing to belong to the flat Vale; they do not give the effect in any degree whatever of being two prolonged and adorning attendant ridges on either side; they represent, rather, a distant and uneven amphitheatre. Here and there, but never on the banks of the river, there were green undulations which showed beauty, and dotted with certain timber, but not large. I saw nothing of striking and indisputable superiority anywhere, though much that was now and then pleasing. Thus I arrived at Sopur, and, somewhat distrustfully, judging from the general aspect around me, I waited for more romantic features.

On the next day—Saturday, the 20th—I continued my course up the river to Srinagar—the City of the Sun—and, as I anticipated, passed through merely the same class of scenery. It was dusk before we arrived at the capital, and here the effect was decidedly depressing. The city lies on both sides of the river, and it presented to me, at first sight, one of the most tumble-down places I ever saw. This feature is never quite alien to the picturesque; in short, very often the least habitable of dwellings look the sweetest and the happiest under the pencil. Comfort and fertility have so little connection with beauty, and are not unfrequently her mortal enemies. No one stops at Srinagar; if he did so, it might not improbably turn out to be a final stop. You here abandon the tow-ropes, and the men take to their mode of rowing, which consists of beating the water with paddles shaped like a broad heart, and with these they push along, varying their measured strokes with an occasional *presto* movement. Thus you mcunt till you get to a large and imposing, but uncouth, building on your right, and this is the Sher Garhi, or Palace of the Maharajah. Opposite to this is the opening of a canal, into which you turn sharply on the left. This is called the Sant-i-Kul, or Apple Tree Canal—why, I know not. This stream connects the Dal with the Jhelum. The word "Dal," I was informed, means "lake;" so of course, *anglice*, we always call this piece of water the "Dal Lake," i.e. the Lake Lake, whereof by-and-by. After about twenty minutes' paddling up this canal, which is fairly dressed with trees, and under some evening influences looks in parts extremely pretty, you pass a Hindoo temple on your left, and come to the "Chenar Bagh," or "Plane Tree Garden," on your right. Here is the regulation settlement of bachelor visitors, who pitch their tents under the trees, and those who bring horses with them stable them up behind. The banks are perfectly flat, as is all the land behind it; and it is most important, as I came to prove, to choose a spot where you are not liable to be swamped when the canal runs high. The trees under which this resting-place is established are fairly handsome, but admit of no sort of comparison with the great growth of the same tribe elsewhere. Here they form a grove of shelter, planted together, and look remarkably well from the opposite side. Beyond the bend of the canal they are more separate and somewhat finer.

Well, on looking back at my diary, here I appear to have passed life in my boat, moving up and down into Srinagar to see Bahar Shah and to other places, spending money on things that were wanted, and throwing it away on things that were not, until the 28th, when I started for my first excursion, which was to Islamabad, completely up the river. But I had not to wait beyond the first morning after my arrival before receiving another proof—and this time an important one—of the benefits I had derived from Sir Frederick Roberts' interruptions. For behold, on Sunday, the 21st, there appeared before me, while seated among my two or three newly purchased wooden chairs under the trees, Ummir Nāth, the Maharajah's representative for the welcoming of strangers, to whom, indeed, on the suggestion of Colonel Lister Kaye, I had previously written. And Ummir Nāth most courteously informed me that, among many others, I was to have a card of invitation to a grand dinner at the Palace, to be given by his Highness the Maharajah Pertab Sing in honour of Sir Frederick Roberts on the following day, viz. Monday, the 22nd, at half-past seven. This card now lies before me, and it is easy to confess that the occasion and the entire novelty of the whole affair quite chimed in with my inclination for travelling, curiosity and incident.

At the proper hour, therefore, on Monday evening, I got on board my small boat—my gig—that here waited on the two large, and was paddled down to the Palace: the boatmen feeling very grand—perhaps almost as grand as I did. But on mounting the high steps and threading through the scarlet-carpeted corridors towards the large reception room, I soon found myself but a very small item in the grand number. On entering the saloon among the assembled there I beheld a long bench, or row, of seated celebrities, occupying the whole width of the upper end; his Highness the Maharajah; his Excellency Sir F. Roberts and Lady Roberts and a son; the English Resident, his Excellency Mr. Nesbitt; Captain Ramsay, the Master of Ceremonies, and many others,

"Whom not to know argues myself unknown."

There was a sort of confusion and irregular grandeur in the whole scene, which was considerably enhanced by the gorgeous dresses of some of the performers, for curiously enough the entertainment preceded the feast. First came the Nach (or dancing) girls, a performance of which I am wholly unappreciative; then came the Thibet dancers, gorgeously arrayed and most hideously masked, to the extent indeed of reminding one of the griffins at the entrances of the Buddhists' pagodas. Heaven send that the gods themselves are not after all like these. Then there was wild howling and clanging music—that is, of cymbals: ugly and confused gestures and postures, and sounds of unearthly portent proceeding from a chorus of vast horns, so vast as to need support over the shoulders of more than one person, and of length as unearthly as the sounds. All this variety of attraction occupied much time, and then came the dinner. My own place was marked, and the card given me, but at the last moment some French lady made a confusion at that part of the table on account of some forlorn friend, whereby I nearly lost my place altogether. But I was happily beckoned by an authority in charge, I believe Captain Ramsay, to come and sit by him at the bottom of the table, for which charitable act I was very glad, and of which I was very, very lucky to be in time to avail myself. Here I was well placed and well taken care of, and I shall always remember, with deep carnal gratitude, that the turkey and in particular the ham were as good as any I have ever tasted.

When the repast was over, and all were well champagned for the inevitable conclusion, his Excellency Sir F. Roberts, the chief guest, made a clear and fitting speech, and we all adjourned to coffee, and presently afterwards to fireworks. These were witnessed from one of the balconies: they were profuse and noisy, and some were handsome. What I was particularly struck with was a very effective background to all. This was composed of a very large and lofty mass of wicker work, thoroughly furnished with an infinity of lamps, which made it look like a long screen of glittering gold. A great effect was thus produced by simple means, and might well be imitated, for it concentrated and intensified all that was exhibited in front. I saw the Maharajah more than once, walking about hand-in-hand with the Commander-in-Chief, and I could not but be struck with the lifeless, worn and discontented expression of his countenance. The not unusual medley of departure on such occasions prevailed in Srinagar, as in other more pretentious places, but I found my boatmen without too much trouble, and, with a lantern at the prow, rowed home beneath a starry sky.

The next day I entered my name at the Palace, and did the same at the Residency for the Resident and for the Commander-in-Chief, and not being able to leave without my tents and other paraphernalia, which Bahar Shah was arranging for me, I walked across the large flat space behind the Chenar Bagh to the small library on the river banks, and subscribed Rs. 5 for a month's entrance. In this district also lies the Post Office, and to and fro I several times repeated this monotonous entertainment. At length all necessary preparations were complete. The boatmen in both boats were clothed by me, as custom required, as also were my other men, Mogul John, the Khidmatgar, or valet; the cook, Bana ; the waterman, or Bhcestie, Camala ; the sweeper, Samdu ; and a very useful and active young volunteer servant, Sedika, or Sedecka, by name. This youth belonged to the boat, but was ambitious for all service, and was a son of one of the boatmen, not by his second wife, but by his wife No. 2.

Thus we all set out together on the 28th of April for Islamabad, and hauled up for the night on the flat bank, at a place called Pampoor. On my way I caught sight of the small stone temple at Pandritan, or Pooran Adi Sthan, formerly the capital of Kashmir. But as the artistic little building was in the middle of a pool of water, and there was only a half-swamped boat at hand, I deferred to trouble myself about trying to examine it until my return. On Monday, the 29th, there was no scenery to excite, the river banks being still towing-paths, and the nearer grounds quite flat; and on Tuesday, the 30th, I completed the boat course at a place called Kanbal, where I spent the night. I must not omit to mention, however, that on the way up I stopped at a place called Bijbehara, and mounted a high bank, attracted by several magnificent chenar trees. On arriving under them I found they represented the broken lines of a very fine original avenue, and wandering up and down I came across another visitor, who turned out to be Lieut. Blenkinsop from Allahabad, in the Veterinary Department. We naturally fell into conversation, and as no visionary was there, we were far from disagreeing about the general scenery of Kashmir, so far as we had realized it. We were equally in accord about the splendour of the chenars. He luckily had a tape with him, with which we measured the girth of one of these trees at about five feet above the ground, and it gave a circle of between thirty-eight and thirty-nine feet. It was of course the largest of the noble broken line.

At Kanbal, by virtue of a letter from Bahar Shah, I arranged a very pleasant pony and saddle, and came on next morning with all necessaries for Atchibal. This was an easy day's march, and the tents were raised under a group of beautiful chenars, with some very pretty sloping grounds behind. Mountains there were in sight, of course, and the road through the strange, stony, straggling town of

Islamabad was peculiar in more ways than one; but beyond this I have no observation to make about the flat scenery. Here at Atchibal are the tawdry remains of the Maharajah's gardens and fountains, which are famous for the cold-water springs. All is very ragged, and gives the impression of having always been flimsy.

The next day's journey, May 2nd, was one of much interest. I visited the ruined Temple of Martand, a word which is said to mean the Sun. Fergusson has a full account of this temple, and a very fair illustration of it. It is by no means large, not so large as the temple at Jerusalem, which, according to Prideaux, was small enough; but it exhibits features of great beauty and elaboration. It is surrounded by a courtyard, fenced in by a beautiful open screen work of stone; and curiously enough, recurring to Pandritan, General Cunningham (whom Fergusson quotes) opines that this inner court was originally filled with water. The temple stands grandly alone, and a most impressive view of it is obtained by ascending a small eminence behind it, and gazing down upon the structure. It stands in a vast flat valley, but here the flatness was effective, for the distant higher hills or mountains round were, when I stood there, covered with snow, and were displaying a most effective amphitheatre. I spent some time hovering about the scene, so glad to feel my interest at last excited, and, to the relief of my wondering and perhaps pitying attendants, at last moved on to Bawan Springs in Mutten.

Passing through the ragged little town, we came to

another beautiful plantation of chenars, shading a rushing crystal stream of water; and here, in a spot fairly picturesque, I dined and tented for the night. And here also I once more reaped a benefit from the visit of the Commander-in-Chief. "What is that affair under the trees?" "Oh! that is Bana's delight. It is a sort of cooking apparatus; it was built up for the Commander-in-Chief when his Excellency was here." And this was the last. And after all, how fortunate, in the main, I was in following Sir Frederick Roberts into Kashmir, and what an unknown debt of gratitude I owe to one who at first slightly injured, and afterwards so effectually, albeit so unconsciously, befriended me.

While at Bawan I was induced to visit what are called the Caves of Bhoomjoo, to which the word "pilgrimage" is attached. They lie about a mile distant from the chenars, and in Ince's Guide Book, edited by Joshua Duke, may be found a page and a half with all particulars; but for myself I have not even a word and a half to spend upon these mere uncouth hollows. The road to them, however, enabled me to obtain a sight of the immediate prospect outside the chenars, which is pleasing enough. There are some folding hills of attractive feature, and one black rock, capped with snow, added character to the general view.

On Friday, May 3rd, I rode to Eishmakam, a pleasant ride, but not calling for special observation. The valley, as all these valleys are, was flat, but the town and its fortress are on an elevation; and having pitched my tent on a pleasant piece of ground under a fine walnut tree, I mounted to the Fort. Hence the view is striking. You behold a good stretch of the Liddar Valley, but it is flat as a table, of course.

In this case, however, it is well wooded, and for the first time I saw some show of the hills sloping down in junction with the valley, a feature wholly wanting in the main Vale. There was also a fine range of mountains, still snowy. You may well imagine that Eishmakam is a strange rocky place; and in the fortress you may visit a strange tomb of a Holy Muhammadan, Jhan Shah, who lies buried in the long recess of a ragged chasm. On the morning of the 4th, I started for the reputed "lovely" Liddar Valley, and was to tent for the night at a place called Pylgam; and, my feelings of "great expectations" not having yet been completely cowed, I was subjected to the cold fit of what I find I have called in my journal, "complete disappointment." I must give my written evidence fairly and honestly, and quote the words: "The valley is of mere third-rate Swiss scenery. It is flat; and in parts full of flooded rice grounds. There are, of course, green mountains and certain winter-snow crags; but, barring one or two grassy slopes and hanging woods, nothing charms or enchains attention. The journey is one of fourteen miles to Pylgam, and Pylgam itself is distinctly ugly. A few ragged dwellings on an ugly stony flat constitutes the town; the river struggles along among the boulders in various narrow streams, before becoming a rushing unity lower down, and tenting space was difficult to find, though here I passed the night." With this extract I must be content to report of Pylgam and the Liddar Valley.

The next morning proved very fresh and fine, and my ride back to my walnut tree was pleasant, breakfasting and lounging in the sunshine on the way. On the 6th, through those tedious rice grounds of Kashmir, I came back to the chenars at Bawan Springs. Here, to my satisfaction, I found two arrivals; Captain and Mrs. Harries were tented under the trees, and we joined tables pleasantly, both quite concurring with me as to the caves I have referred to. Towards evening a beautiful white bird flew tamely close before my tent, which Captain Harries told me was called the Bird of Paradise of Kashmir. But in reality it is no Bird of Paradise at all, though very beautiful. It is covered all over with long white feathers, and has a long tail following behind it like a comet's. I could not get the real name of it, and so must leave it hallowed by belonging to the unknown, and with the impression, which the astonished sense of sight has left upon my memory, of having seen a winged comet among the trees.

Returning on the 7th to Kanbal on the river, I purposely walked on foot through Islamabad, which, for its curious people, mosque, and general character, is worth that trouble, if you go through it at all.

I was now to return to the Chenar Bagh, and, on my way down the flat-banked river, I visited some very scant remains at Wantipur, and afterwards made a more successful effort at Pandritan than I had done in coming up. By the help of Camala, my waterman, and Samdu, my sweeper, I managed to get the awfully cranky boat baled out, and as the dead duckweed pool that surrounded the little temple among the willow trees was only forty yards square, we succeeded in the voyage to and fro without shipwreck. The structure is a hollow square, each of the four sides having an open arch, and the centre forming a cupola. There was just room to push the boat quite underneath, so as to view the centre. The little affair is deeply and elaborately adorned, and is in its way quite a little gem ; so that our small duckweed enterprise with a leaky boat was rewarded by the sight. And here stands this comparative speck of architecture, solitary among its willows, sole remnant, if legend be believed, of the once capital of Kashmir. It lies only some half hour's walk from the Ram Munshi Bagh, close by the Chenar Bagh, and may thus be easily seen by any of those few who may care for such a visit. This Ram Munshi Bagh is the Bagh set apart for families. I walked through it instead of continuing in the boat, without regretting that I was not qualified to dwell there ; it seemed to me to be shut in, and not to be well supplied with water. As we walked along from Pandritan, Camala shook me down a quantity of small mulberries from time to time from large trees. But I had far better mulberries than these later on, Kashmir being deservedly famed for that delicious fruit of mournful association.

The weather had been wet and unpleasant, and my boat matting had flapped much during my return ; and when, on the evening of the 8th, I reoccupied my tent, that flapped in concord. Indeed,

I too well remember that about this time the weather did begin to be very uncertain, or rather certain to be rainy and windy and unpleasant, and on the night of the 10th I find I have marked a very heavy thunderstorm. The tent that I had travelled about with was now changed for a new one, and until the 16th I passed a not very joyous time under my adored chenars, while, with very little intermission, their heavy foliage flung quantities of water down upon my double roof, and amid unmusical tones of droppings, my waterman was employed in cutting and keeping clear an improvised earth gutter round my canvas walls.

This bad weather was enlivened or darkened by a small discovery that somewhat concerned my domestic economy; for word was brought to me by my cook and waterman that my "bearer"—a corruption, as I believe, of the word *behrá*—Mogul John, was habitually getting partly or wholly tipsy, and that he had boasted in his cups that he could rob me of my whisky at night, by getting hold of the bottle under the pegged sides of my tent; indeed, that he had done so more than once already. I therefore enlivened the monotony of water by a private examination of the accused, as to spirit. He began to equivocate, and persisted, till I threatened to throw him into the canal. Thereupon he roundly denied the charge, whereupon the witnesses were called, and confronted with him. The trial took place, and "Guilty" was then with perfect facility pleaded. I had more than once suspected him of drinking, and I had now to add lying and theft. I don't suppose he has ever offered himself again, but it is best to record his name and character; add to which, on declining to settle his book except through Bahar Shah, a deduction of what the Stock Exchange would call five-eighths was made of his bloated total. All the rest were honest and straightforward to the end; but travellers should be upon their guard. Yet, even so, they may be deceived; for this person was on Messrs. Cook's list. Muhammadanism had not kept Mogul John pure; whether he was Sunni or Shia, he worshipped the bottle more religiously than he did the prophet.

One fine afternoon was too tempting to be lost, and I accepted an invitation from Mr. Gordon, a barrister from Allahabad and a tented neighbour in company with Lieutenant Blenkinsop, to take a row round the Dal. Anyone who has read Moore's exquisite nonsense about the Dal in his Lalla Rookh—that blind product of "the encouraging suggestions of friends"—ought to anticipate disappointment; and by thus meeting that enemy half way, he is not likely to be too keenly overcome. The water, as it rushes out from the entrance, is of a lovely crystal, and so it is inside wherever you can catch a good view of it—beautifully crystal. But where do you see it? Even the guide book persuades itself to have courage enough to tell plain truth here. Its main surface is covered with dense belts of gigantic reeds, bulrushes, and floating gardens, these last with something of a pretty name, being, as I had once found them at Mexico city, ugly and shapeless lumps of dirt bound roughly together.

The feature that attracts attention here is that exhibited by the mountains which encircle the lake, particularly towards the abandoned palace, called Peri Mahal, not far from which stood one lonely tree, like a mourner o'er the dead. Here the slopes are charming, and the crystal water has been somewhat spared, to reverberate the sun and shade, and to repeat these pleasing shores downwards on its thus attractive surface. So also there is some fine grouping near a spot called Chashma Shahi, or "Royal Spring," of which I shall speak more at length before I leave Kashmir. In companionship the afternoon passed pleasantly enough ; we manœuvred our way through all impediments, and the evening concluded with a quiet tented entertainment.

XVI.

MY next excursion was to include the Sind Valley. This lies upon the road to Lay, the capital of Ladak; and I followed it to somewhat beyond Sonamerg—merg signifying meadow. But there were other spots to be visited on the road thither and on the return. It was on the afternoon of Wednesday, the 22nd of May, that I made my start; but the early morning of that day I had already devoted, at the earnest desire of Camala, to a climb to the Temple called Takti Suleiman, or Throne of Solomon. Here, I must ask you to believe among other matters told of that same monarch, that King Solomon used from time to time to sit "in all his glory." The climb is smart and rough enough, as many paths have been to many thrones. And when you get to it, the Temple is as little worth the trouble as has happened to be the case with many thrones. The height is 6000 feet above the sea, and 1000 above the Chenar Bagh. When there, you cannot fail, in some respects, to be impressed with the view. In the distance you see many folding hills, and winter-snow mountains; while below you cannot but remark the very curiously sinuous course of the Jhelum, displaying a pattern on the ground, to which an oft-repeated legend attributes the invention of that well-known pattern on the old-fashioned Kashmir shawl. And, so far as this pattern is concerned, the extreme flatness of the Vale well serves to exhibit the effect of the laid-out shawl. The colouring of all the view was charming at that early hour, for I had started at about five o'clock.

In the afternoon, then, in spite of there being some grand out-door entertainment by the Maharajah, which was open to all, and my stores and all other necessaries being on board, I started with my two boats, but in cold and comfortless weather, for Aloos, on the north bank of the Woolar Lake. This was to be my to-morrow night's station, and an anchorage down stream was to serve for the night, and my first visit was to be to the Lolab Valley. Leaving early on the following morning, I found we must diverge from the passage by the Norū Canal, which lies on the way from Sopur to Srinagar, in order to get to the lake, which we reached at about three o'clock in the afternoon. Here, in a marshy, weedy corner, the boatmen proposed to stop. On my naturally expostulating they talked of "hawá" upon the lake. This is a very dangerous and well-known storm of rain and gusty, high wind, funnelled through the surrounding hills and mountains, and working up shallow and confined waters to the destruction of flat-bottomed boats. But all was peace and quiet now; and it was only a corresponding state of quietude, vulgarly called laziness, that reigned within the boatmen's breasts. They were, however, soon roused by a not very tempestuous vocal breeze, and we crossed the lake at leisure, with which I will not pretend to have been greatly charmed, though it is not wholly without feature. The water is shallow, and was very muddy and weedy, and Aloos was little better than the spot whence I had worried the boatmen. But there is some show of folding hills and valleys round about.

Ponies and coolies were ready at early morning, and I was glad to get away and begin to ascend. We were to mount a considerable ridge in order to descend to the Lolab Valley on the other side, and it was a very stiff and not very interesting mount. But my eyes and ears were now and then regaled by the well-known whitethorn in full bloom and by the far from unknown voice of the cuckoo. At last but came to the summit; and there, in a small but beautiful woodland scene, at a turn to my left into a path that led to Sopur, I breakfasted under a very fine old forest tree.

A little farther on I was to pass out of this broad belt of shade, and to look down on Lolab, far below. Accordingly, I walked through alone, in order that I might enjoy alone the promised opening. Shortly I issued from the wood, and all was before me. What was my sudden, but enduring, impression? Simply that I would go no farther. Below me, strikingly far down, lay the valley, flat as a floor; and not only so but flooded with rice cultivation ."Oh!" I was told, "certainly, yes, there is much rice; but Lalpur has some very pretty walks." Very good; but I did not undertake Kashmir for a "pretty walk," nor surely for the guide-book's entertainment of "*ten or twelve days, marching about from village to village.*" Right or wrong, I turned from flooded rice-grounds. The surrounding hills were commonplace to me, and

I am quite content to be abused for my something more unpleasant even than indifference. "Where can we go now?" said I, in not the best of moods, and intending inwardly simply to go back. But Camala saved me this. "There is Nagmerg," he said; "that lies up here." We had turned back into the wood, and he pointed to a rising ground to my then left, and therefore in a direct line opposite to what had been my breakfast-ground. "Anything," I said, "rather than doing nothing, except going down to the Lolab." So that path we took, and I certainly do not repent it. We were soon in the midst of a very undulating—indeed, almost precipitous—forest, well clothed, but not too closely so, with fine trees; and on an extensive bank, rising before me, I presently beheld an immense sheet of forget-me-nots in full bloom, offering a spread of flowering azure that was quite new to me among these flowers. But this was adventitious. The general scenery was standard and permanent, and I could recommend any one to visit Nagmerg, though the climb is severe. It presents a fine, widely undulating surface of mountain meadow, beautifully fringed with forest edges, not of merely pine, but of fine round-headed timber; thus calling to mind the description of the picturesque which Gilpin gives in his "Forest Scenery," where an irregular base forms bays and promontories of foliage. From both sides, that is, front and back, the views are most striking. The one looking towards the Vale I saw. The one looking in the opposite direction I did not see; for my weather was very unpropitious, and I consequently lost one whole day, not only in tent, but, for the greater part of the day, in bed. It was of no use to get up.

From the northern side, the great mountain Nunga Purbat can be seen; but him I saw afterwards, of which anon. Towards the Vale the view is really grand. You look completely down the vast gorge you have been climbing, and the lake and all its shores are visible far below. In the very farthest distance you get a long range of snow mountains; and between them and the lake you have the intermediate flats, effective from this point, because decked out specially by the River Jhelum, which trails directly towards the eye in one long approaching line of distant silver. Short was my evening view, however. For the next morning the weather was at war with everything; and thunder and lightning of the mountain's force, loaded with violent hail, swept the whole country round, and made it quite impossible to move. While it lulled towards the afternoon, my solitude was enlivened by a visit from a Captain Balfour, who kindly walked towards my tent to make inquiries, and who gave me certain useful hints about Lake Manasbal and the Sind Valley, confirming me also in the wisdom of my determination not to descend to the Lolab.

On the morning of Sunday, May 26th, I came down again to Aloos, and took to the boats: and down indeed it was. My men and pony coolies recommended it, the latter naturally, for I had to come on foot, and now and then on something else besides. But the green rugged scene was extremely picturesque. On turning out of the river, the next day, to get to Manasbal, the scenery became extremely pretty. The surrounding hills sloped pleasantly towards the water, which was of a perfect crystal, and our tenting-ground was under some handsome chenars at the head; and here I had the good fortune to meet again my neighbours of Atchibal, Captain and Mrs. Harries.

Here I stayed four days, moving about in one way or another, and was one day much amused by attending a fishing excursion, where the fish were caught with nothing more nor less than mulberry bait, which they eagerly snatched. What they were worth when caught, I am not competent authority to say. But talking of mulberries, for which Kashmir, as I have said, is famous, there was an old Fakir living below our chenars at the lake-side, who brought us every morning, before breakfast, some of this delicious fruit, fresh gathered from his own garden. It was daintily set out in a little wicker saucer, lined with fresh chenar-leaves, and decked with blossoms of the wild single rose, carefully sprinkled on the purple fruit. We went down to pay him a visit, and to walk through his garden; and he showed us, with much quiet satisfaction, a long natural tunnel, made longer by his labour, in the hill behind his house, which was to be his tomb. Nor are they merely Kashmir Fakirs whose vanity extends to tombs.

The weather had been unsettled, but was improving, and on the morning of the 30th of May my attention was attracted by a small group of shepherds driving some thousands of sheep up the mountain for pasture. This, I was informed, showed they considered the weather might now be depended on as settled, so I followed its expected example, and began to settle my own mind ; this time, for a start on my excursion up the Sind Valley. And this I made on Saturday morning, the 1st of June.

The excursion, as far as Sonamerg, comprehends four stations on the road from Srinagar to Ley in Ladock. There are altogether (Duke's Ince, p. 239) nineteen of these, and the whole distance given is 260 miles. The same book says that "many visitors," even those "who do not care for sport" (which will take Englishmen anywhere) "simply" (very simply ?) "march to Ley for the benefit of the exercise." Considering the sort of country to be travelled over, and to be repeated on return, such a proceeding might be termed a strong application of the principle of exercise, at the end of which it is quite possible the "visitor" might find himself very much "exercised" indeed. That my good host, Colonel Lister Kaye, went many days into the mountains, I know by his messages into Srinagar. But he went to shoot the ibex, and, from what I gathered, had been successful. For myself, had I been in every respect, perhaps, different from what I was, I might have ventured on the same arduous enterprise, but in no case would I have gone to Ley for mere exercise. The little run to Sonamerg—some forty-five miles—was all I went for. It is so easy to write things in books. I was told by a recently returned sportsman that the road becomes fatiguing, tedious, and monotonous in the extreme.

To Sonamerg, then, let us go, and tent at Kangan,

at about twelve miles' distance. Thence, next day, to Gund, another fourteen. Then, next day, to Gagangir, another nine. And thence, on the fourth and last day, to Sonamerg, another ten. Here I found an extensive undulating rocky meadow ground, dressed on some of the slopes with timber, but altogether somewhat naked; surrounded at greater or lesser distances with mountains, which were somewhat interlaced in the direction of Ladakh. Here an entomologist, who had been with me, and of whom I will speak anon, left me at once, as he was pressing forward on his far longer journey; and here my solitude was enlivened by the presence of Mr. and Mrs. Blisset, he, I believe, being at the head of the telegraph service.

Of this my journey to Sonamerg, I wish to say that it was by far the most generally interesting and engaging of all my Kashmir wanderings. There are, of course, many of us who want to see everything, wherever we may go; and, not only so, but who measure the beauty and curiosity of everything they see by the distance that it lies from home. To these I do not speak: but to others I should say, Content yourself with this visit to Sonamerg, or if you will add, add Nagmerg. Of Gulmerg I say nothing, because I did not go there; but from what I gathered, its recommendations, without unnecessarily detracting from its features, are more noted for society than for scenery, and this must always be a great object in Indian furloughs.

One great advantage in the Sind River or Valley excursion is that as you advance the scenery culminates. When I first turned into the side valley, after about three-quarters of an hour's ride, I fell into a dead stretch of those interminable flat, wet rice-grounds that deform Kashmir, and which illustrate, in the most forcible manner possible, what I have repeatedly affirmed, that fertility may present ugly landscapes; and if rice-fields do not, what does? But in this present case there was a fine apse of mountains before me, not gigantic by any means, but large; and towards these one may direct the eye. In perhaps two hours you leave these undelectable and unwholesome spreads, and arrive for breakfast on grass, and under trees. Thence onwards the scenery improves; the ground is rough and picturesque, and presently there opens a remarkably striking perspective of the valley before you, with heavily wooded slopes. In a short afternoon ride of three hours we came to the evening's halt at Kangan, and tented on a charming spot. The slopes on the right were densely wooded, with very varied foliage, and on the left were bulky grassy lumps of almost mountains. One great companion in this journey is the noisy, rushing river Sind. And what a companion a really running river is! Even if it is running against you it is one; and how much more so is it when it runs with you and beckons you on with "follow me," as so many of us have long since proved, through the beautiful slopes among the walnuts and sweet chestnuts of the Italian Switzerland.

But during these two or three days I had another companion also—I mean the entomologist I have already mentioned. He was travelling for a Society, and he had come out into these remote districts, and was bound for a certain altitude, far off still, in order to investigate and report upon a certain question: whether a certain given butterfly was to be found at that altitude. This may sound trifling to some; but it was an inquiry into nature, and worth a great deal more than many erudite wranglings. He was wrapped up in his research, and full of information in his sphere. He had also secured several varieties, which he showed me, in gazing on which (reminding me of rougher sport of this class in almost schoolboy days) I wondered not more at the specimens than at the artistic method of the packing. A pursuit of this kind carried to this extent might seem unaccountable to some; but to me it seemed far and far more entertaining than walking 260 miles to Ley, and back again, for exercise.

At 7.30 on the following morning we started for Gund, still following up the rushing stream, now milky with snow and glacier water; and with scenery always improving, and satisfying the craving thirst for Kashmir gorges, without flats and rice-grounds. And here I may call to mind the constant companionship of wild flowers. The rose of Kashmir sounds more romantic and suggestive than the Kashmir rose; but the blossom itself, by whichever name called, is pleasing in its modesty, and grows in modest places and on a modest bush. At all events, it is far more engaging than the Rose of Sharon, or the flower that was shown me in Syria under that name. It shows of course a single blossom only; but how much more of sympathy there really is in the speaking countenance of a single blossom, with its smiling eye, than in a pursed-up double one, without a countenance at all! The difference between the two I have always interpreted to myself as this—the single blossom says, "I'm looking at you," while the double says, "Look at me." But a quite peculiar feature in the Kashmir bush is that the blossoms grow on the long straight branches from end to end in a regular row, one after another, so that by bending one of these into a circle you have at once a perfect and unpretending chaplet, which, in all its simplicity, might strikingly adorn a lady's brow. I could not but recall four French lines I have read in one of Isaac Disraeli's charming volumes—the first of his "Curiosities of Literature." He quotes them from among those many that were written on the famous "Poetical Garland of Julia;" and although it is the violet that speaks them, they might, with a little indulgence, if not strictly, be spoken by the Rose of Kashmir:—

"Modeste en ma couleur, modeste en mon séjour,
Franche d'ambition, je me cache sous l'herbe;
Mais si sur votre front je puis me ver un jour,
La plus humble des fleurs sera la plus superbe."

Which let me thus translate:—

Modest in my colour, modest in where I grow,
Free from all ambition, 'neath the grass I hide;
But if I, one day, should find me on thy brow,
The humblest of the flowers would, then, the fullest be of pride.

But besides the modest rose-bushes, there was a

white clambering rose. High and wide, and in some of the plants strikingly so, it clung to the trees, and blossomed abundantly among their leaves and branches, as if belonging to them. The effect was charming; add to which at early morning the air was perfumed with just the most delicate aroma. The hawthorn must again be added, and one or two shrubs of the dogwood. Nor were specimens of the blue iris wanting.

In addition to the general class of scenery I have described, the camping ground at Gagangir showed some fine curving rocks in the direction of the next day's journey; while those on the other side of the rushing river were splendidly clothed with forests of varied fresh green foliage. On the last day the scenery was, perhaps, the finest; and at length emerging on the rocky meadows of Sonamerg we beheld a cragged, double-headed mountain, exhibiting two or three glaciers on its slopes and precipices.

It was the same afternoon of this arrival that the entomologist left me for the next station. After that, I met Mr. and Mrs. Blisset; he being somewhat disappointed that a grizzly bear had escaped him and had been seen afterwards crawling up the mountain. On the morning of the next day, June 5th, before breakfasting with them, I rode for about two hours, going some way down the path towards Baltal and back. Beyond Baltal begins the Zogila Pass that leads into Ladak; and after breakfast, all tents having been already struck, I was on my way back to Manisbal Lake. As the scenery on coming had culminated, so on returning it deteriorated; and this was one disadvantage of having to return. Rice-grounds reappeared, and the foul mud-ploughing, and the shout of the muddy plougher to his muddy oxen. How different from the healthy furrows of our Surrey hills! Yet this is the grand growth in Kashmir, to come to join in which has been recommended to English farming emigrants. Well, indeed, and with a pang of absence, they might remember,

> "How jocund did they drive their teams a-field."

It was in the course of one of these day's marches that a curious incident occurred, the peculiar feature of which might have by many been overlooked, by mistaking it for a mere exhibition of common timidity. As I was quietly riding along, I suddenly saw a black snake, of no great size, crossing the path. Instinctively I threw my crop at it, and called out to my guide who was behind. The moment he saw what I pointed at, he made three or four short, measured jumps back. This would very naturally be attributed to fear. But it was no such thing. I instantly detected a reverential colouring in his attitudes; and I am confident that there was here figured the latent sentiment of the old Nâga, or snake-worship. Nothing could have induced that man to hurt the snake. And this is the reptile which the Christian holds to impersonate the enemy of all mankind. Thus have minds or brains differed throughout the world; and, in particular, to what thoughts and facts has not the serpent, or snake, given rise? I distinctly witnessed his influence here in a very humble case; and later on I saw a very grand one in the vast temples in Cambodia.

On Saturday, the 8th of June, I arrived at Manisbal, and on crossing the new bridge, on my return, noted that there were some rather striking peaks and shelving valleys far away to the right as I turned down to the left towards my destination. Happily I found Captain and Mrs. Harries still there, and that they had been joined with their friends, Captain and Mrs. Brown. The space under the chenars was therefore rather largely occupied; but as I was to start at early morning, I became, at their suggestion, their guest at dinner for the evening, and slept on board my boat below. I must add that the lights and colours of the general landscape were particularly effective in the course of this afternoon and at sunset.

After having thus seen the Sind Valley, I should naturally have returned to Srinagar; and so I should have done, had I been favoured with fair weather at Nagmerg, and been able to see Nungar Perbat from those striking and engaging heights. But as this was otherwise, and that I was determined to get a view of him, I was bound to go across the somewhat dreary Woolar Lake again, to a place called Bandipur, for Tragbal. This I did on the 9th, and made my way through foggy, sedgy, weedy, and muddy water, and thence up a canal to a coolie station. Here we were furnished with ponies and attendants, and were to go to Kralapura. But the pony-boy, by a blunder, took us up another road, and we found ourselves brought for a meal and a night's halt to a merely wretched, ruined, empty cowshed. Fortunately a Kashmir cowherd was on the spot, and explained to my men the mistake; whereon Sedeeka "turned to" and thrashed the pony-boy. Cuffing is often appealed to out there, especially with coolies. But not much harm was done; for the charming touch of evening that I enjoyed in going across two wooded heads or ridges of no great distance in order to redeem the error, more than made up for the mistake. In the first rather scanty wood we were overtaken by just the fringe of a small thunderstorm, the intervening sunshine silvering the rain-drops, and on descending from this and mounting the other, the evening sun came out bright and warm upon us, and all things glistened. But chiefly, as the effect of all this, there was a wondrously fine evening double rainbow, which for some meteorological reasons hung close upon us; and while Kralapura lay in deep bird's-eye view immediately below us, it thus gilded the scene as Constable himself would have joyed to see it. Moreover we were here wholly among the hills; the flat, insipid Vale being quite excluded.

At early morning on the 10th came our climb, and fortunately for me, I had a very clever pony. The height from the lake—itself some 5000 feet high—is called 4000 feet; and if it is not so, it seems so. The coolies and the men came a shorter but a sharper way, and arrived some little time after me with gestures that betokened something not very unlike fatigue. We were all landed under some large pine-trees overshadowing a piece of water, and here I breakfasted But this was not yet the top, for that lay another 2000 feet above. However, here I tented, and shall not readily forget the truly pastoral scene I witnessed. As I came towards the trees I saw before me two large flocks of goats, reposing with their two tall shepherds. The goats were themselves of unusual size, and very long-haired. But their tameness was quite as singular as their appearance. I got off, and walked among them, and they would scarcely make way for me; in those solitudes I confess to have felt companionship:

"Their tameness was *charming* to me."

After breakfast came the second climb to see the mountain, and through the forest to a wide, ungainly, undulating plain we came at last—Camala and I. Here, to our right, we caught a full view of Haramuk, rearing his snowy range to about 17,000 feet above the sea, to some 11,000 feet or 12,000 feet above the vale, and to some 6000 feet or 7000 feet above us. But I did not come specially to see Haramuk. The afternoon was very fine, but where was Nunga Perbat? "Ah!" said my waterman, who was on a pony with me and spoke just enough English to be generally misunderstood (though not so in this case) —"behind rain cloud." And truly, there gloomed a centre storm in the far middle distance, a large dark separate curtain across the otherwise blue sky. I turned my pony to the right towards Haramuk, caring not where I went, when lo! through an opening of some crags and crests, the corner of my eye caught a startling object. It was really Nunga Perbat, and the storm was really miles away from him. Hastening forward I called to Camala, and gained an eminence and gazed. He stood out far distant and quite alone without competitor; and he was snowy white throughout. The sun was full upon him with his map-registered height of 26,629 feet, and he looked supremely fine. His form, from my point of view, was perfect: two vast shoulders with an aspiring head between them; the whole body to correspond; and all alone. This mountain scene was truly impressive, and all the more so from its chief feature having come upon me by surprise. There stood he; Haramuk and his high range were to my right, and over the ridge to the Tragbal Pass—11,800 feet high—which lay to my left, for I had diverged—I saw the long snowy mountain-path leading onwards down to Zedkusu on the road to Gilgit; and along that snowy path there was approaching one small, slow group of one man with his one laden donkey; a perfect Bewick winter colophon. I sat gazing on Nunga Perbat till I perceived the effect was changing by the movement of the sun. A shade was just appearing on one side, with a slight mist into the bargain. I did not wait to drink the lees; but with the last taste of the sparkling wine I quickly rose and departed.

Two facts should here be noted: you do not see Nunga Perbat at all from the common path; and you should see him at mid-afternoon. As regards the path, I met two young sportsmen on the road who had killed there ten bears together—seven for one, and three for the other; and who had just come up from Zedkusu. But they had seen no more of the mountain than I had seen of the bears. This bear-shooting, by-the-way, of the common black bear is now belittled in Kashmir. "Oh! bears, yes." And I confess the sport does not, as described to me, seem very grand. These animals are as fond of mulberries as are the fish, and are shot down while enjoying their schoolboy plunder, squatting on the branches. With the grizzly and grisly gentleman the case is somewhat different, and the sport is rarer. Kashmir for other sport, has, by all accounts, been shot out altogether. From the forest tent I came down, and down, on the following morning, and was towed up the "charming" mud-banks of the Jhelum; landing and tenting again at the Chenar Bagh on Wednesday, the 12th of June; but, this time, higher up and beyond the crowded trees. Thus ended my second excursion. My third and last was to be to the Pir Panjal Pass.

XVII.

I HAD heard of the glories of the Pir Panjal Pass into Kashmir from Lahore so long ago as when on board the "Ganges" coming to Calcutta; and I had heard of them again at Murree; and being myself purely an excursionist, with my time my own, I could not have dared to leave the Vale without seeing the Pir Panjal Pass. Accordingly, I made my arrangements for starting on the evening of the 18th, and in the meantime I employed my few days in walking across the wide flat to the reading-room and in paying another and a fuller visit to the Dal, especially in order to see something at least of the remnants of Moore's "splendid domes and saloons of the Shalimar." The illusion that any such features could ever have existed there must be dispelled by a visit. But, then, Lalla Rookh is not a guide-book; and they who desire to think of Shalimar, as he wrote of it, should not go there. What remains shows that the whole affair must have been put together in such a manner as common sense must see was alone possible in those remote and then quite outlandish districts; I mean that the quality of the remains, to the vulgar mind at all events, thus shows that in its original condition the building and its surroundings must have partaken of the tawdry. The canal leading up to it is to-day of dismal aspect truly.

The Nishat Bagh (or garden) may follow suit in my description; but the Naseeb Bagh is well worth a visit, for it is a palace of nature merely, consisting of no artificial bagh and buildings, but of a fine grove of old chenars like a small Windsor forest. Save for the inconvenience of access, it would be the choicest of the Srinagar tenting-grounds. I was again depressed by the absolute suffocation of the waters of the Dal; there is even a causeway (as we call it) built into the lake; but the sloping banks and mountainous hills around improve upon better acquaintance.

Well, in undertaking the Pir Panjal Pass, I arranged to put all my people on ponies, to their great delight, reserving one of the boatmen to come on foot, in order to look after the coolies with the tent and stores; and on the evening of the 18th I started for the Pass, going round in the boat to the Post Office on the river. Thence, next morning, I was towed up to Karkapur, arriving about two o'clock p.m. This was a desolate-looking place, but at about a furlong onwards there was a fine chenar-tree to tent under, which, in turn, afforded a fine, though distant, view of mountains with undulations; but these also far away. A beautiful burnish of virgin gold attended sunset, and this tint is very characteristic of Kashmir. In coming up the river I thought the hills in certain parts looked better than before, but the banks were but towing-banks still.

Starting at six next morning I had a ten-mile ride to Rama, and tedious and ugly was the ride. Rice-grounds and coarse grass were its adornment, and the flatness was of the Isle of Dogs. The weather was hot, my thermometer, both yesterday and to-day, showing 88° in the shade, where we could get shade. Though we arrived at an early hour we were obliged to halt, which we did under some fine walnut-trees. But we were not quite solitary, though perchance would have rather been so. For we were regaled with what at home would be called "rough music." Here, however, the occasion was the exact opposite. So far from its object being, as with us, to accompany the wranglings of husband and wife, it was here intended to celebrate their early harmonious junction, before the luxury of love had been succeeded by the luxury of quarrel. My people were somewhat astonished as well as amused at the barbarism of my objection; and at my explanation of how we understood such sounds at home were rapt in wonder.

An early start next morning brought us, after an eleven miles' ride, to Shupyan, where there was some show of timber, but only a poor tenting-ground, and the ride was again flat and ugly. Afterwards, another night brought us to Hirpur, whence the ascent is considered to begin, though this is not strictly correct; and here it was that the general hire of horses took place. The spot itself is more or less engaging, and I tented by a stream's side under a large walnut-tree. The bungalow (so called) was of so doubtful an appearance that I left it in doubt.

On Saturday, the 22nd, I sent the coolies forward with their guide, getting up at early dawn to free my tent for them, and at a later but still early hour all our riding party mounted our ponies. There was myself and cook, the waterman and the sweeper, the under boatman and volunteer waiter; and off we all trudged together, to get to a spot on the Pass called Aliabad Serai for the night.

What we were to see I could not at all make out. In the Chenar Bagh there was a near neighbour of mine, a young doctor, who had come over rather too early in the season, and was suffering from a much-frozen lip in consequence. But I could not possibly get from him any distinct description of what he had seen, though I am quite sure he did his best to give me something of the sort, and was very indulgent of my cross-questioning; but he was only an exaggeration of too many travellers: they cannot manage to describe what they have seen, so as to prepare you for it. In this case, however, that peculiarity was strong, perhaps because I always found him reading mathematics. Thus it was that my curiosity was great, and my distrust, perhaps, was scarcely less.

Well, we began with a very pretty ride through the Hirpur woods, though by-and-by the path became almost too picturesque in rocky ruggedness and unmitigated ups and downs. At length there was a decided down, and we came forth upon a low bridge across the rushing, boisterous Rembiera. There the real ascent began through the forest on the opposite side. Out of this we presently emerged, almost equally impressed with roughness, and came upon the coarsely green and shapeless gorges of the Pass, while the Rembiera now roared far below us on our left. This unpicturesque gorge continues in long perspective, and you see your future path in certain broken lengths for a good way ahead, roughly cut out upon the harsh, dry cheek or slope. It is as bad as bad can be in places, and I believe I was the only one who escaped the ineffable bore of continually getting off and on. But my pony was very clever, and only wanted his fair chance given him, and this served for both of us. What else could you expect on the Pir Panjal? Perhaps we saw more than usual of this class of the so-called picturesque, and I was told we did, for by the breaking of some bridge we were forced into an unusual divergence, and were driven over a ragged round. What chiefly proved this was that our breakfasting hour happened during the divergence, and we bivouacked on a shingly slope of perhaps 60°. On we afterwards continued, and I soon discovered that, whatever the Pir Panjal Range may look like at a distance from the south, the Pir Panjal Pass, or vast gorge of the Rembiera, is, as compared with grand mountain passes, ugly, confined, and coarse. There is not to be seen one single glance of a good, real, craggy peaked snow mountain. You are for the whole way to Aliabad Serai—to speak of nothing farther at present—under the brows of that lower class of mountain known as the round or clumsy-headed, and there is only coarse grass, some rock, and dissolving snow to show for itself. The bareness of the slope you travel on is extreme, though this of itself need not have destroyed attraction.

At length, in the midst of all this, hope jeering at me as we went on, I heard the welcome, yet most unwelcome words, "Aliabad Serai," and there it was among the same shapeless slopes, showing itself at a curve about two miles away in front. Thither we came in time, and I then found myself upon a wide, exposed and undulating maidan, or meadow, with a profound apology here to that beautiful word for this application of it. Around us were unattractive mountains, but the most unattractive object of all was the most filthy Serai itself. "Hardly fit for a lady," says one of the guide-books, somewhere, in which passage I have scratched out "lady," and inserted "pig." If the Maharajah's feeling as regards the visits of strangers to his dominions is to be tested by the state of this building, he must be held to abhor their presence.

I tented out in the pseudo-meadows under a blazing sun; and be it the turn of sun or of high wind, either of which can arrange to worry you or both can assault together, there you must take your chance. Hitherto I am bold to say that, judged by this class of excursion, there was nothing whatever worth coming for, nothing at all, so far. But the view from the Fakir's house down on to India was a point much spoken of, and this lay still some miles further on, the distance to be undertaken on the early morrow varying in report from five to seven.

Assuredly I was not going down to Lahore at midsummer, and therefore my continuance to and from the ridge was matter of mere faith. And faith in what? We are told that faith is tried. It is, indeed, and very often too, and too much, though sometimes (as must be the case) it is rewarded. I felt mine tried here, but nevertheless I meant to face the trial, and to see whether joy would come in the morning. But behold! there is another arrival from the very spot. Who are they? Two young officers from Lahore. Now then for information, unless (by-the-by) there are mathematics. But I got none, though for a far better reason, and my disappointment was much softened by my amusement at the *naive* reply. I naturally walked to their tent and bid them "good day," being received, as I always was by officers in India, with pleasant frankness.

"You have come from Lahore?"

"We have, indeed, and glad to get away."

"Of course stifling?"

"We could not sleep indoors and scarcely out; even there it seemed hard to breathe."

"What did you think of the road up to the top of the Pass?"

"Well, we were not much impressed with any particular part of it, and it was very hot and fatiguing."

Then came my real point. "And the view from the Fakir's house—I propose riding there to-morrow morning—is there anything really striking there?"

Alas! there had been no Eurydice behind Orpheus in this particular escape from corresponding regions.

"*We didn't look back,*" was the reply. We could not but all laugh together.

As I was determined on two points—one to see the ridge, and the other to leave sweet Aliabad Serai on the same day—I had to start very early for the first object, and I and my waterman were both in our saddles very soon after four o'clock on Sunday, the 23rd, the pony coolie coming with us. What the real distance was I know not; what it seemed I know.

The coolie insisted it was four Cos, or eight miles; for me it might have been eighty. Long, dreary, monotonous, commonplace, and seemingly interminable did I find that "lovely" ride. At last there appeared the building at the crest; and towards this I made at once in haste.

How was my faith rewarded? Did I see anything worth coming for? Yes, indeed I did. All that there is to see I did not see; the enormous flat stretch, including even Lahore, was curtained off by gloomy mists; but in this there was perhaps something gained in the dark charm of half-mystery that hung about, without concealing, all that lay immediately below. I stood upon a seeming precipice. Poschiana lay six miles down by path, and through the sombre atmosphere I saw Poschiana, and a gloomy depth yet lower still, and the misty outline of the rising hills immediately beyond. It was all impressive to behold, and rests upon the memory.

I am very glad I persevered. It is in reality a Surprise View. How, then, should it be recommended to come into the Vale by this Pass? I should answer for myself that such advice is wrong. For what is the descent into the Vale for which you will lose this great surprise? It is nothing. Even if you saw the Vale you would only look upon a flat. But you do not see it at all, or only just a small distant, ineffective peep, perhaps in the direction of Islamabad. Even were there anything to see, the obstinate folding of the dead-coloured buttresses of pine in this "lovely pine-clad valley" would shut out everything below. Yet "kaleidoscopic effects" have been declared! But there is not even variety in ugliness. I have a small but very sensible pamphlet which was published in 1887 by a "Mr. Charles F. Gilbert, Executive Engineer on the late Kashmir Railway Survey," who came upwards. After saying that some of the scenery on the other side is "very ordinary," he thus sketches it from the crest to Shupyan: "Monotonous maidan for four and a half miles, monotonous valley for six and very ordinary wood and water foreground beyond," . . . "no foreground, no background." For, myself, I must boldly dare the responsibility of asserting that the only feature—and that is a grand one—worth looking for on the Pir Panjal, for anyone who has ever seen really fine mountain scenery, is the Surprise View on going into India; "the rest is silence."

My only deviation on returning was from Rama to Chrar; to see Shah Nur-u-din's Zearat, a road described by Ince to run "amidst beautiful scenery all the way," but, as described by me, "ugly ride, ugly place, ugly mosque, and ugly Zearat."

XVIII.

WHEN I found myself at the Chenar Bagh again on the evening of Friday, the 28th of June, I found it very full, and therefore moved up to nearly opposite the entrance to the Dal, and next door, as great good chance would have it, to a Mr. Garrick, well known in India for a very remarkable translation of a Native poem. I was myself now getting rather tired of travelling and tenting, and on the night of July 3rd my canvas was drenched with rain, and I was forced to sleep in the boat. And here was my good luck; for while lying there on the 4th, another boat was suddenly pushed in alongside of mine by someone who had come to call on Mr. Garrick and mistaken my boat for his. Mr. Garrick had left that morning; and this fact leading to a few words, behold, I was recognized as the stranger who held the very short conversation at Domel. It was Mr. Collett's self who spoke. And behold, again, he told me I was looking fagged, which no doubt I was, and that I must come up to his house on the Dal and spend a few quiet days there. And behold again, after a very noisy night of Muhammadan "Merry Marriage Bells," in the course of the morning of Friday, July 5th, I arose and struck my tent for the very last time in Kashmir, and went in my boat to his landing-place, where I was met by his servants and carried up in a rede to his quiet dwelling called "Chashma Shahi," or "The Royal Spring," which lies beneath one of the very prettiest of the mountain groupings round the Dal. Thus, the first slight chance of my few words at Domel, which I need not have exchanged, and the second small chance of my being driven to an upper portion of the Bagh, and the third of my being next to Mr. Garrick, brought me into contact with Mr. Collett, and found me really a most timely and beneficent refuge with the owner of Chashma Shahi. There I remained, enjoying the quiet hospitality of my friend till I left Kashmir, lounging about his garden, and gazing on the mountains round, or listening to the birds, including the varieties of the mocking-bird, and the beautiful note of the golden oriole which had always cheered me in the Bagh. Nor do I forget the sight of a mute beauty that is your companion everywhere, although without a voice, I mean the hooppoe. These charming birds, with their exquisite crests and their curved bills, are most familiar, and will take little or no heed of you while hopping about and piercing the grass for whatever food it may be they are in search of. Here at Chashma Shahi, with Mr. Collett, I enjoyed "somno et inertibus horis," the "jucunda oblivia vitæ" of his retreat, until I bid him a most grateful farewell on the morning of Wednesday, the 24th.

Then I was again carried down to my boat (though now I could have walked), and embarked upon the Dal, passing out into the well-known Sant-i-Kul Canal, paddling by the Chenar Bagh with a last farewell, and thence to settle all things with Bahar

Shah, who presented me with a small shawl on parting. Thence I was punted through the last of The City of the Sun, with its weedy, grass-covered roofings, and afterwards towed almost as far as Sopur for the night. The next day I continued to Baramoola, passing at one time through a long space of shallow water covered with weeds and flowers. At night there was a general assembly of the crews of both boats, and the usual farewell assembly and distribution. My cook, who had now become my travelling servant, and Camala, my waterman, came on with me to Murree, and two of the boatmen as far as Hattien, where, to my great relief, I learned the Tonga road was already open all the way to Kohala; and they who travel now will never know the ups and downs and crags that from time to time were encountered by those who travelled in 1889. Thus I came back again to Powell's Hotel at Murree, passing coldly through all the stations where there had been greetings on the coming, but where the dwellings were desolate on the return.

Now in leaving the Vale I made a point of coming out by the old road, over the Baramoola Pass, in order to see that first view which has been so much spoken of. I found very much what I expected; it is striking to a certain extent, but the, to me, radical defect is there: the dead flatness of the Vale, and its paltry river-banks. On turning to come down into what I call the Entrance Valley, or gorge, I must confess this appeared to me to be much more striking, though the winding, and the there rushing, Jhelum is not actually in view. The fulsome and clumsy exaggerations of the scenery in Ince's Guide-Book speak for themselves, and carry their own refutation ; and to show how such books are written, even the author shrinks from repeating Moore's obvious nonsense about Baramoola being an "earthly paradise," and dares to suggest that "*Moore must have seen it at its best.*" Moore in Kashmir !

When Hamlet says he sees his father "in his mind's eye," he at all events had seen him with his real eye. But Moore had no such solid memory of Kashmir to recall.

What I had expected to see in Kashmir was a beautifully wooded and undulating valley, with flocks and herds, and hanging forests, adorned by a river with ever-varying banks—I will say such a landscape as might compare with that beautiful description of The Isle of Loves which is to be found in the IXth Canto of Camoens' Lusiads. I had expected a beautiful diversified Vale, where the mountains, seeming to belong to it, combined with it, adorned it closely, and appeared to grow out of it. In his Introduction to the "Fortunes of Nigel," Scott refers to Lady Mary Montague as saying "with equal truth and taste, that the most romantic region of every country is that where the mountains unite themselves with the plains or lowlands." Of this I found nothing in the Vale of Kashmir, though I found it abounding in Java and Japan. Indeed, how do geologists describe Kashmir? They opine that the Vale represents the dry bottom of a gigantic lake that eventually broke through and left only the sluggish river. I can but talk by my own brain ;

and I have already said enough to show why, as regards Kashmir, whatever else may be the views of others, I entered hoping and departed disappointed.

And if this was the case as regards the scenery, so was it as regards the "lovely virgins." Not quite so much, perhaps; because I was too old to be able to persuade myself that where poverty, hard work, and poor nourishment must of necessity prevail, fairylike beauty and complexion could possibly abound. I could discover no more of that among the brown-skinned and well-featured females that I saw than I could of "kaleidoscopic colourings" in the rough Pir Panjal Pass; and the real Kashmir woman, moreover, has all the bearing of being rather cold, proud, and distant towards strangers. It is quite possible that if they ever lose one sort of character they may lose the other, but that would not serve to enshrine them in fantastic poetry.

XIX.

I WAS not left long at Murree, for scarcely had I arrived when I received a very kind letter from Miss Ommanney, asking me to repeat my visit to the Colonel, and to come and add Nathia Gali (or Gully) to my experiences. Therefore, on a fine morning, on the 13th of August, I got into the saddle, and arrived about four o'clock that afternoon. Assuredly there was no flatness here Thickly and handsomely timbered gorges, running in all directions, one with another, mainly constitute the features of these gullies; while the picturesque dwelling of the Colonel and his two daughters in the midst of a wood exactly corresponded with the surrounding scenery. Here I passed six pleasant days, enlivened by a periodical succession of lawn-tennis parties on the artificial ground, and looking over several water-colour sketches by the Colonel. On the 22nd I returned to Powell's at Murree, to leave on the 25th for Powell's at Rawl Pindi, and on my way I found the rains had made all green since my arrival; so much so that I could scarcely recognize the road.

Being now on my way to Simla on a visit to Colonel and Mrs. Nicholson, I made no stay except to buy one or two required articles among the dispersed mansion-shops of Pindi, and came on to Lahore, still hot, but now much cooler than when the two retreating Pir Panjal officers had not looked back at it. Thence I took rail to Umballa, where a tonga was then necessary to Kalka, at the foot of the mountains. There I slept, continuing my next day's journey up the mountain to Simla.

There must now be a railway to Kalka along the flat, for the works were well advanced when I was there, and this will be a great boon. There was also a talk of carrying the line up to Simla, but this great advantage, in one sense, would rob the traveller of a most exciting and interesting tonga drive. Both in going up and coming down, and particularly in the down, your attention is kept alive at every turn; not much less so by the skilled driving than by the character of the road. But take care of the heels of the horses when you get out at the changes. As regards Simla, I must confess to have been much surprised when my driver pointed out to me the first view of the city. It seemed to be hanging on a precipice, and not to be adorned by any attractive features as to its buildings. In short, when I came to know it more, I felt convinced that had I arrived there an unprotected and unrecommended stranger, I should not have remained in the place—as Simla—for four-and-twenty hours if I could have got away within that not very prolonged period. But, as it turned out, my stay was of very many twenty-four hours, for I had sent on my letter from Colonel Busk to his brother-in-law, Colonel Nicholson, the Military Secretary of the Commander-in-Chief, whose coolies and jinrikisha were waiting at the station, whence I was carried still farther up, and received a hearty welcome from the Colonel and Mrs. Nicholson at their charming residence of Armadale.

I was not long in practically proving what was in reality the configuration of Simla. On the day after my arrival I accompanied Mrs. Nicholson to the shooting-ground at Annandale, where she figured quite in the first-class among the competitors, and I took my aneroid with me to test the level. It was one of Adie's, and has from first to last turned out singularly correct according to all officially registered altitudes. Accordingly, I pointed out that, measured from the high crown of the town, which is considerably above Armadale, down to the shooting-ground, we had descended just 1000 feet, and, as a natural consequence, had to clamber up it again before we could get home.

Simla is altogether precipitous, and the Viceregal Lodge stands up like a kite in the sky. You may drive about in your carriage and four, but then your carriage is a jinrikisha, and your four are four coolies. No wheels, as we understand them, are allowed to any but the Viceroy and the Commander-in-Chief. All the rest must go as I have explained—in which conveyance I confess to have felt as shy at starting as I had on striding a donkey for the first time in Cairo. Or you may ride, or you may walk. But I don't think officers are expected to salute from jinrikishas. In point of fact, if carriages were allowed there would assuredly be pushings over precipices here and there, or barriers of safety would serve to impede traffic. There is, to be sure, one round of about five miles for riding, called the Mall. Make the best of it.

It was on the 2nd of September, about the close of the rainy season, that I arrived at Simla, and the weather was superb. The sharp edges of the great snow range are visible at intervals from the high level of the Viceregal Lodge, and their buttresses and independent lesser mountains in all directions offer an immense variety of form.. But life is carried on in perpetual warfare with the laws of gravitation, and thc place is toe and heel for ever.

Being a guest at Armadale my time was varied with much society. My first duty was, of course, to enter my name at the Viceregal Lodgc, and Mrs. Nicholson took me to call on Colonel Ardagh, the Viceroy's Private Secretary, where I was highly interested in his paintings, for they were of views in Dalmatia, where I had been with Sir R. Burton. Of course, I called on Lord William Beresford, and the remarkably tantalizing task of getting to his dwelling reminded me of my discovery of that of the Commissioner at Mandalay. I must also mention Colonels Quintin and Hennessey; and Colonel Pole Carew, who entertained me at dinner at his romantic dwelling, "Shady Dale," down to which I had almost to jump. Colonel Warburton, to whom I was indebted for my visit to the Khyber Pass, also reappeared; and many ladies diversified the scene. Thus was I in enjoyment of life at Simla till the morning of the 13th, when I left on a journey to Narkanda, departing under the command of my indulgent host and hostess to come back to them and give an account of myself. Happy "exam."!

XX.

ACCORDINGLY, I started after breakfast in my carriage and six. That was the number required. My first halt was at Fagu, at a distance of twelve miles, and at 1000 feet above Armadale. My next at Matiala or Mutteana—what a wonderful freedom in orthography there is out here!—this was only 900 feet above Armadale. And my third, Sunday the 15th, brought me to Narkanda, 1650 feet above Armadale. Here my solitude was enlivened by meeting Colonel Harvey, of the Wilts Regiment, who, seeing my name, claimed me as a relation of his friend, my nephew, formerly of the Bays, and gave me very useful information about my return road. We passed the evening in gazing on the grand range immediately in front of the long verandah of the bungalow; but though I saw this fine range, I saw also that I had not seen it at its best. In the first place, the magic mantle of these mountains, snow, was scanty; I was told it was unusually so. In the next, the grand moment for the view is towards sunset, when the rays fall full upon them, but at that hour they were cloudy. In the third, at early morning when all the black, sharp edges were quite clear, the sun was exactly behind them. To see the Narkanda range to perfection you must have a fine clear evening. Still, I had seen them and can recall them. But if I admired

O 2

the aspiring tops of these Himalayas wherever I caught sight of them, not less was my wonder excited at their buttresses and outworks. The extent and magnitude of these is most surprising, and hence indeed it is that so much difficulty is found in getting so good an approach to the main range as will enable you to obtain a long and uninterrupted line of ice and snow. There is a view of the above description at Fagu, which is, in my own idea, worth going for alone.

But I did not stop at Narkanda; I went on to Kotegarh, in the valley of the Sutlej, where I found I had come down to the level of Armadale. Here I had the good fortune to find Colonel Hammond, C.B., of the 5th Punjab Cavalry. We therefore could dwell and descant upon the scene together. The whole country was of course vastly mountainous, and it was gloomy; and the dark river, winding in the most delusive manner to the sight, was gloomy. It lay, perhaps, 2000 feet and more below us, and though to the eye it was boisterous, to the ear it was completely silent; and onwards thus it foamed and flowed alone between its rocky banks, rushing as one of the five godfathers to christen the Punjab, and to fall at last into the mighty Indus, which, as another godfather, has served to christen India.

I stayed the whole of the next day at the little bungalow at Kotegarh, and in dutiful memory to Colonel Warburton I buried a chicken, to the subsequent delight of Colonel Hammond. You may ask me what this means. It refers to an excellent hint of the Colonel's. Bury your chicken for a few hours in good mould, before you cook it: plucked or not plucked. On the next day, the 18th September, the Colonel came with me to Baghi, and we both enjoyed, particularly I myself under his guidance, a delightful ride through a rocky forest. This brought us to some 1750 feet above Armadale, and I mention all these altitudes as illustrating the style of the country.

On the 19th we went to the top of the Hatta, 10,000 feet high, whence the mountain view is grand; and here Colonel Hammond left me to return, while I continued to Narkanda. The remainder of this ride was again through forest till I at last dropped down into the Narkanda road and came along soberly to the end. Returning to Simla, my path seemed yet more impressive than before, and on Sunday, the 22nd, I was at Armadale again for breakfast. If, on approaching Simla, anything particularly struck me, it was the host of Sunday folks coming out to Mashowbra, close by, in jinrikishas, in saddle, and on foot, to enjoy the air of heaven in the place of dogma. If in their countenances of thanksgiving I detected any slight latent frown, it evidently meant, What infidel is this, going into Simla on such a holy morning!

On arriving at Simla there was a renewal of entertainment; and finding that Lord and Lady Reay, who had been so kind to me at Bombay, had arrived on a visit to his Excellency, I performed the pleasing duty of immediately entering my name in their book. Between that day and my departure I had been honoured with a dinner and a concert at the

Viceregal Lodge, and an invitation, through Lord William Beresford, to a ball given by the Viceroy's staff. Thus was Simla gilded by means of my friends' letters from England, and by my entertainment at Armadale. After breakfast on Sunday, the 29th, I bade farewell to my generous host and hostess, where I had passed so many pleasant, and indeed luxurious, days, and swung down my fifty-eight miles to Kalka in a rapid and exciting tonga journey. Alas! for those who will enjoy the barren luxury of a railway.

My next point was Mussuri, in order to obtain a long backbone view of the Himalayas, which Mussuri, from a proper point, affords. On the 2nd of October I reached Rajpore, at the foot of the very steep climb to my destination, and rested at the New Rajpore Hotel. The journey was very tedious, for many horses had died, and slow-paced oxen only were available over several miles. But the Mohun Pass, rocky and wooded, and varied, in a certain way, by the dry bed of the sometimes torrential Bindal, served as a diversion. The next day's climb was very trying and tedious; and it required a nine miles' hard pull to get to the Charleville Hotel, whence the views are fine and varied. But the hotel was crowded, and all sorts of English pastimes were going on, including a luxurious luncheon. Bearing a letter from Mrs. Nicholson to Sir George Greaves, I lost no time after breakfast in going to his house, which happened to be close by, though by a rocky approach. I found him at his solitary meal, but he asked me to dine with him, which invitation I accepted, conditioned on my getting a refuge at the hotel. This, I afterwards found, was impossible on my return thither, so that I had to put myself off on that account, and receiving his verbal "salaam" in reply to my note, I took my luncheon and counter-marched to Rajpore, with a certain feeling, for the first time, of being an outcast in India.

XXI

Now I had made up my mind to revisit Darjeeling, for the purpose of making the journey to Sundukfo, and seeing more of the mountains. I therefore struck for Allahabad, having learned on inquiry that I could get across to Darjeeling without returning first to Calcutta, a necessity which, I fancy, would have altered my resolution. On my way to Allahabad I passed again through Delhi and Agra Fort, revisiting all the now old scenes—so soon do we become acquainted with what we have seen—and confirming former impressions; and from Allahabad I found my way, at some cost of fatigue, to Darjeeling. The connections, or quasi non-connections, between the various lines involved many tedious waitings; and in crossing the Ganges from a place called Sahebgunge, where we had to wait from morning till afternoon, to another called Manihari Ghat, a straight-line distance of some four miles, we were forced from some nautical mysteries to compass fifteen, up and down on the river. Altogether this journey, which was to relieve me from a return to Calcutta, cost me, night and day, from the morning of the 15th of October to the afternoon of the 17th, and covered 660 odd miles; but I got to Darjeeling at last.

A good many might think this journey worth while for merely a second sight of the magnificent mountain view from Darjeeling before finally leaving India; and I would not readily dispute their judgment; certainly I should prefer so doing to walking 160 miles to Lay and back again for exercise. Kanchinjunga from Darjeeling is of surpassing grandeur; and Mr. Roberts' comfortable hotel is admirably situated for a contemplative gaze from one of the best positions. But for myself, my chief object in returning was to arrange a journey to Sundukpho; the usual time occupied in going and returning being five days.

The great point gained in this excursion is the freeing of the whole mountain view from that middle ridge which hides all but three comparatively insignificant peaks from the top of Tiger's Hill. But there was here necessity of companionship for a special excursion of this kind; and the first not unlikely person that I encountered was a jovial-looking German, of nearly middle age, but stout, who began talking about undertaking the exploit, but in a negative sense. This might have so passed; but he kept repeating the same thing so often that I made up my mind he was really making up his own to take the daring plunge after all. I was in no hurry myself, for I was expecting at leisure that the weather would get quite cool enough for my intended jaunt into the Madras districts, and thence across to Ceylon; so I waited patiently till the egg hatched.

This worthy gentleman was a Mr. J. W. Krüger, from Rangoon; and he was soon joined by a young and active Englishman from the same city, Mr. John Reddie by name. The enterprise therefore ripened, and we made up a party of five. There was Mr. Krüger, Mr. Reddie, a young Mr. McDonell (who was staying at Woodlands with his mother), myself, and the fifth traveller from another hotel, a Mr. Cooke, being a friend, I believe, of Mr. Reddie's. Three days were required for getting horses, things, and attendants together, and these, under the command of my mounted cook and servant, Bana, were despatched in order. "What a noise your people made leaving early in the morning," we heard when we returned. No doubt they did, for they were many. Besides my own cook, there was another and a waiter, eight baggage coolies, five ponies with grooms or sâìs, and one most important and indispensable individual, the sweeper, without whom there would be no admission at the mountain bungalows. For ourselves, we took the train to Ghoom, where we were met by our ponies, and thence we found our way, riding and walking, to Jore Pokri, for the night. This was on Thursday, the 31st of October. On Friday, the 1st of November, we slept at Tongloo, and on Saturday, the 2nd, at Sundukpho. This was the limit of our journey, and it was here that we were to enjoy the fullest view of the mountains which the fairly practicable paths of these districts afford. The excursion fully repaid us, which I believe I can say was our unanimous opinion.

On the next morning we were all up at the very peep of dawn, and hurried on to the eminence, which was of easy access, lying immediately behind the bungalow, and there, in the fresh and sparkling air, and in our loose but sufficient clothing, we had our rough hot coffee arrangement put together, and sipped our cups and watched for glowing sunrise. All the folding icy groupings lay uninterruptedly before us in long retreating perspective, and though it was immediately obvious that the largest of the three peaks seen from Tiger Hill belongs to a comparatively near snow crest, called, I believe, by the absurd name of the "Hooded Monk," yet it must be understood that it is at first difficult to pick out Mount Everest from the rest; and it must also be understood that the guides were quite unable to assist. The fact is, he lies to the north of the range in Thibet, and, after all, you really do not see a great deal of him; the form of what you do see resembles that of a diamond or lozenge, so far as the nearer mountains permit that much of him to appear. What his exact distance might be from our position the various calculations do not enable one to state with exactness, but it would be quite safe to say that a straight line of eighty miles would be the very smallest figure admissible. Popularly speaking, a round hundred might be ventured.

It will thus be evident that, seen at such a distance, it would be unfair to judge of his particular appearance; but certain it is that the eye, so far as it can judge, entirely misgives the notion of his presenting anything like the picturesque and varied form of Kanchinjunga. Being curious on this point, I have since my return conversed with my friend, Dr. Inglis, on this subject, whose report confirms my doubts. Some ten years or so ago he made a real mountain excursion among the ridges, and ascended one which lies on the western boundary of Sikkim, and is an offshoot of Kanchinjunga, which brought him to almost the same distance from Mount Everest as the former mountain stands from Darjeeling. He was at a height of some 15,000 feet, and there lay only one other ridge, perhaps some 3000 feet higher still, between him and the 29,000 feet of Everest. He had a fine, clear, open view of the mountain accordingly, and the description he has given me is, that it rises quite conspicuously, as it naturally would do, is very large in appearance, but of the plain and simple form of a huge sugar-loaf; and therefore it must be far inferior to Kanchinjunga in variety of bulk and outline.

Even as regards his height, viewed from our distance, the eye was quite unable to distinguish him by any prominence of that kind. He did not appear to dominate the group. But mark; as light came gradually growing on, and a glow in the sky gave token of fast approaching sun, there appeared at length a sudden proof that, far away as he was, he was nevertheless the real monarch. Kanchinjunga lay strikingly close to our right, and while the sun was just tipping his crests the long-reaching perspective still lay in cold and slatey atmosphere, till, in a moment, the farthest-away peak of all was lighted up alone; and thus the lofty Gaurisankar was made manifest among the group by the early golden crown with which the monarch of the morn adorned him. Speaking for myself, this decided singling out of the veritable peak by a living coruscation was quite electrical, and, say what you will, this feeling was enhanced by the recollection that I was gazing at that moment on the highest mountain in the world.

We spent a certain time at Sundukpho, and wandered for a certain distance down the road towards Phallut through the undulating pine forest that hung upon the slopes to our right. But Sundukpho was our intended limit, nor can I doubt that it offers the most striking view obtainable in those regions. Certain it is that the further we went the less we saw of all that had so engaged us in the early morning, and as Phallut was wholly inaccessible on account of broken road and bridges, we were quite content to return to our bungalow at Tongloo, and on the following evening, Monday, the 4th of November, to find ourselves again at Darjeeling.

Our entire journey had been propitious, and we had all been well attended to in all things. The road is altogether exceedingly picturesque, the forests being copious. But there is, no doubt, much fatigue at times, because the ups and downs are very arbitrary. The formation of the ground continually involves a mount which you know merely necessitates a descent, and so on to the last. To mention the main altitudes : Darjeeling stands at 7000 feet, Tongloo at 10,000, and Sundukpho at 12,000. As to danger, the word is worth mentioning only because it has been printed, and therefore should be contradicted. It is more difficult of discovery than is Mount Everest of discrimination. When we were well at home and at the dinner-table, my health was drunk with compliments for having "gone so straight." Indeed, we were always all well together, though now and then young Mr. McDonell would dare me to follow him in short cuts, for of course there was a great deal to be done on foot. And so farewell to Darjeeling and its grand excursion.

We dispersed at once, and on Friday, the 8th, I found myself again at old quarters at the Great Eastern Hotel, which I had left just ten months before, to undertake my Indian and Kashmiri "wanderings and wonderings."

Yet one last note about Darjeeling, which I must choose to record for my own satisfaction, though trite in itself and purely personal. In that now again far-distant land I suddenly observed a notice, "To Banstead Cottage." Banstead I had known since memory began; it was the next parish to Chipstead, my father's rectory, and his unmarried sisters, our worthy aunts, were for ever sending for us all. But both were in olden times two very quiet villages, Chipstead particularly so, among the Surrey Hills. What could Banstead have to do with Darjeeling?

"Who lives at Banstead Cottage?"

"Oh! a Mr. Gibbons."

"That won't quite do—"

"Ah! but he did not build it."

"Who did?"

"An old gentleman, now living at so-and-so."

"What is his name?"

"Crommelin, Colonel Crommelin."

"That will do; a name as familiar to me as my own, and of a twin Huguenot family of old times."

So on Colonel Crommelin I at once called, and saw his daughter, he being rather unwell. But the name was at once recognized, and I was begged to call on the morrow without fail. This I did, and suffice it to say that, although I had not known him personally among others of his family there, yet during our long interview I was at Banstead in my early youth again, until I left the house, when I was at once in Darjeeling again. Thus readily can thought adapt itself and wander where it wills, or where it must, but would not. The Colonel had passed his ninety years; and it was about the time of my early days that his brother, "Tom Crommelin," was a very well-known name among sportsmen, nor can it be yet forgotten by many now living.

XXII.

ALTHOUGH my circle to Calcutta was now complete, I had still something more to do in India, for I could not leave without visiting the Madras Presidency; and as I had resolved to sail for the city, I secured a cabin by the British India Company's steamer, *India*, Captain Hall, and was in hopes to have been piloted down the Hugli by Mr. Hudson, with whom and Mrs. Hudson I had dined a day or two before. We left upon the 18th of November, but were detained in the Hugli by signal, on account of threatening weather, which our captain could not profess to see any real signs of. However, on the morning of Thursday, the 21st of November, the foul weather signal was down and we got away, and passed out of muddy water into blue ocean.

Beautiful weather attended us, and we arrived at Madras at 4 p.m. on Saturday, the 23rd. We had touched here in heavy rain coming up, and though the sun now shone, the flat place looked only a trifle less uninviting than before. The works of the harbour seemed to be all to pieces; and as to its protecting power, I was told that the signal for bad weather, so far from meaning "*fortiter occupa portum,*" was a warning to get out of it and go to sea. My object, however, was inland, and as soon as possible I found my way to the Madras Club, by the help of a boy whom Mr. Rowlandson had kindly sent to meet me. There I saw Mr. Hamilton Holmes, the Secretary, who at once made me at home; and very fortunate I thought myself; Mr. Rowlandson calling shortly afterwards. These introductions are indispensable in India. Two more letters were also of great service to me which General Scott Elliot had given me, among others, one to Colonel Gunning, and particularly one to Colonel C. J. Smith, R.E., who marked me out a most successful march on my way south as far as Tuticorin. At Madras, where, nevertheless, I drove about and admired the lordly houses of the English quarter, this was my chief thought, and especially the getting to the island of Paumben, as advised by Sir Guildford Molesworth, to see the corridors of Ramisseram. No one, however, would give me much hope of doing this by way of any road out of Madras; for at best a long and next to impossible bullock-track would take me only to the shore, whither I might never arrive, and then, as to a boat? But by dint of asking—"by asking you can get to Rome"—I was at last introduced through Captain Simpson to Captain Street, who gave me no new hope, but gave me a letter to Winstanley Carlyon, Esq., Port Officer in Paumben, to be used if I could get there. This turned out to be of vital importance; and by-and-by I will tell you how I did get there, and how you can get there whenever you like to go. But don't forget the letter.

On Monday, the 2nd of December, I left Madras, and my first march being to the Nilgiris, or Blue Mountains, I went as far as Mettu. On the following day I took a tonga to Coonoor, or Kunur—spell as you please the name of any place you please—and drove to Davidson's Hotel, lying about a mile out of the road. I made the height of this hotel to be 6300 feet, and was throughout the drive delighted with the bold mountains and the wooded gorges through which I passed. On the following morning I continued my drive to Outacamund, or Wakamand; and be its orthography what it may (nor do I care), there can, at all events, be no doubt about its attractive beauties. Who would ever stop even to spell the word Simla—as Simla—if he could reach the fine, open, picturesque, and charming scenery of Outacamund? Here I lodged at Sylk's Hotel, after admiring, I think, every inch of the road thither, mounting to 7000 feet. There were the blue hills in verity, and the impressive Dodabetta Peak, of 8000 feet, and an air that seemed to breathe immortality. A fine evening drive round the lakes is one recollection that strikes me among many; nor must I omit a visit they took me to the Foda People, as they are called, with their long black hair, and in their huts. I do not, however, profess to have conversed with them; and can give no information as to their beliefs and social lives. Hooded carts and waggons with pairs of beautiful white oxen were continually met with, and added life and beauty to the surrounding scenery. One spot seemed to tempt you to go to another.

On leaving Outacamund, I made for hot Trichinopoly, passing through Seringam, where I was quite disappointed with the great temple of which the general view in Fergusson is so impressive. He, however, somewhat prepares you for this, and the warning is apt. Besides which, strangers are subjected to much hindrance. "Trichi" (as they call it) was very hot, and its great feature is a great hot rock, once part of a now entirely demolished fortress. Up the hot sides of this you may climb, if you like, in a blazing sun, to see a great flat panorama round you, called by the Guide-Book "one of the finest panoramic views in India." For myself, mere extent is not synonymous with beauty, and very often quite inconsistent with it. I coolly (as coolly as I could) declined the rock, even with the last tempting promise of the guide "that I should see all the railway station." Hence I visited Tajore and returned, examining both the Great Pagoda and the Temple of Soubramanya, both of which are illustrated and fully discussed by Fergusson. But I must confess that I found all this Hindoo architecture fall short in its attraction when compared with the dignity of the Muhammadan, and the exquisite pillars and porches of the Jains.

All the detail on the Gopuras and elsewhere is so crowded and confused, and so eminently trifling (to say nothing more), that the structures bespeak a far inferior people by their own far inferior conceptions; though this need not interfere with a great deal of interest and curiosity attaching to these productions. Even a certain amount of this species of disappointment attaches to the exterior of the Great Temple at Mádura; but the structure itself is vast and varied indeed; and where the interior is not choked and bedaubed with barbarous splashing of colouring, the courts are full of majesty. Nevertheless, disfiguration predominates, and destroys far too much of what would otherwise be stately and majestic. In one part of the edifice I was astonished by the extensive and busy bazaar that was being held ; though there was a certain living picturesqueness produced by the varied colouring and the clamour. Come to the south for clamour. It would be too bad to say these people were "a den of thieves ;" and indeed nobody had yet intruded on them to call them so, nor to overthrow their tables. In what is called the Tirumulla Nayak's Choultrie there is a splendid corridor ; but I had to see one yet more splendid. From Mádura I continued to Tuticorin, whence I was by-and-by to sail for Ceylon ; but being detained there by irregularity in the boats, I made the best use of my time by a visit to Tinivelli and its two temples ; they were, however, so hideously disfigured by paint and whitewash and brownwash, and the following and howling people were so jealous of my intrusion, that I came away without satisfaction, but wholly without reluctance, and do not recommend any one to go there.

At last, on Saturday, the 14th of December, the *Java* appeared for Colombo, and when this was well certified I made all things ready and went with my servant on board, thus finally leaving India, just thirteen months after I had landed at Calcutta.

XXIII.

WE did not sail till the Sunday afternoon, for certain arrangements had to be made with the Port Officer, one of which entailed the disembarking of a host of coolies, already taken on board, for the vessel was declared to be overloaded. This host of parti-coloured males and females were uncivilized enough to go back as quietly as they had come out, and left us to depart at three o'clock. Our passage was propitious, and at seven o'clock on Monday, the 16th of December, I landed at Colombo, where I had set foot on the 20th of November, 1888.

I did not come to pay a visit to Ceylon—the Taprobána of Camoens and afterwards the Taprobane of Milton—which used to present itself so fancifully in our young geographical studies. I did not picture it as the island of palms and spices, and as a land endowed with all those recorded beauties and attractions that made the East, even in those days of only yesterday, a region of the imagination. For if facilities of locomotion make travelling easy, it must be at the expense of ideality and of losing the charm of absolute novelty. I have before mentioned the constant intrusion of Europe wherever you go, and that you never can get rid of her. Here at Colombo is a striking example, and you begin with abundant proof. You will not land with difficulty on a "palm-fringed" shore, breathing spicy gales, but you will land with vulgar facility, because the late Sir John Coode devised a magnificent breakwater and protected a spacious harbour; and though the waters are crowded with natives in their hollowed-out "Catamarans" or "floating trees," aided by their open one-sided outrigger framework, and ready for everything, yet there is the welcome, vulgar steam-launch to take you, western-like, to shore; and when you get there you will seek your comfort in a European structure called "The Grand Oriental Hotel."

I arrived in this beautiful island full of intention and desire to see the most of it within a reasonable time, and I occupied just four weeks and three days traversing some part of it and steaming round it. This latter course occupied ten days, and was forced upon me by my determination to see Ramisseram. How was this last to be accomplished? I soon found out there was just one way and one only, viz. to get on board the steamer that made periodical journeys quite round the island and always called at Paumben on the way. On learning this I immediately put myself in communication with the Steamship Company, and was introduced to the captain, Captain Whitley, of the *Lady Gordon.* He was starting in two days on his then next passage, going "south about"; but he recommended me by all means to wait for the next turn, which would be "north about" and one much more agreeable, considering winds and currents.

Following his advice, which I offer to others, I

made my arrangements, and at once decided to start for Kandy. This I did at 2 p.m. on Tuesday, December 17th, and reached my destination, "The Queen's," at 6.40, four hours and forty minutes on the train.

The almost overwhelming fertility that surrounds one, especially at starting, is the first impressive feature of this journey. I am not about to descant upon "palm-fringed shores," for I don't at all like them; they are extremely flat, marshy, and unwholesome, though crowded with vegetation to please the eye; and for two hours after leaving Colombo you travel through this style of country: flags, cocoa-nut palms, and all manner of thick-growing, moist-looking creepers; and rice grounds and their specially offensive features, though I concede the vivid green when the young plant is growing. Then you begin to mount, and at Kandy you reach an altitude of some 1680 or 1700 feet. Thickly-covered hills and dales and distant mountains are the general characteristics of the scenery, interspersed with large patches of cultivation, the whole suggesting a garden climate. The line now and then crosses the old road, and though the journey in its time, now gone by, might have been tedious, it sometimes seemed tantalizing to be snatched with rapidity by steam over spots where one would fain have lingered to receive an abiding impression. The gorges are in general deep, and the sides abrupt, and the features of the landscape seem all very close together. I was also astonished at the quantity of close-growing forest, but in a map of the island published in

1884 by Mr. J. Ferguson, of the *Ceylon Observer*, there appear these figures :—

	Acres.
Total area of the island . .	15,809,280
Total area cultivated . .	2,997,100
Total area of good forest land	2,680,000

Kandy is a sort of Buddhist "Mecca," and has its great Buddhist Temple, called Maligawâ. Like the Pagoda at Rangoon, this covers (without any irreligious parenthesis of, "or is supposed to do so") a tooth of Buddha. Infidel scoffers have attempted to deride the tooth, and pretend that what has been shown for it might belong to a crocodile. I still remember those I saw at Junagadh; but so it is, that no sooner does Faith blossom than Disbelief attempts to blight it. Besides which, the tooth cannot be too large for either of the huge recumbent figures that I saw, one at Rangoon, and the other at Bangkok in Siam. I have no more difficulty, however, in believing in the tooth for Buddhists than I have in believing other revered curiosities for others. The temple itself, however, did not interest me so much as those I have already referred to. It is greatly reverenced by the Believers, many of whom, however, are complaisant enough (in the words of Mr. Ferguson of Colombo) "to accept a new religion so long as they are not asked to give up their own."

The drives and walks in the neighbourhood of Kandy present the same class of scenery as I have described, and the immediate Lake is a charming object; nor is the course round its shores among the least attractive, a turn which I enjoyed one very fine, indeed lovely, evening on my way to dine with Mr. Gordon, whose hospitality, as well as that of all others who entertained me, I choose for my own satisfaction to immortalize in these, of course, immortal pages—immortal, that is, until the next glacial period shall again freeze up the surface of the world, and destroy for another space all that therein is.

I could not make up my mind to leave the great Buddhist centre without attempting a journey to Anuradapura, one of the buried cities of Ceylon. It was rather an undertaking, because although there was the vulgar convenience of a railway for sixteen miles as far as Matale, and a less vulgar but less convenient coach thence to Dambulla, yet thence to Anuradapura was to cost me a whole night's travel, and, of all things, in a bullock coach or covered cart. However, people had done it, and I followed the usual mode, strongly recommended by the authorities, of booking this whole coach for myself (it would contain only two), and placing a board down the centre; this was to be covered with every wrapper at hand, and I was to dream (dreaming, that is, without sleeping, which many of us seem often to be doing) that it was a bed. Accordingly I telegraphed to Dambulla to secure this luxury for the night of Saturday, the 21st of December, astronomically the longest of nights, as it was likely to be experimentally; for the distance was forty-two miles, and I was not to arrive before the lazy sun had risen, starting soon after his early setting. Let me make a passing observation about this sun which is so often pointed out to all of us as an example. The earlier he goes to bed the later he gets up, and the later he goes to bed the earlier he gets up. How can mortality follow so absurd an example?

Well, I embarked on my railway, content that all was arranged in order. But on getting out at Matale I was pleasantly hailed by an obvious clergyman, comparatively young. "Good morning; I conclude you are going to Anuradapura; so am I; I'm glad we shall be fellow-passengers on that trying journey."

This is what you are liable to. So much for certainties! I scarcely had the heart to disclose to him my own selfish but indispensable arrangements, but was however obliged to do so. "The fault is mine," he said; "I ought to have inquired, as I generally do." And here was what is commonly called a "fix," for there was no train back, and he was on duty and I was on necessity; for the journey with a squeeze of two was for me impossible. As he was a thorough gentleman and quite sincere, I shall not shrink from the phrase in which he expressed his dilemma: "Dear, dear," said he; "I am under a solemn engagement to preach, and I only wish to please God Almighty."

The result was that, as I intended to stop at Dambulla on returning to see some Buddhist caves, I suggested the chance to him that I would reverse this plan, and stop to see them on going, if he could secure me with the post-master the whole wagon for the next night. So we both got on the horse coach together, and so far I was exceedingly glad of his company as the bullock luxury was not now at all in danger. I trace this anecdote through because I here experienced an exhibition of the missionary mind, such as pervades what we call Pagan countries, lying in outer darkness, i.e. not following European Faith; and I do so without misgiving, because in this case my companion was (as I have said) sincere and courteous. The truth is, that he instinctively spoke in missionary style, but free from cant. Thus we kept up an entertaining interchange of views and thoughts, and I was reminded of an observation attributed to the late Archbishop Whately—so good that it ought to be his—when he said to a young missionary clergyman, about to embark on his religious enterprise: "When you are trying to convert anyone try to answer your own difficulties." It seemed to me, sometimes, that this was what my very candid companion was doing. But when the coach at last stopped at Dambulla, at the end of its twenty-nine miles, his final observation disclosed the tone of his own mind, and is instructive, I think, as regards those who really believe that what they themselves believe is the only real belief: and not only so, but that they are bound to bring others to the same belief. "I quite appreciate all you have been saying, and have discussed these things with myself, but what I have been at last permitted to attain to, and what I hope for you, is that, in the language of St. Paul, you may rise to a spiritual understanding of things." There was a good dash of poetic enthusiasm in the mind of my companion, and is not the religious sentiment essentially poetical? No one who knows Ceylon will fail to recognize, in this interview, the Rev. Mr. Garrett.

After all these theoretical discussions there now came the rude and practical one: How was faith to be kept by the preacher as to time, for no one was at hand to work a miracle? So Mr. Garrett immediately went to the Post Office to arrange, if possible, what I had suggested; but alas! he returned with an unfavourable reply, whereupon we both remained with our mouths open, but quite as silent as open. Fortunately, however, someone else spoke and said, "You have not been to the head man." How often is the subordinate more absolute and obdurate than the head? This was the case here, and I cheerfully altered my plan, Mr. Garrett thus getting away with the coach to himself, and his pulpit being furnished as was promised. I remained under only one misgiving, that somebody less congenial might come up the next afternoon and present the like difficulty by making the like request, and so on *ad infinitum*.

However, I took my rest, and on the following morning visited the Buddhist temple. As Dambulla can show "the largest and most celebrated rock temples in Ceylon," it may be worth visiting by many on this account, and there is a very welcome pamphlet on the subject, written by Mr. S. M. Burrows, M.A., Oxon., entitled, "The Buried Cities of Ceylon." But I must wholly dissent from the expression in his preface, where he talks of a nation that "could carve a mountain into a graceful shrine."

The mountain itself is certainly ungraceful enough, though there is a splendid view from it; and the caves are in truth but little less so. To a certain extent they are, I suppose, carved, but the leading character of all the five that I visited is, that vast, as well as small, ugly natural cavities in the mountain have been adapted. They are most curious to behold, but they are not elegant, nor were the priests one whit more so. But you ought to go and see them, even if you don't worry yourself and the bullocks as far as Anuradapura. The whole visit comprehends a strange exhibition of piety and of picturesque rudeness of art amidst rude features. There are Buddhas of all descriptions: of small there are many, and of large there is one; and belonging to this large one there are a pair of naked feet showing the soles, standing square together upon the heels, and justifying, to my surprise, a drawing of such things in Ferguson's book.

Evening now came on, the horse coach had arrived, and I was to dine and prepare for my bullock journey by half-past six, expecting no further interference with my arranged movements. But, behold, as I entered for my repast a half-caste figure stood at the door. Like the ghost of Monk Lewis' "Alonzo the Brave"—

> "He spoke not, he stirred not, he looked not around,
> But eagerly gazed"—*upon me!*

I felt certain of his intent, and took no external notice of him, but inwardly from the first determined, like Sterne with the Monk, to resist any request.

Therefore, when I had finished, and I found him still standing in the same place, it required nothing to make me firm. But had this not been so, he would himself have settled the question, for at last he persuaded himself to make his appeal for a seat to "my *Christian* consideration." This was not only enough, but too much; it was of the too frequently encountered slang, a strong specimen of which in a newspaper boy I had encountered at Coimbatore, so I shortly denied him, and told him why, as already explained, besides which a small boy servant was indispensable to me. But as he persisted in his phrase I had to meet it with a round untruth, and straightway declared myself to be a Buddhist, in order to be rid of him. This shut him up, and the driver allowed him to "hang on" somewhere up to a certain distance. Meanwhile I got through the night upon my plank bed as best I could, rather cheered than disturbed in fitful sleep by the bugle and the bells, the former assuring me that we had reached yet another change, and the latter that the oxen were trotting. By daylight to Anuradapura we came. I spent the Sunday and Monday there, calling on the Government Agent, Mr. Murray, who asked me to breakfast on the Monday, where I again met my friend Mr. Garrett. Mr. Murray then very kindly drove me about on view of all things.

I cannot say I think that the general traveller would feel greatly gratified with what Anuradapura has to show him. With the purely historical and professionally architectural it might be otherwise. The more attractive drawings in Ferguson give promise of much more size and importance in the originals than they possess, and of the old palaces absolutely nothing remains but what appear to have been the under peggings of various stone columns or pillars. The most surprising group of these belongs to what is called Lowa Maha Paya, or the Great Brazen Monastery, and their number is given as 1600. They stand about twelve feet high, and I walked to and fro in this stone forest with a curious sense of novelty. There are also several of those ugly and unsightly things called dagobas, and, as a variety, these are generally surrounded with carved pillars with capitals. But the great natural curiosity of the place is the Bo' Tree, reputed to be the second oldest historical tree in the world. It is said to have been planted 245 years B.C. from a branch of the Sacred Bo' Tree, under which Gautama sat on the day that he attained to Buddhahood. Here is the story, as recounted by Mr. Burrows; it is worth quite as much as many others. "The Royal Missionary Mahindo had converted the Rajah and people of Anuradapura to the tenets of pure Buddhism, and with miraculous rapidity. Queen Anula and thousands of her countrywomen with her became converts. Mahindo, feeling unable to administer so many vows of self-devotion, suggested that his sister Sanghamitta should be sent for to do what he could not. She came, and with her the King of Pataliputua sent a branch of the Sacred Bo' Tree, under which Gautama sat on the day that he attained to Buddhahood."

My curiosity and interest having been gratified, I encountered the necessary return midnight journey to Dambulla ; and on Tuesday, the 24th, Christmas Eve, found myself again at Kandy, walking along the row of trees that border the attractive lake.

After another whole morning spent on the beautifully wooded hills of Kandy, instead of returning direct to Colombo I diverged to Nawara Eliya, to enjoy that fine air, upwards of 6000 feet above the sea. From Nanu Oya there is a fine coach drive of about four miles, which adds to the pleasure of the journey. Here I walked through a tea estate called "The Scrubs," and was shown some of the mysteries of a tea factory : how they turn a slanting perforated cylinder to separate the small young leaves from the large, and how the black tea is produced by fermentation ; and how the green is the unfermented ; and lastly, to my surprise, how all is close packed in the chests in a dry piping hot condition. And having thus satisfied this curiosity, as I had satisfied another at Anuradapura, I returned to Colombo.

Here I was to prepare at once for my passage round the island, made necessary, as I have said, by a determined visit to Paumben, in order to see the Temple of Ramisseram. On the afternoon of the 31st of December I accordingly embarked on board the *Lady Gordon*, with her pleasant captain, Captain Whitley, Mr. Pace, the Company's agent, accompanying also. After sunset on the 1st of January, 1890, we landed at Paumben in boats for a certain small distance. I had previously telegraphed to Mr. Carlyon, the port officer, as to my letter from Captain Street ; and while on our way we were met by his servant, bearing a letter to our captain on the subject.

He returned with us; and I use the plural because Mr. Pace, and the first officer, Mr. Porter, a planter, and another passenger, determined to make the venture of coming with me. I delivered my letter, and we took Mr. Carlyon quite by surprise; but a more hearty reception could not have been offered; and well indeed it was that this was so, for otherwise we could not have managed Ramisseram within the limited time of stopping. We really invaded the house, and forthwith all sorts of preparations were made for feeding us and lodging us. Tins were opened, beds on chairs and sofas were improvised, bottles of wine and beer were opened; in short, we gloriously ate and slept. But time was running against us, and that he should not go too swift for us and run us ashore, Mr. Carlyon called out all his dependable people to furnish bullock carts for us in the very early morning. These were to be ready at the door by four o'clock, and not till we were assured they would be so could we lie down to rest.

As surely as four o'clock struck there were the carts, and there was the hot coffee; and without scalding our mouths, off we were. Mr. Carlyon of course came with us; we should have lost much pleasure could he not have done so. We had seven miles to go to get to the temple, and the road lay tolerably easy under a constant canopy of an avenue of trees. The bullocks trotted famously; they were of the small white active kind, and the carts were light. Still some small anxiety disturbed my mind about the steamer, but this was at once most easily allayed: "Oh," said Mr. Carlyon, "I am the pilot; they can't go without me, and the tide won't fit till ten." And hence we were at peace. In went the prods, and on went the bullocks, and to the temples we came. Like Abu, the outside was nothing. We were to go to the proper entrance, and drove round the building. I hastened in. I had certainly been somewhat prepared for what I was to see by the engraving and descriptions in Fergusson; and yet was I quite unprepared for what I did see. These corridors are almost overwhelming. On each side you have a corridor, with from twenty to thirty feet of floor width, and a height of about thirty feet to the centre of the roof, and these are flanked on both sides with large massive integral and elaborate pillars, lighted by an inner small aisle; and the whole uninterrupted length extends to no less than 700 feet. Well may Fergusson say that no engraving can convey an idea of the scene. To stand at the end of this unexampled perspective provokes a desire to walk down and through it to the end, and when at last you have arrived at the end, you have but to turn to find it all before you again, provoking a repeated traverse. Grandeur can here speak for itself, but it likewise commands your wonder for this very Labour of Hercules that must have been here performed.

Fergusson's engraving gives only the centre corridor, which is the shortest; to give the two side ones would be impossible; but I have a photograph which I bought at Madras in which the 700 feet of length has been attempted. In this photograph the beautiful play of light has been very successfully caught, while one most deplorable blemish in both is

RAMISSERAM : ISLAND OF PAUMBEN

not apparent. To use Fergusson's too trusty words, "within the last few years these corridors have been painted" (splashed) "with a vulgarity that is inconceivable on the part of the descendants of those who built this fane; they have been dosed with repeated coats of whitewash so as to take off all the sharpness of detail, and then painted over with blue, green, and yellow washes, so as to destroy and disfigure the effect to an extent that must be seen to be believed." This very strong protest is too well founded, though not so fully applicable to the grand side corridors as to the central of which he especially speaks. But the side corridors have suffered also, and the majesty of the stone has been almost everywhere basely defiled.

> "Nihil est ab omni
> Parte beatum."

There is always a "but" somewhere. Perhaps the gods were jealous of the fane, and set mortals to defile the work of mortals. But such was and such is Ramisseram. My companions in part amused themselves with those ugly dances, and still uglier instruments, belonging to Nach girls, who were allowed inside the temple. A young elephant was also allowed to intrude his trunk. These utterly ugly shows of the Nach girls are to me offensive anywhere. I thought them blasphemous among the corridors of Ramisseram, where I wandered and pondered until it was, all too soon, full time to go.

Safe with the pilot, I cared not how long I stayed. We jogged back safely with our faithful bullocks, and at ten o'clock precisely were on board and off for Jaffna.

At Jaffna we disgorged four missionaries; they were appointed to do work there, and as they departed in their boat they broke forth in hymnal choir upon the waters. They had asked and obtained permission to hold their service on deck, and in this case no inconvenience was caused, as none could be interrupted or offended; but I have been on board one or two of our crowded English steamers where this illegitimate intrusion was unbearable among different beliefs.

The next point of interest in my compulsory voyage round the island was the far-famed harbour of Trincomalee—the most important naval station in these regions, and among the chief harbours of the world. And that it has been so regarded is made evident by the repeated contests for its possession. From 1639 to 1795 it five times changed hands between the Dutch and French, until in the last year it was taken by the English, and confirmed to England by the Treaty of Amiens in 1801. As regards the scenery it is remarkably pretty, the water being circular, and the surroundings consisting of green hills. I should not deem it worth going to see, though certainly worth seeing, but how Mr. John Fergusson, of Colombo, in his highly interesting lecture before our Royal Colonial Institute, on Ceylon, can for one moment talk of its being "more beautiful" than the splendid harbour of Rio de Janeiro, I do not understand. He does, however, qualify this by "I believe;" and as we all know the power of "belief," we may let the patriotic phrase go by. The harbour, however, can add its great natural and national importance to its appearance; and therefore can command a special interest as belonging to our great maritime power. For these reasons I am very glad to have visited and realized it, though I may hope never to have occasion to recall it on any too interesting and alarming an occasion. We entered at night on the 4th, and did not leave till the afternoon of the 6th; but I did not go on shore, simply for the sake of going on shore. The view was the best from on deck, nor had I any introduction to the resident naval commander-in-chief, who, I understood, was not there. The rest of our passage was comparatively uninteresting, though we touched here and there, till the vast lighthouse building at Dondra Head attracted our attention. Galle was our last touching point, and we rode into Colombo at early morning on Friday, the 10th of January, 1890, having completed a very pleasant round of nine days and a half with our pleasant skipper, Captain Whitley.

Once again at Colombo, I was bound for Java by Singapore, and had just five days at my disposal. But I was to leave Ceylon without picking up any pearls; and also without ascending Adam's Peak, the head of which I had again caught sight of from some point in our passage round. And this latter neglect was wilful, though I must confess to have long felt an interest in it from its being pointedly mentioned in The Lusiads of Camoens. Thus runs the first half of stanza cxxxvi. of Canto x., and my translation:

"Olha em Ceilão que o monte se alevanta
Tanto que as nuvens passa, ou a vista engana;
Os naturaes o tem por cousa santa,
Pela pedra onde está a pégada humana."

"See in Ceylon so high a mountain rise
It caps the clouds, or doth the sight mislead;
The natives hold it sacred in their eyes,
For there's the stone with mark where man did tread."

This man, of course, was Adam; and as the mountain is only 7352 feet high there is a spice of exaggeration in the poetry; but as most prose travellers are (so to speak) prosaic, or prosers, in their exaggerations, Camoens may be pardoned as a poet.

The man, as I have said, was Adam; he and Eve, whom I have always suspected he falsely accused, having sought amidst these enchanting island scenes a refuge that might, in some sense, recall that garden whence they had been expelled when all was lost, and when

"They hand in hand, with wandering steps and slow,
Through Eden took their solitary way."

Hence Adam's Peak, and also Adam's Bridge that intercepts the passage to Calcutta. These two traditional first human beings were apparently allowed repose after their transgression, while Pilate, after his, was driven to Monte Pilato, and there, I believe, committed suicide, as well indeed he might, so far as I remember that uninviting dwelling. But all things change according to surrounding influences. And I am given to understand that this footprint of Adam's is now entirely claimed as that of Buddha, and so revered by all the thousands of Buddhist pilgrims that labour up the mountain with their priests. What the size of the footprint may be I know not, but from what I have heard it might belong to one of the gigantic Buddhas. Indeed, who can believe that Adam would ever have toiled up that mountain, having come so far as Ceylon for the blessing of repose? And it is not to be believed that he was so gigantic a man as was the Noe, whose lengthy tomb many of us have seen in Palestine. So far as an ascent of the mountain is actually concerned, the morning and evening Shadow must be the attraction, besides the view which must be grand. But I had ascended the 12,200 of Tenerife as published already, and nothing here could have been otherwise than a diminished exhibition. Otherwise, as I may now safely enough say, I should have ventured the fatigue.

Fortunately I had met at the hotel Mr. and Mrs. Burnett, who had been fellow-passengers from London to Calcutta, he having constructed the waterworks at Colombo. I therefore had the advantage of driving about with them, and in one of their drives we went to the head of his works. The rush of splendid water through certain ingeniously arranged courses excited my interest and curiosity, but equally defied my criticism. Not so one of the ugliest of towers I ever saw—not due to Mr. Burnett by any means—which had been extolled for its beauty by high authority. The view over the city, swallowed up, almost, by trees, is very striking. Another drive was to the Cinnamon Gardens; a phrase which sounds engagingly poetical. But, in truth, the cinnamon is produced from a somewhat commonplace looking shrub, not very much unlike a very poor laurel, this in its real form being a beautiful shrub. The garden also is quite flat, so that although the visit is highly interesting, not much beauty should be anticipated. Another excursion was to the oldest Buddhist Dagoba called "Kelamy," presenting the usual bulging lump of curious ugliness. In all these drives we continually passed through roads overwhelmed with foliage, and continually bought green cocoa nuts to enjoy their juice.

But the last day came at last, and on Wednesday, the 15th of January, 1890, I went on board the Bremen steamer *Braunschweiger*, Captain Störmer, bound for Singapore on my way to Java. Yet must I recount a curious fact that happened in the harbour a day or two before I left; a fact inseparable altogether from the ludicrous, and yet mixed with the regretful. A Brazilian man-of-war, the *Almirante Barroso*, which had been out on a long cruise, rode in, carrying the Imperial colours, with one of the princes as second lieutenant on board: Don Augusto, son of the Duc Saxe Coburgh, and the Princess Leopoldina, second daughter of the late Dom Pedro II. Then, for the first time, the prince was made aware, with the captain and officers and crew, of the revolution which had driven his grandfather from the throne and country, and established a republic in the place of an Empire. The young prince was in the coffee-room once or twice, and seemed as he might have seemed had such things not happened. His person I should call pale, and somewhat delicate; and his small voice was exactly that of the late Emperor. If the Empire is ever to be restored, it must be so in the person of the Prince of Graõ Pará, the son of the eldest daughter, Princess Isabel, and the Comte D'eu, son of the Duc de Nemours. But Brazil will choose for itself, and I have every sympathetic reason to hope that she will do well.

XXIV.

A PASSAGE of six days, without incident, brought us to Singapore—I believe they still spell it so—and I went to the Hôtel de l'Europe. The approach to the place is remarkably green and pretty, but all is very flat, and the wharfs where you are landed are some three or four miles' drive from the hotel. There was nothing here I cared to stay for, and on the following day, the 22nd, which curiously enough was the New Year's Day of the city with all things closed for the holiday, I managed a ticket for Batavia by the French boat of that evening. On going on board, however, at 4.30, I found our departure was delayed till the next day. This was a question of mails, and therefore ought to be noted. The *Oxus* from Bordeaux had not arrived. However, at 11 a.m., on the 23rd, we positively sailed, and after a holiday passage arrived on the 25th at Tanjong (Port) Preok in Java, curiously called "The Netherland Indies" by the Dutch. This passage is, I believe, always fair and placid, in evidence of which our steamer carried a wooden awning. Nobody stops in Batavia, so that on meeting the Commissioner from the "Hotel Java" at Weltevreden, at a not inconvenient distance, I drove thither with him and found a very pleasant French landlady, though hampered sadly with Dutch colonial modes of living.

After settling down, however, in a large bedroom opening on a large verandah, I found a notice had been put into my hand which the slow Commissioner ought to have taken care of at Batavia. It was an evidence of the Dutch jealousy and timidity as to strangers. I should at once have given notice of arrival, and asked permission to remain for four days, I believe. The landlady suggested I should call on the Resident, and explain the case, the late hour, nine o'clock, not signifying. Accordingly, I wrote my letter to be presented, and drove off to present it. The whole affair, and what presently occurred, reminded me somewhat of the ancient style of things as they recounted them to me at the Cape, where the Dutch martinet system for years ruled triumphant. The Resident's name was Metman, and the Resident's house was a good pretentious one, surrounded by a white pillared outside corridor. I was walking up the broad steps to it, arranging my card and letter to send in when I had rung, or clapped my hands, when a solemn voice invaded my ear, and looking up I beheld a large figure, who was evidently the Resident himself; he had come out to meet me, and proved to be as pretentious as his house.

"La première chose qu'on fait ici," said he, addressing me in French, "en entrant dans une maison est d'oter son chapeau ; c'est une grande faute de politesse de ne pas le faire." Had he held a scimitar in his hand he ought to have chopped my head off in conformity with his rebuke. I could not provoke him very safely for (as I erroneously supposed) I had come to ask his pardon for an omission ; so I controlled my sense of the ridiculous, as well as some small offence, by politely reminding him that his corridor was yet outside, and in truth that the "première personne" I had expected to meet was "la domestique" and not "son Excellence" himself. He gradually softened, read my letter, asked if I had a passport, and fumbled out something which meant, more or less, that I must appeal to the Governor of the Island, and went in, leaving me staring. So the next day, though it was Sunday, I called on our Consul, Mr. McNeil, who received me very pleasantly, somewhat smiled at my account of the interview, and enlightened me on two points: first, that the Resident was quite the wrong person to go to, for he had no authority whatever in the matter; and secondly, that he was not entitled to "Excellency," both of which small mistakes on my part fully accounted for his assumed comical self-importance. The next day all was easily arranged at the Police Office; but my friend, the Resident, had actually privately sent to the hotel to inquire about a stranger who was travelling about the island "sans papiers." The anecdote may seem trite, but it means a good deal. The authorities are exceedingly jealous, and fines are imposed unless rules are strictly attended to; though escapes were recounted to me. The difficulty in these last cases is that the captains of the steamers are held responsible, and are therefore quite on the alert to defend themselves in case of need.

The grand object of my coming to the island was to see the famous Buddhist Temple, or Pagoda, known as Boro Buddor; and in order to accomplish this in the easiest mode, I had to take the steamer to Samarang. But it did not leave till the morning of the 30th, so that I took occasion to make other intermediate experiences; and one was to taste the Mangostine, a fruit concerning which I was very curious, and which I was delighted to find was in full season. I never could get anyone to describe it to me, so I shall now describe it to you. It grows in clusters on its short branches, of which I eventually bought in plentiful quantities, hanging them up in my bedroom. The fruit is of about the size of a small orange, the outer thick rind being of a very dark crimson, quite inedible, and quite separate from the very delicate fruit inside. This fruit lies perfectly white in a hollow, in concentric pieces, like what we call the pigs of an orange. You pick out each of the pieces separately, which are sometimes with and sometimes without a stone. They are almost entirely liquid and crush into nothing in the mouth; and if I am asked the flavour, I scarcely know how to describe it. The prevailing feature is great delicacy, and it is a compounded delicacy. It is delicately sweet, delicately acid, delicately aromatic, and has delicately something of its own, perhaps produced by the above combination. On cutting the dark purple rough outside, the white centre presents a curious contrast, almost recalling the contrast of Beauty and the Beast. The gross opposite to this fruit is the Dorian, which I smelt, but tasted not. I did not indeed get a fair opportunity of doing so, and therefore must escape a charge of cowardice on that plea.

I availed myself of my two days to make an excursion by train to Buitenzorg, and on the following day continued to Soekaboemie and returned. This took me among the wooded mountains, but as the weather was cloudy—it being now the wet season—I did not see so much as on a second excursion later on. I saw enough, however, to prove to me that the Javan scenery can show what the Vale of Kashmir cannot—the beautiful effect of the long mountain slopes combining with the valleys. This characteristic I observed throughout.

On the morning of the 30th I started for Tanjong Preok, and went on board the *Pambora* for Samarang, and suffered the ordeal of bad weather along a coast, and Dutch Colonial food into the bargain. Lots, but coarse. We thought ourselves advanced by not being able to touch at the intermediate ports, seeing that we therefore arrived in shorter time; but we paid for this on coming back, pains following pleasures, as usual. Moreover, when we got to Samarang, "The Blue Flag" was flying, which meant we must lie to outside, and could not have the steam launch to land us. On the second day, however, the 2nd of February, we were relieved, and I went to the Pavilion Hotel. Here I lunched, and immediately took the train for Ambarawa or Willem I, arriving at 6 p.m. Here it was necessary to hire a carriage for my course, but alas! the only word I could get understood was Boro Buddor; and even this was spelt in some other manner, which I shall, however, accept as the inevitable. At last, when despair was at its depth, there appeared a young Dutch officer, who had just one or two more words in English than I had in whatever it was they talked at the hotel, and a carriage was ordered to be at the door at six in the morning.

And punctually it came—a carriage and four; and punctually at 6.30, after breakfast, we started. The road was extremely hilly; indeed, mountainous: we were at one time, by my aneroid, 2000 feet above the sea. The driving was excellent, and when we had to walk we hired bullocks, sometimes joining them on, and sometimes taking out the horses and putting in the bullocks instead. Intercourse, when needed, was carried on by pantomime. At last, about half-past one, we arrived at Magelang, and stopped at Mr. Unglaub's German hotel. Here I gave tongue, and after a consultation with the host, decided to take carriage and horses for (let us see) Djocjacarta, sleeping at Boro Buddor, which was not far off. This time it was to be a carriage and six, and I was to get to "Djoc" (that will do) by early afternoon on the next day.

I therefore left the hotel—most picturesquely situated, fronting on a large, green, well-timbered space—immediately after luncheon, again experiencing excellent driving and fine mountainous and cultivated country, until at last there appeared among the trees a huge, dark brown, massive structure of a wholly novel form. This was Boro Buddor, and driving up to it, and almost round it, I was landed, shortly before four o'clock, at a most convenient small hotel, built there solely for the entertainment of travellers to the spot.

The dark massive Boro Buddor, a terraced pyramid, was now clear before me. Fergusson calls it "a seven or a nine storied Vihára." Its square basement, he says, measures 400 feet, but the real temple is only 300 feet from angle to angle. The form is of a perfect square; and for a full architectural description of it recourse must be had to his pages. Its date he assigns to the interval from A.D. 650 to 800. It has five square independent procession paths, one above another, pyramidally diminishing in circuit, and connected with one another by steps. And on mounting these, you come upon a large open surface, still showing increasing open altitudes, which may or may not be called storeys, towards the very centre, where the former solid dagoba, or dome, once stood, and where a wooden scaffold for the general view has been now constructed. But the detail of ornament and the variety of figures on this great mass is almost incredible. As I stood upon the top scaffold I counted seventy-two perforated small dagobas, each containing a Buddha: and as both faces, right and left, of the procession paths are sculptured, Fergusson counts that there are nearly two English miles' length of them altogether. Add to these independent figures of Buddha in every available position. The whole building seems to bristle with canopies. It may be readily understood that all these *bassi relievi* relate to the whole life, historical and legendary, of Sakya Muni; and even were they in a fairly readable condition, they might occupy an erudite for—how long? But the stone is dark and discoloured; here and there it has fallen out of form, and almost everywhere a quantity of lichens of various colours are growing on the surfaces. Even to such an one, therefore, the task of close examination would be prolonged, while to the ordinary traveller it must be one of despair.

Be all this as it may, it yet remains to wonder, after all, how the temple still stands as it does today, mouldering only under the hand of time, and spared by that iconoclastic barbarism which is so sorely prevalent between opposing faiths; for in Java the religion of Buddhism has been long since abandoned for that of Islam. This sparing is explained by the fact, as stated by Fergusson, that "when the Javans were converted to Mahommedanism it was not in anger, and they were not urged to destroy what they had before reverenced."

The position of the Temple is romantic: it was no doubt artistically chosen. Mountainous country extends on all sides: immediately on the left are serrated ridges, and below, mixed with meadows, there are extensive handsome forests. I lingered on the top till after sunset, and watched large flights of white birds winging home to roost for the night, amidst a certain large group of trees. Then, by-and-by, a few more belated ones followed, and by-and-by again some single stragglers, one by one; but all came in at last, and all to the same wooded resting place. And then I also left the now neglected fane with its abandoned faith to darkness, and, like the white birds, came down to roost, myself.

In the morning I was on the top again for sunrise, and for a long survey of all the marvellous detail—all to fall to pieces by degrees. My carriage and six was quite ready in good time, and I came as far as "Djoc" visiting the Temple of Mendoet on my way; small but remarkable for its three colossal figures and its refinement of execution. This, if I remember rightly, stands in the very midst of a wood. At "Djoc" I found the hotel full, and came thence, by rail, to Solo, and thence next day to Samarang, in expectation of the steamer from Tanjong Preok. Here, however, there was delay arising out of some confusion as to steamers, and I had to pass a dull whole day at Samarang, adding but one new fact to my gatherings, namely, that those same Java sparrows, slate coloured with white cheeks, for which some fifty years ago we paid ten shillings per pair, are in their own country as common and as mischievous as our own house sparrow in England. "What on earth are all that host of small chattering birds just come in to roost?" "They are the Rice Thieves." I passed a good deal of rice, by the way, after leaving Boro Buddor, but in several cases it was being cultivated on the hill sides in terraces. There was great fertility throughout.

On the morning of the 7th of February I got on board a British India Company's steamer for Batavia, and having to stop extra time at the various ports, because we had left them out in coming, I arrived only in time to know that I had lost my return steamer to Singapore; and I landed only to return to Weltevreden. Availing myself of the interval before the next boat started I made another journey to Buitenzorg, going this time to the Hôtel Belle

Vue and securing a room with a full view of Mount Salak and his glorious sloping wooded sides, forming with the valley below a charming picture. To this scene was superadded the colouring of a supremely fine sunset. Returning in the morning, both Salak and Gedé were clear: the former rises 8000 feet and the latter 10,000 feet. But Salak is the finer of the two, as Kanchinjunga is finer than Gaurisankar. From Thursday the 13th to Sunday the 16th I was on board the *Javára*, Captain Pot, landing, on the latter day, once more at undelightful Singapore, with its undelightful Hôtel de l'Europe.

XXV.

My next object being Bangkok in Siam, whither I was tempted by Fergusson's volume, I was obliged to wait for the steamer till Sunday, the 23rd. I had also to make up my mind to visit the astonishing Cambodian Temple Nakhon Watt, and the ruins of the vast city Nakhon Thom, which, geographically speaking, I ought to have managed on my way to Hongkong from Bangkok, and of which Mr. Watters of the *Glasgow Herald* had given me full information in my passage from Calcutta to Madras. But having communicated with Saigon upon the subject, I was informed by the agent of the Steamship Company that I was too late for this year, the river Mecon being now too low; so that this visit was for the present hopeless. They were kind enough to admit me to the club for a few days, which relieved me in my uneasy stay; and, moreover, we had at our table Mr. and Mrs. Siegfried, fellow-passengers from Batavia whom I afterwards met at San Francisco; and Mr. Wright, also a fellow-passenger, representing Messrs. Siemans. With this latter gentleman I visited the botanical gardens, of which one is bound to speak highly. These gardens are remarkably well kept, and very pretty in themselves; and there are some really fine fern and orchid houses. When, however, the day for leaving came, I was not sorry to say good-bye to Singapore, and particularly to the Hôtel de l'Europe.

On Sunday, the 23rd of February, I left for Bangkok in the Ocean Steam Navigation Company's ship *Hydra*, Captain White, with three other passengers: one was the well-known American Missionary of Amoy, Dr. Ashmore, whom I met more than once afterwards in his busy peregrinations; M. Pina de St. Didier, of the French Consulate at Bangkok, transferred from Mandalay, of which we had some talk; and in particular, two young Germans, who were afterwards my companions to the ancient capital of Ayutia, Alexander von Roessing and his brother Lieut. Freiherr von Roessing. There was nothing of maritime note in our passage except that we rolled rather more than seemed quite justified by the sea; these steamers, however, are built rather flat-bottomed because of the bar at the mouth of the river Me Nam.

But one fact, trivial at first sight, though to a certain extent of natural import, attracted my attention, namely, that scores, or rather hundreds of hard, round, white cabbages were suddenly spread out on the fore-deck by a group of Chinese. Captain White and Dr. Ashmore were both much amused at my notice of such a circumstance, but showed me how these cabbages illustrated the astonishing trading character of the Chinese. No cabbages grow at Bangkok, and these had actually been brought all the way from Swatow to Singapore, and were now going thence to Bangkok, thus covering a distance of about 2500 miles at sea. And all this for a mere cargo of cabbages and for the profit of but a few pieces of silver!

On the 26th we came in sight of the lighthouse built out on the shallow waters, and here we anchored at eight in the evening. At six on the following morning we started up the river, wide, winding, and lying between two quite flat shores; but these were thickly dressed with trees, and in that respect the Me Nam is more agreeable than the Jhelum. Green thick shrubs and palm abounded on both sides. Presently we came to huts and houses on the very edge of the water, some being built even on piles and standing over the water; and these increased in number till we came to the very bright and busy scene of our anchorage at the beginning of Bangkok. Here we were "visited," and afterwards a missionary who had come to meet Dr. Ashmore very kindly took me and the two young Germans in his steam launch to the Oriental Hotel—this lay some twenty minutes away—and we landed on its river frontage, in bright sunshine, of course, with life and boats and trees and buildings all about us.

At Darjeeling I had made the acquaintance of our Minister Plenipotentiary and Consul General at Bangkok, Captain Jones; and to him I had telegraphed from the mouth of the river. He was, therefore, expecting me, and I forthwith took a boat, the shortest mode, to his large and stately house, with its garden in front abutting on the river. I had come only to lunch, for, as he had warned me in his letter, he had as yet scarcely an extra chair in his large rooms. But how cool and lofty these were, and how often I enjoyed a few hours of day repose in them. In the course of the afternoon he took me a drive through the city, and the first structure we visited was Wat Sekest by name. I have no particular note of it, except the remark that it is ugly and rugged. But I here obtained from the top my first general view of the city and the river. The chief feature to remark in this is, how thoroughly it is hidden in the crowds of trees; and the next, how many small canals there are. Perhaps it was this last feature that led the early Portuguese and Dutch travellers (as Fergusson tells us) to call Ayutia (the ancient capital, about fifty miles up the river which I afterwards visited) the "Venice of the East."

The next scene—indeed scenes—that we visited were scenes of cremation. There appeared to be a certain district of the city devoted to these operations. And assuredly had cremation been hitherto practised in England as I saw it practised here, the aversion, indeed horror, with which many of our innocent brethren have brought themselves to view it might not only be pardoned, but applauded. In principle, this system involves the question between the living and the dead. Which is to inherit the land? Mr. Gladstone, in an interesting literary article on libraries in the *Nineteenth Century*, humorously hinted at our books pushing us into the sea, and the daily list of publications might really almost make the timid tremble. But what will our corpses some day do for us? Strangely enough, religion is lugged into the discussion, and the chief prejudice against the process appears to be ecclesiastical. On this point I remember reading in the *Times* newspaper, some time ago, a synopsis of a sermon preached against cremation (I think at St. Paul's Cathedral) by the late Canon Liddon, in which that highly gifted man wound up with this most strange anti-climax:—"Finally, my brethren, what if our Blessed Lord's body had been burned?" The mere shutting up of church-yards points but to one conclusion in the longer or shorter future of the question. For the cemetery is only a new invasion.

Well, what do they do with their dead at Bangkok? Burn them—really they do not. Look at this ceremony close in front of you, now going forward. We have already talked together about the Towers of Silence at Bombay. There the vultures are at all events left to do their ugly Jezebel work in solitude. But here they come boldly down among the people, and demand admission among the dogs as equal guests. Your pyre is on the ground; it is clumsily put together, and it is clumsily fired; but fired enough to cause a sort of underdone roasting. In goes a dog and tears out a morsel; but it is hot enough to burn his mouth; he shakes his head and shakes it out of his mouth accordingly; growls at it, lets it cool, and devours it, and then repeats the trick. So other dogs, and so the vultures, too, except the growling. That last bird was too audacious rather, and resents the scorch with an indignant screech. And so things go on, and all as a matter of course. Bad enough, you will say; but what if common burial went on with corresponding hideous imperfection? And so we leave Bangkok cremation. That all their so-called holocausts so take place it would be exaggeration to assert. But these are of every day. *Que voulez vous?*

The next day I again lunched with Captain Jones, and again spent the afternoon with him; and rowing up the river we landed to see what, I must confess, had first attracted my attention to Bangkok by the print of it in Fergusson, "The Great Tower of the Pagoda, Wat ching." This was indeed an object wholly and entirely different from the solemn pile that I had so lately visited in Java. But it was highly interesting nevertheless. Referring to the same volume, there is what he calls "The Hall of Audience," but I saw it as the Gateway to the Court of this Pagoda. The structure as portrayed at p. 634 must speak for itself. Even broken crockery ware is arranged for blossoms, and I don't know that I can do better than quote Fergusson where he writes that this Pagoda "is covered with an elaboration of detail and exuberance of coloured ornament that has seldom been surpassed" (has it ever been equalled?) "nor is it desirable it should be, for it is here carried to an extent, truly barbarous." I confess to have been exceedingly interested in conning this quite novel style of architecture, and by mounting to a certain height, not only because I thus became more and more intimate with it, but that I also enjoyed an impressive view of the noble river and the city. On the water, moreover, large rafts of teak were floating down the stream, adding yet more life to the living picture.

Lunching again with Captain Jones, we went

afterwards with the Roessings in the afternoon to Wat Po, where we saw a most remarkable compound of almost every kind of pagoda, including a huge reclining Buddha, which occupied the whole length of a large dark Temple. Then to the Gardens : and then we dispersed till morning, when we were to make arrangements for our journey to Ayutia. This we did with Mr. Andersen, the proprietor. We were to have a steam launch and attendants. We arranged our lists of provisions, and my servant, as cook, was of course to go with us.

Accordingly, on Monday, the 3rd of March, I was called at a quarter to four, and all being ready, I started on the dark river amidst the small stars of the lights among the vessels, and stopped at "Markwaldts," a short distance up the river for my companions. But the premises being large and the buildings irregular, I had the misfortune to commit that never-forgiven crime of waking the wrong man. We soon got away, however, with the right two, and the daylight broke rapidly upon us. Sails and boats were scattered everywhere, in busy movement ; the winding river's banks were everywhere clothed with trees, and the gable-ended houses of wooden villages opened to us in constant succession. Five hours and a half brought us to a place called Bang Pa-i, and here the interesting features decreased. But here a new interest arose, for there was a King's Palace and Garden of which Mr. Alten, a German, was the resident guardian, and to whom my companions had a letter. Here we therefore called, and Mr. Alten came on with us to Ayutia, which lay just two hours more up stream.

Constant temples and pagodas appeared as we went along, picturesque but not important; till at last we came to a large old one. Here we again found a huge recumbent Buddha, and (what was novel) all the walls were fairly honeycombed with tiny recesses, in which were placed tiny Buddhas: these being brought, as we were informed, from time to time by pilgrims. Then we came to the Old Royal Domain and Palace, which showed "splendid wrecks of former pride," for Ayutia (says Fergusson) "had for three centuries been the flourishing capital of one of the great building races of the world." To the top of this old Palace we mounted to obtain a general view of the ancient city itself. It was most striking. All was now one flat mass of thick growing trees, out of which at various intervals arose the tall naked ruins of the ancient pagodas, towering above the trees in exactly the shapes given by Fergusson's engravings. Never was there a more perfect picture of the results of abandoning Art to Nature in a fertile land! This, for me, was the real view of the old city, but my companions desired to walk through it, which they did. They could tell me no more, however, than that they had walked along paths and gone from tower to tower, but as the whole ground was a mere dead level, they had caught no general view at all. This was to be had only from the Old Palace, and I lounged about that abandoned structure and mounted to the top again while they were gone. On their return we dined under an open canopy, and steamed back to Mr. Alten's where we comfortably passed the night.

Before leaving after breakfast in the morning we were taken over the buildings and gardens, the usual feelings and expressions of grateful satisfaction following, and then we embarked for Bangkok, not, however, without visiting a place of worship built by the King, which he had fantastically had erected as nearly as possible like a Christian church. The whole day brought us down to Bangkok, the journey occupying from 10.30 a.m. till 4.30 p.m. on Tuesday, the 4th of March.

I had yet to see the King's Palace and Compound, or Private Domain, and I had also now to arrange for my departure to Hongkong. I had also to obtain some photographs from Mr. Loftus, the photographer, and in doing this I was offered the attendance of his brother, who had the license of admission to all that was ever permitted to be seen. The opportunity of beholding his Majesty himself I missed, for he was absent. The nearest I could come to this was only the Crown Prince's tutor—a somewhat remote German cousinship—whom I met on lunching again with Captain Jones, and also the Netherlands Minister, Mr. Morant.

On Friday, the 7th, I was to be on board the *Mongkut*, Captain Fowler, belonging to the Scottish Oriental S.S. Co., so that I had just one entire day to visit the Palace of Bangkok, and this I accordingly did with Mr. Loftus *frère*. A truly Oriental mass of gaudy buildings and bewildering ornament I found; and if Fergusson chooses to call it all tawdry I suppose we must not contradict him. But I do not at all feel inclined to depreciate the style after this fashion. It is intensely novel and picturesque; look at the entrance to the old Palace; and it makes you feel that you are among new people. Moreover, it suits the atmosphere, and appears to be perfectly in place. So much was this the case with me that some palladian buildings which had been, for convenience sake, introduced for offices did, by the side of all these Siamese kaleidoscopes, appear heavy, cold, coarse and vulgar. One feature that astonishes is the elaboration of the roofs and of the jutting eaves. Not only is their unnecessary extent vast, but curves and colours, and gildings among the tiles are studied in every variety, and even though a rigid Sir Christopher Wren would have called it worse than Gothic, and a mere baby show, I must confess to have been baby enough to enjoy the sight. There is even the Golden Temple, with its gilded vestibule and peristyle, its interior and, so to speak, high altar. In short, what is there not of Siamese Art and Fashion? If all would not suit in London—and certainly it would not—still it is equally certain that St. Paul's would not suit at Bangkok. Brain, atmosphere, and region work together everywhere; and architecture is only another tree or flower. But talking of England, I must not omit to mention my surprise at finding so much English written about the city. There appears to be a decided tendency in this direction, though whether there is any suggestion of education connected with it I did not learn. There was one object among the rest, however, which none could criticize or cavil at. It was a huge model of the Great Snake Temple of Nakon Wat, round which you could even walk ; and this considerably whetted my desire to visit that spot on some future opportunity, which I did.

Full of brain pictures of green, blue, red, yellow, and gold, and of sheets of gorgeous tiled roofs, curving down into tremendous corners and overhanging eaves, I came for the last time to lunch with Captain Jones. Nakon Wat was the subject of our conversation, and I took a last inspection of the splendid illustrations in Lieut. Garnier's two volumes, lying on his table. I had to look to him for an introduction to the authorities. He, however, told me that he had already obtained for me a letter from the Foreign Minister, Prince Devawongse, addressed to the Governor at Nakon Wat, recommending me to his care, which he had forwarded to Consul Tremlett at Saigon, to await my arrival whenever I got there. Moreover, he recommended me to call, in his name, on General Sir Allen Johnson, whom I should find at Hongkong, and who had actually gone across country to Nakon Wat from Bangkok, out of season.

On the afternoon of March the 7th I was on board the *Mongkut* for Hongkong, and found Nakon Fowler with his remarkable black Chinese dog, and Dr. Ashmore again, also on his way thither. We dropped down to the bar and lay there all night. Moving off by daylight, and leaving a trail of disturbed mud and sand behind us, we anchored opposite the wooded island, Kohsichang, which is the resort for change from Bangkok. Here we remained all day, and were joined by Mr. Gordon, whom I afterwards met with at Shanghai, connected with the public works at Siam. On the 9th we sailed again with five days of fine weather. Then came a change to rough, with rain and mist and seeming chillings, though my thermometer still stood at 78°. At night on the 15th we anchored in Hongkong in smooth water, but entirely missed the promised view on account of both fog and lateness.

The morning of my landing, Sunday, the 16th of March, was again dull and chilly, but Victoria Harbour looked all alive, and the hills all round insisted on showing in the picturesque. Chinese junks lent novelty to the general view, but they were not of the large order, though the ridiculous painted eyes upon the prows stared with wonted giant aspect. Then, again, there was the great Dragon Flag, to frighten all beholders, as should the figures that guard the pagodas. It took us about twenty minutes to row from our anchorage to the Hongkong hotel where I was very comfortably housed; and shortly afterwards Messrs. Melchior et Cie., to whom I had a letter, were good enough to enter my name at the Hongkong Club—a notable advantage indeed.

The day being dull, I was not disposed to move about much, and therefore immediately made my call upon General Sir Allen Johnson at his hotel; for my visit to Cambodia was one of my leading thoughts. On introducing myself, as recommended by Captain Jones, Sir Allen received me very kindly, and furnished me with abundant information, including photographs, all of which was subsequently of considerable use to me. How he could have undergone the overland passage from Bangkok to Battambong at all, and afterwards visited temple and city, and then found his way to Saigon, and all out of season, was a matter to me of astonishment. The feat deserves the name of "General Johnson's March."

My next call was on Messrs. Butterfield and Swire, to whom also I had a letter, and I was received by Mr. Mackintosh, who at once put me in the way of getting to Canton, and thence to the Portuguese settlement of Macao, which latter my connection with the name of Camoens made it equally inviting and imperative to visit; for here the poet had resided as Commissary of the Estates of Deceased Persons; and here he is recorded to have completed his Lusiads,—probably the last three cantos.

I was to leave on Thursday, the 20th, at eight a.m. The weather was now decidedly improving; and the beauties of Hongkong were brightening to the view. The scenery is of course limited, because the island, though remarkably picturesque in form, is small, the whole circumference being given at twenty-seven miles. No doubt, to many bound by occupation all becomes very soon monotonous; and ledgers with a good amount on the right side afford a more generally entertaining aspect than repeated rocks and vales; though these may still be preferred to too large amounts on the left. While to me all was new, all was no doubt pleasing; and as Messrs.

Butterfield and Swire's office is on a hill, and owns an open balcony, I ventured a note of admiration to Mr. Mackintosh: "What a beautiful view you have here, when you come of a morning!" Perhaps I ought to have anticipated the reply: "Yes, if one had not seen it so very often."

I had to come more than once to Hongkong—the meaning of which is Good Harbour—but was never there long enough at a time for its beauties to cloy; yet I soon began to find the air in the city itself depressing from the close surrounding hills; though nothing can be cleaner and neater than the streets. On Tuesday I took one of the many long-poled chairs that threaten your viscera every time you leave the hotel, and mounted to the flagstaff, returning by the French convent. There is a railway also, but I preferred the chair. The view from the top is supremely fine. From a height of 1774 ft. at the Victoria Peak, you look down upon the splendid harbour and free port, where the value of the annual trade is estimated at 40,000,000*l.*; and where, as usual, British tonnage immensely surpasses all others. The spread of water is intensely blue, the effect of which is greatly enhanced by the russet colour of the mountains as a contrast, stretching the long tongues of their bases out into the richer colour. I was fortunate, moreover, in having a day of fine weather mists, and thus of enjoying a series of dissolving views, appearing and disappearing as these gauzy veils from time to time passed over the scene to intercept and permit by turns the sunshine of a brilliant sky on all that lay extended far below.

A highly successful and interesting passage took me to Canton, on the Thursday morning, the scenery being all more or less mountainous, and the Tiger Rocks very striking. Of what I was to see at Canton I had formed no clear idea; and now that I have seen it I am by no means sure of conveying any clear idea about it. The first feature that struck me from on board, on arriving, was the vast number of crowding boats, or sampans, upon the waters, and it seemed almost incredible when I was told that the population who live upon these boats is numbered at something like a quarter of a million. I at once boated to Shameen, where all the Europeans live, and called on Mr. Detmering, to whom I brought a letter from Messrs. Melchior et Cie. He advised me to take up my abode across the river (the Chao, or Choo, Kiang; or Pearl River), in the small Oriental Hotel at Honan; and there to rest for the night, and start for the city with a guide in the morning. This I accordingly did, amusing myself by a visit to the Honan Temple, which is quite devoid of any architectural attraction; but it displayed at the moment of my visit a solemn religious Buddhist ceremony, wherein the procession of priests reminded me exactly of the Roman Church. Vestment, ceremony, and dignity predominated.

From Canton I was to go to Macao, and return thence to Hongkong. My luggage was therefore dispatched at once to the Macao boat, and at ten a.m. on Friday, the 21st, I came across with my guide to Canton. The crowd of residential boats again attracted my attention. They extend for some four or five miles in front of the city; they are of all sizes, hooded of course, and even in the small craft are occupied by whole families; these include geese, cooped and uncooped, and coops of ducks and chickens. Somewhat apart are handsomer craft, occupied by the more wealthy, and devoted to more wealthy and less public purposes.

We each got into the lifted chair, and were paraded through the city. One word immediately springs to my lips. Canton is a glorious kaleidoscope. There are no streets, they are all broad flat paved passages; all are crowded with variegated Chinese walking to and fro, and very busy about something or about nothing; the shops are open on both sides; some gorgeous, and all well ornamented, and every trade and calling makes appearance. Among the number, mark the butcher with heaps of pork roastings, and a few black dogs into the bargain. Among other glitterings, one most remarkable, and indeed I might almost say gorgeous, effect is produced by the peculiar mode of hanging out signs: a custom pursued by every one. My guide began by leading the way in his chair, but I shortly altered this in order to enjoy the perspective. Large polished black long parallelogram boards are hung out vertically; and in large Chinese character, which is very handsome, the name and the trade are emblazoned on each in very marked, broad, golden characters. So that, what with the open shops and the rich gold lettering of the sign boards, and the moving crowd, in variegated robes, the effect is dazzling. As you are being carried along on high, the views, as may be imagined, which you thus command are extensive; and in various parts an open wicker work is arranged above to protect the more exposed passages from the sun.

This is really the sight of Canton for the passing stranger, and I should suppose a more striking one he would not note in China.

But spots and buildings are to be visited, the most singular of which I found to be the Temple of the 500 Genii. All these figures, sitting down, are gilded from top to toe, and all are posing with their hands, and among all the 500 I could not find two posing alike. Where one or two were intended for the Great they were represented as very stout and corpulent. The Chinese God of War—Kuanti—is always represented as corpulent. That is their idea of strength, and certainly some people should be strong enough to carry about with them what they are possessed of in this respect. All keep looking at you more or less pleasantly, none angrily, so that when you come out you feel to have left a pleasant crowd behind you.

But if this be a pleasant visit, what shall be said of its contrast in the Temple of Horrors? It may be called the Hell of the Wicked, over illustrated. Then there is the Examination Hall, where there is not much for examination, as you are not a student; the silk weavers; the Courts of Justice; and, lastly, a long walk to the Five Storey Pagoda, which I held to be the last *and* the least. It is far from impressive in itself, and the view from it of Canton is disappointing. Through Canton once again, rather for a visit than for a dwelling; and then to our boats. This time we were met by golden marriage processions, carrying all things in golden glitter, and at last, through the sampans again, I came to the Macao steamer.

There was, after all, very little that I found closely associated with Camoens at Macao. Grotto there was absolutely none; nor is it easy to trace where there ever was one. The garden you are shown into is a very pretty undulating piece of ground, and is rather heavily timbered; and in a picturesque part of this there are some rocks, in the midst of which there is planted a small bust of the poet, with certain extracts from the Lusiads, engraved on stone. These, however, are scarcely legible, partly from the decay of the material and partly from the growth of lichens on the surface. Nor does the state of the case rest here. More than one admirer, or desirous of being so called, has taken occasion, for his own sake, to hitch his name on to that of Camoens by writing unneeded eulogies on him, and, in particular, one Frenchman has mutilated a large face of one of the rocks by inserting a huge black stone tablet with a huge number of stanzas. I could conjure up no associations with the poet, nor gather any inspiration from the scene. On the following day I was again at Hongkong.

XXVI.

I was now to make arrangements for getting to Shanghai, which was to be my starting-point for Japan; and I again availed myself of one of Messrs. Butterfield and Swire's boats for the passage. This I did by sailing in the *Anchises*, Captain Lapage —known as Captain Lappidge—and went on board on a cold, foggy, windy morning, it being Wednesday, the 26th of March. On this passage we touched at Amoy, and took in Mr. Marshall, Inspector of Consulate Buildings, and whom I afterwards met at Shanghai. This entrance to Amoy is very fine, the rocks are remarkable and the water spacious, offering a secure and commodious harbour. This is the port for Formosa, which I held in prospect for a visit, if only to gratify an old schoolboy's curiosity, but it was not to be now, if ever. We started again the same evening and came into yellow water, which marked Woosang at the entrance of the Wangpoo, on which river Shanghai lies, and there we anchored for the night.

The extensive fortifications at Woosang not threatening to blow us out of the water if we attempted to steer up the Wongpoo with audacious intent of landing at Shanghai, we ventured on that proceeding, and assaulted the Shanghai quay at the auspicious hour of eight o'clock in the morning, without however having spread any insane alarm in consequence; and after quietly breakfasting with the captain on board, I quietly came on shore and put myself under the paternal and maternal protection of Mr. and Mrs. Jansen, at the Astor House Hotel. The town was in perfect repose, and indeed everything was shut, for it was Palm Sunday.

On Monday, however, the vulgar world's every-day work began again, and temporal thoughts superseded eternal, and then it was that on going to my bankers' for money, I found I had to make out the receipt in taëls, which is not a coin but a fanciful weight, and this weight continued to press upon me when I went to take my cabin to Kobe, for the measurement by the aristocratic taëls knocks the poor dollar into second-class value, and enables companies, dentists, and other professionalists to charge by the higher denomination. Of this, however, Mr. Bois, of Butterfield and Swire's house—here they are everywhere—had forewarned me, so that I paid without a groan, or at allevents, without letting one be heard.

At Shanghai, on this my first visit, I passed only two days, but returned more than once again. Already, however, it was easy to see that in its grand European aspect it is a fine-looking city, with grand dwellings. Carriages are plentiful, and so are jinrikishas. But these have not yet obliterated the old-fashioned wheelbarrow, though they have relegated it to the use of the lower classes. It is exactly a wheelbarrow in the mode of locomotion, but the body is like that of an Irish car. A division stands in the middle; the man sits on one side, and his baggage

—in the shape of his wife or otherwise—is on the other. And when the cargo is very heavy, a man pulls in front to help the pusher behind, with his two lifted handles. The jinrikisha is also ubiquitous ; and is at first very likely to give you a cold, or the ear-ache.

On Wednesday, the 2nd of April, I went with my servant on board the *Yang-tse*, Captain Lormier, and was now at last bound for Japan, which I had begun to think it was a shame to have not yet seen ; for I had been provoked to go there so long ago as 1873, and even then had been warned that the country had been already spoiled some years before. This was the warning and information given me by the Rev. Dr. Smythe, whom in that year I met at Buenos Ayres. He had been practising as a physician in Japan, and had since then entered the Church, and was resident, at the time I speak of, in the Argentine Republic. It does not, however, happen to us very frequently that we can choose exactly what we shall do and where we shall go. In travelling I have proved this—that if you will not go to one place merely because you have not yet been to some other, it very often happens that you will go to neither. I know, for example, for myself, that it happened to me to drive into Rome with a friend behind four horses, and even to see the glorious Bay of Rio, long before I could get circumstances to allow me to see Holland. And I know, moreover, that when I did go there by rather a forced arrangement, I met with an unexpectedly early winter, and spent my time in suffering sciatica and lumbago, and drinking curaçao at every station I came to. The Fates said "Yes"; the Furies "No."

I never found a fair and natural chance of getting to Japan till this last date I speak of, and I confess myself now to have been perfectly satisfied with what I saw, notwithstanding all the spoiling. I saw much more by means of the intrusion of Europe than I should otherwise have done; I saw plenty that had been unaltered by Europe; and after having seen all that was Japanese for entertainment and instruction, I was quite content to fall back into what was European for the enjoyment of reflection and repose.

The French steamer, the *Yang-tse*, was advertised to go through the Inland Sea, and that was the first object to be enjoyed. The weather, it is true, was very dull, but, independently of this drawback, I must profess myself to have been quite disappointed in this one particular passage. There were on board two ladies, Mrs. Watkin Wingfield and Miss Smith, who had been staying with their relatives, Sir John and Lady Walsham, at Peking (which city I do not ruthlessly rob of its legitimate and essential G), and I am quite sure they would say, and indeed they did say, the same; nor had they, as I afterwards had, the chance of amending this first impression. The truth is that the going through the Inland Sea is a mere matter of course, for Kobe, or Kiogo, has to be touched, and that lies on this sea; but the mere phrase itself does not mean seeing that sea. From Kobe runs the passage to Yokohama, and that is the business of the French Messageries and of the English P. & O. But these companies take the shortest cut and go through the Inland Sea by day or by night, just as despatch requires. The consequence of this was that on this occasion we saw only the entrance, the beauties of which were very soon steamed through. Later on, I found other means of realizing the real charms of this exquisite piece of water. Be it noted, moreover, that the French steamers do not even touch at Nagasaki, though the P. & O. do.

We landed at Kobe early in the morning of Saturday, the 5th of April, and went at once into European quarters at the Oriental Hotel, a French house which I would recommend; and the wet, cold weather found me quite content to remain under its European protection.

The next day was fine, and I went as far as Osaka with the ladies, who continued on their way by train to Tokio. My object in a special journey to Osaka and back was to see some specimens of the Japanese cherry blossoms. These I found very striking of their kind. They come out before the leaves, and they grow thickly and very closely on the branches, as closely as if they were on a child's garland. And they are but a childish show at last, for they give no fruit at all; thus exemplifying the well-known national taste of the Japanese for the cultivation of flowers. There was nothing at all picturesque in the position of the trees I saw, and the cherry tree, moreover, is one of very stiff and unpicturesque form. There was nothing particularly striking in the hour's journey, as regards country, but a singularly adventitious effect was thrown over vast extents of the prospect by the accident of the rape, grown for oil, being at that moment in full feather of its well-known golden blossom. Certainly I have to confess that at the station, both coming and going, I was made to witness one spoiling of Japan by European intrusion. The Japanese, as a matter of every-day courtesy, keep continually bowing in a sort of bobbing manner, to one another ; no one makes a curtsey. This species of politeness may pass in the robes of Japan, but when the performance takes place in European garb, as it often must where people are more usefully and energetically employed than in growing fruitless flowers, the gesture has lost all possible national grace, of which I have seen it sometimes exhibit some traces, and verges on the idiotic.

My friends, Messrs. Butterfield and Swire, were again at my side to help me ; for on going to their house I was introduced to Mr. Baggalay, the son of an old member and acquaintance, who gave me much assistance and information. And here I immediately found that something of old Japan had not been quite destroyed, but only wounded and yet surviving. For instead of being wholly forbidden to go out of a city, all were now to procure passports of permission so to do ; nor was there any danger of having the head taken off because you had omitted to take off the hat. But these passports were to be strictly regular ; no railway tickets could be bought without them ; and no deviation from the strict course they were requested for would be permitted. I obtained a separate one for Kioto on the spot ; but the general one was to be prepared at Tokio and sent for me to Kioto; for without it I could not stir beyond that city. After arranging this indispensable matter, I was well pleased to take a European lunch with Mr. Baggalay and to meet a nephew of Sir Austin Layard. And if I remember this lunch particularly, it is because I was greatly struck by suddenly seeing a most striking portrait of the late Lord Justice; a face which I had first known young in Lincoln's Inn, so far back as in the thirties, and which I now saw out here in far Japan, as that of yet one other dead and gone.

After a scrimmage about my servant's name not being on my passport, I got away for Kioto, and according to advice drove to the Europeo-Japanese Ya-ami hotel. But the drive was in a jin-ri-ki-sha (or strong-man-carriage),—that peculiarly Japanese vehicle, on which Municipal Licence fees are paid in Tokio to the respectable number of 39,000—and the distance was somewhat considerable, rendered seemingly yet more so because it was late and the streets were dark. In the morning I found that the position of the hotel was very picturesque, commanding a bird's-eye view of the town in which, however, seen in this fashion, there is a considerable predominance of brown roofing. The day was spent as usual, in wandering about and making casual observation; and as the Mikado happened to be there, the streets were more than usually adorned, particularly with large and variegated paper lamps. In the evening I was induced to go to the theatre; an experience which I was not likely to repeat. It was by great favour and with difficulty that I obtained a ticket to join a private box, and it surely was with great difficulty that I persuaded myself out of compliment to remain; but I take great credit for my courtesy. Anything so prolonged, dreary and monotonous I had not yet imagined. Yet I read in Mr. Caine's "Round the World" that the author spent several evenings in going to the theatres! In a pleasant and instructive book, Chamberlain's "Things Japanese," there is a paragraph about these theatres, and lectures and other holdings forth. And in particular as to sermons (of all things) the missionaries tell the author they never can be "prolix enough to stay the insatiable appetite of their converts." That is not European, certainly; and Mr. Chamberlain attributes this to the virtue of patience; patience surely reduced to a vice. In Japan, therefore, beware of theatres and of—sermons; no great friends, these two, anywhere, for people are so good; but here, *in pari delicto*.

I had a pleasanter entertainment in view; the descent of the Tanba River. I started with my guide at 8.30 on the 10th of April, and a jinrikisha was, of course, the vehicle. Fifteen miles took me to Taaba, to embark on the river, and a long, straight, picturesque street, crowded with suspended variegated paper lamps, was the beginning of my road. After that the rest of the line was through flat and indeed ugly country, with hills to the right; but this suddenly changed when we came to the river, the banks of which from first to last were lofty and pleasing, and now and then aspired to be rocky. But it is not for this alone that you take the boat—a good flat-bottomed one. It is the excitement of the twelve miles down stream over so many rapids that constitutes the special delight of this excursion; and it is one well worth while. The river is not nearly so large as either of the other two which I shall by-and-by have occasion to describe; but, as these do not fall within the scope of everybody's travel, this river ought by no means to be overlooked. The rapids are rocky, and skilful management is indispensable. Moreover, at the end of the hour's rush, which is about the average time occupied over the thirteen miles, the far-famed Arashi-yama, or Stormy Mountain, rewards the exploit. Here, the steep and lofty hills that clothe the right of the river are covered thickly in quiet spring with all the well-known soft foliage of Japan, and these blush all over in their higher plumes with spreads of the pink wild cherry blossom. Far more pleasing is this blossom thus seen than on the stiff branches of the separate trees; striking as that sight is. A grand and comfortable tea-house greets you here; and six miles more of jinrikisha take you back to Kioto.

I should have left Kioto at once, but my passport had not yet arrived, which delay cost me two more days. And dull they were in weather. Still I went to the "gardens," or rather a wilderness of trees, mixed with other features belonging to a country where nature cannot help being beautiful. The maples, in all their variety of virgin green, are a real charm in Japan. In autumn they can show more colour; but give me the young growth of spring where all shows sign of fresh and beaming life: of Nature waking up again to live; and where there has been rain, and sunshine follows it, mark how the virgin foliage of these trees festoons before the background of the dark wet bark behind. Perhaps it was the weather that made me find Kioto and its people more colourless than I had expected. The small children seemed to me to be the only gaily-dressed among all others; and then there seemed to be a striking number of women with black teeth. This was explained to me as signifying marriage. We often hear of women losing their looks after marriage, but in Japan it would seem they take artificial pains to disfigure themselves forthwith. What reason could my guide give me? It was a short and decisive one: to keep people off. Very effective, in that respect, one might readily admit; but capable, one might also misgive, of presently keeping the husband off among the number.

On Sunday, the 13th, I got away, and came as far as Nagoya, where I slept. And here I had my first experience of real Japanese manners, though the hotel was Europeanized to some small degree. The first I approached appeared for some reason inaccessible; but the mystery arising out of an interchange of unknown tongues was at last dispelled by a young Japanese Missie being fetched from above to squeeze out the two words (laughing, of course) "No room." This was the Shiukinro hotel, whence I went to the Shinachu; very different names, these, from "The Lion" and "The Bear." Still they were hotels; and at this latter house I found both bed and board. It was one of those curious little buildings which belong to Japan, but it was not wholly

Japanese. Built almost like workboxes, these present the most opposite possible character to the heavy-beamed structures that one used to find in Switzerland. They are so slender that when night comes on, an outside set of panels are adjusted. Everything was neat and clean, and the walls of the little square rooms were daintily ornamented with colours; and here I may mention that I was never really troubled with any insect but the obscene and pertinacious house-fly. The dinner was served to me by four young girls, who were most delicate in their attentions, and like curious children put their snatched and repeated questions, full of laughing amusement, at everything that I said in reply. Certain English words, funnily pronounced, they knew. That I came from England was enough: off they all went, and on they came again; and off they went again. The whole scene was a novelty indeed; one or two broken words (as I have said) sufficing to keep up the giggling intercourse, whether they quite understood or not.

I was called at four the next morning, and after a slight breakfast, not served by the young ladies, I left with another passenger for the train. The day turned out wet and foggy, and I found no refreshment during the thirteen hours' journey, beyond what was by chance in my pocket. What the particular features of the view were, if there were any, I know not. But I saw a quantity of rice in slush close at hand, and now and then I almost thought that we were stopping to take up frogs. Fuji no Yama was quite out of sight when we ran under him. One feature of the journey reminded me of India, the multitudes of third-class passengers, which were now and then startling and amusing at the stations. But I would rather talk about this line of country later on. Suffice it to say we arrived safely, but not till seven in the evening; and at length I was well content to find myself at the European Grand Hotel at European Yokohama, and to have had the great advantage of travelling through this journey in European form.

My first duty in Yoko was to call on Mr. Brooke, the proprietor of the *Herald*, whom I had met at my friend Mr. Gassiot's house in England. I was at once invited to spend the rest of the week with him and Mrs. Brooke on the Bluff, and willingly made my way thither, where, besides a charming house and host and hostess, I found a beautifully arrayed garden, and the grounds artistically planted with trees; the view from the windows being correspondingly pleasing and attractive. My name was also put down at the Club, and thus Yokohama became a pleasant resting place. The Exhibition being open at Tokio, an early day was of course devoted to a visit thither, where every possible variety of articles as usual, confounded attention; and this was moreover almost entirely distracted by the hustling crowds of other mere curious inspectors. One effect practically wrought upon me was that I was induced to give orders, in town, for china and cloisonné; and in another point of view I must mention having been greatly struck by the difference between the two styles of Japanese paintings that were plentifully exhibited: one in the well-known style of their own peculiar body colour (so to call it) where a few light touches serve to suggest immensity, and the other in oils, where, on the other hand, the pigment is laid on in lumps and masses.

Altogether, I spent exactly two calendar months in Japan, from the 5th of April till the 6th of June, though I came back for a few more days, later on, to Nagasaki. My weather was by no means propitious during all this period, nevertheless I saw the few leading points that I came to see, and was fortunately favoured with fair weather on these occasions, excepting on my Nikko excursion. April is one of the wet months in Japan, and in 1890 it was cold also. But on the 21st I made bold to start for Nikko, and dined and slept at the Tokio Hotel. The next morning I marked "wet," and had to wait till the second train for Yusunomiya Station; the journey to which, for some three hours or a little more, showed me nothing calling for remark except flat rice grounds, and these not being pleasant features in the dry time are certainly not so in the wet. From this station to the hotel at Nikko (which I was told means "sunshine,") the distance is twenty-five miles, and it was then necessary to hire the inevitable jinrikisha for the journey. Two, therefore, I took, each with two men; one for myself and the other for my guide, Awoki. But now there is a railway all through, a great relief in one respect, but destructive of the most impressive part of the journey in another. I refer to the road that runs for miles under an avenue of large and spreading cedars, forming, no doubt, the original approach to the Temple. There are, of course, interruptions in this surely unexampled length of avenue, partly by the total disappearance of some of the original trees, and partly by younger ones of stunted growth, planted in various spots; but the effect produced is grand; historically and devotionally as regards their planting, and actually so as regards themselves. All this is, of course, lost in the railway, though for some length the line runs close by the side of the trees. On my own journey I saw that it was nearly complete, which fact, by the way, cost me not a little; for of course nothing more was being laid out to keep the road in order, out of which it had hideously wandered. If it did not shake every joint out of the socket that is about all I can say for it; and oftentimes I had to get out and walk along the path close by the large stems, thus somewhat varying the picture, and very much varying the shocks. Time, to a certain extent, was lost, and when the dusk approached the pines increased the sombre: nor did I reach the hotel till nearly ten at night, and in the absolute dark.

The next morning I was rewarded by miserable wet and fog. An American lady agreed with me that indoors was therefore the only proper place either in Japan or any where else; but four others defied the weather, and started in their palanquins up the mountain to see the well-known lake. They were very wet when they came back and they were very silent too. "What did we come for?" they had said when starting. "What did you go for?" we asked when they returned. I suppose the lake is worth seeing; at all events it must offer a pleasant day's excursion. But some photographs that were shown me lead me to suppose that that was the limit, and decided me not to spend an extra day on it in doubtful weather. Indeed, the next day would not have suited. It opened fairly in the early hours, but threatened to lose its temper very soon; so I shot off at once to the Temple, and was just in time. You come to this by a straight approach, and are at once much struck by the magnificence of its position, to which it owes so much; for immediately behind the group of structures below, including a rather lofty pagoda, there rises a towering and precipitous broad screen of rock, densely covered with forest trees of various kinds, hovering, as it were, over the sacred edifices both for adornment and protection.

As you approach through the Torii, or outer gate, and mount the steps, you become aware of the elaborate work within, and you pass up three terraces from court to court, astonished at the detail outside and in. The predominance of roofs and eaves, and the great labour bestowed upon them, as before observed at Bangkok, is particularly apparent here, not forgetting the cornices inside. Far from the least impressive view of all is obtained by walking up the 200 stone steps in the forest behind, and gazing on the Temples through the vast stems of the trees that clothe them. This is an addition to the examination of the Temple that ought not by any means to be omitted, though there is nothing worth seeing at the top. Scarcely had my walk concluded when the sunshine ceased, and rain coming on, I sought my European shelter for the remainder of the day.

The following one was fine. I did not care for the lake, but enjoyed the very varied lights and shades that adorned the avenue of cypress on my return. Both in coming and going I had experience of the tea houses and their amused and amusing attendants, and from time to time caught sight of real shrubs of the cultivated azalea, completely laden with scarlet blossoms, whole branches of which are gathered, seemingly without stint; and in one particular case the sun was shining so brilliantly on a particularly loaded specimen that I was reminded of the favourite device of one of our kings, "The Rose in Sun." Indeed I stopped my jinrikisha to enjoy a long contemplation of it in unadulterated light, while I myself was under the shade of the avenue with open pupils.

Finding on my arrival at Tokio that the Honourable Mr. and Mrs. Napier had gone down to Yokohama with H.R.H. the Duke of Connaught, I had no motive for making a halt at the former city, and went straight down to the "Oriental." Two chance meetings here turned out very fortunately. On looking at the visitors' book, I found that Mr. Tremlett, our English Consul in Saigon, had arrived, to whom Captain Jones had forwarded the official letter that was to secure me every facility for visiting the Cambodian Temples. I was of course well pleased to make his acqaintance, and obtained much information as to my projected visit towards the end of the year. The other was the chancing to open a conversation with a young and energetic traveller and his wife, Mr. and Mrs. Needham Wilson, who had seen a great deal of Japan as well as other places, and who particularly recommended me to the two rivers, the Fujikawa and the Tenriugawa, as presenting, in their opinion, the finest scenery they had witnessed in the country. This was exactly the class of scenery that I had come to see, and not to run from one place to another for the mere sake of seeing what you could see elsewhere. There is, indeed, a great deal of very plain and commonplace scenery in Japan—I speak of the main island ; and Mr. Chamberlain himself says that "padi fields of vivid green (not always) separated into squares by low mud dykes form the most characteristic feature of the Japanese landscape." One, or if possible both these rivers therefore became my two leading objects before my return to Koby, and by perseverance and marshalling my time and forces I accomplished both.

The run from Yokohama to see the Daibutsu or "Great Buddha" at Kamakura was a matter, of course, of one day. It happened to be a holiday when I went, and crowds were (as everywhere else) idling about, enjoying the air. No great movement in amusements was visible, but among the number was one that attracted my attention by its humming noise. The puzzle was solved by discovering that this sound belonged to several coloured kites, some in the shape of fish, and some in the shape of birds—

but not much resembling the humming birds of Brazil—that were being flown on high; these were so constructed as to catch the wind and hum, a characteristic of Japanese ingenuity and innocence. Then came the huge Buddha, which Mr. Chamberlain says you must see more than twice before you can thoroughly appreciate "the calm, intellectual, passionless face which seems to concentrate in itself the whole philosophy of the Buddhist religion—the triumph of mind over sense, of eternity over fleeting time, of the enduring majesty of *Nirvâna* over the trivial prattle, the transitory agitations of mundane existence." I have copied the whole sentence in order to confess that having paid only one visit to it, that is to say two with the interval of an hour or two I wholly failed to trace all these characteristics in the gigantic countenance. Nor can I defend myself upon the above excuse; for I have seen photograph after photograph of the original, vividly recalling its exact form and expression, and yet have still remained unperceiving as before.

For myself, if I compare this countenance with that of either of the three—but they are marvellously identical—gigantic figures of the great Rameses II., sitting side by side, in a sublime repose upon their thrones outside the Temple of Aboo Simbel, the Daibutsu must retire altogether. Yet it did not require, in this latter case, a second visit, and scarcely more than a second gaze, to feel fully impressed with the majestic beauty, the excessive sweetness of those faces, which I must say, without attributing to them all that would appear to belong to the Daibutsu, I infinitely prefer. The total height of these, as sitting figures, is given as of sixty-six feet, and (according to my own observation) the flat open hands, laid out upon the knees, impart a very magic of placidity. It is true I saw them to the very best advantage. They look calmly out eastward over a very broad part of their river. We fortunately moored there for the night, when the scene far surpassed that by day. It happened to be a full moon at rising, which therefore shone full upon them ; and three or four of us, clambering on to the enormous masses of golden gritty sand which are banked up against the Temple, lay there and enjoyed the magical effect which it may be imagined so fine a moonlight would cast upon those countenances. I do not attempt to work out any compound group of sentiments that would appear to occupy their brow, but simply speak of their sweet and majestic placidity. I am no great believer in these elaborate analyses of countenances after you are told to whom they belong. I always remember, while at Rome, some thirty-five years ago, the ingenious analysis of the various expressions made manifest in the countenance of the then supposed portrait of the Beatrice Cenci, in the Barberini Palace. I never could appreciate them, and an Italian reviewer, some few years ago, published an article, showing that the figure is no Beatrice Cenci at all.

I was now to prepare for an excursion to one of my rivers. Which was it to be ? I had engaged an active and intelligent young guide for the rest of my sojourn in Japan, whose name was Sosuke Yamamoto, and whose residence was 213 Gochome Motomachi, in Yokohama; I could cordially recommend him. On consulting him, I decided I should at first try the river Fujikawa, as being the nearest, and the one from which I could return to Yoko, including the usual round by Myanoshita, in the course of a week. The scenery also, he assured me, was quite on a par with that of the Tenriugawa, the latter being grander but the former sweeter; while both were magnificent. This was a true description of the two.

Accordingly, on the morning of Thursday, the 8th of May, having arranged all necessary provisions, my guide being, of course, the cook, I and he started by railway as far as the forty-five mile station of Kodzu, and there we took the tram-car to Yumoto, on the road to Myanoshita. We lunched at the hotel Jamanoyu at Tonosa, and came on to the Fujiya hotel, with all its spread of glass windows, at the end of our day's journey. Throughout this march I was constantly charmed by the delicate foliage on all sides, by the wooded gorges and river, and temple; and began to obtain a decided introduction to the particular character of Japanese scenery. One occasional feature particularly struck me. From time to time you come upon a group of tombs, utterly isolated, attached to no temple, to no building whatever. The sanctity of the churchyard for the repose of the dead is totally unknown. As their temples are not for congregations, so are there no surrounding enclosures to protect their tombs. Respect is, however, always shown.

The following day was naturally devoted to the Lake Hakone. The view of Fujiyama from that hotel is well worth gazing on. He is not naked. His snowy peak stands up behind the foldings of middle distance mountains, and the water in the foreground, fringed on the right by hills of hanging foliage, though those to the left are somewhat arid, combines, as a breast of water often does, to enchant the eye. Here also is a temple that can boast its planted avenue. The row across the lake, on the return home, served to disclose its attendant woodland ornaments, but on the other side were opened fatiguing stretches of uneven sulphur grounds, of which I had rather more than enough before I found myself again in the glass house of Fujiya.

The next day's journey was in another direction; towards the river I was bound for; and my resting place was to be Subaschidi. I had been recommended by no means to miss the Otoma Toge Pass, in order to see the finest full view of Fuji no Yama that the island affords; and happily my path lay exactly over it. We mounted, as it were, the side of a long stiff screen, seeing nothing before us but the ridge we were to attain to; until at last we got there, and stood upon a narrow neck, before again descending on the other side. But at the instant of arriving, and sitting down on a bench outside the tea-house for a moment's pause, my attention had not yet been arrested by any striking feature. In a few moments, however, I was up again, and walking but a few paces to the other edge, really only a few paces, there suddenly opened before my eyes what I must honestly call an astounding view. It was a "surprise view" altogether. On mounting the neck I saw nothing, on crossing it with a few paces I saw everything. A varied and enormous valley lay before me and far below me, just fifteen hundred feet below me where I stood; and covering up the very whole of the far-away background there was spread forth the full 12,500 feet figure of Fujiyama, staring me in the face like an enormous pyramid, or taking rather the shape of a vast protecting flat tent curtain. That this view has been seen by many and has been already set to the grindorgan by many, may be true. But that makes no difference to me; I saw it for the first time, and shall ever remember it as one of the leading glories of my travels. Nor was I deceived by my aneroid, for I afterwards compared its register with one of the Company's engineers at Gotemba station. I stood at a height of 3000 feet above the sea, and Gotemba, which lies in the valley, is marked on the railway map at a height of 1499. What the real distance was from the ridge I stood on to the snow-crown of the mountain I had no means of ascertaining; and perhaps for the picture's sake it is best left in mystery, on which the astonished senses love to feed. Down to Gotemba we had to come, and there at once were found two first-class jinrikishas, in which we started at full speed for Subaschidi, occupying from 4 to 6 p.m., and mounting just 500 feet more, i.e. 2000. Here I received a check. The road to Kofu, a distance of one day, was broken up, and of course the first misgiving that arose was that I could not get there. But that was not the case, the vexation was limited to my being driven into two. Misfortune, however, turned out fortune, and the toad's head bore yet a precious jewel; for the road we were obliged to take on the following morning, besides being always beautiful, and leading past two temples, brought us down upon the splendid Lake of Kawaguchi, which we should not otherwise have seen. Here again was hanging foliage, and rocks and water, truly Japanese. But the grandest of effects appeared when, turning the head and looking across the water, there rose seemingly almost out of it Fujiyama's self. In short, we kept going round the base of the mountain and had it almost ever in view. On the borders of the lake we rested for the night.

The two temples we thus had to pass were those at Yamanaka and Yoshida. Of the former, architecturally speaking, there was not much to say, though, as usual, the gateways, roofs, eaves, and soffits, formed the most elaborate features. But the position was romantic, seeing that it was surrounded by a grove of fine timber and foliage, the beautiful camphor tree predominating, as it is said to do round the many temples of Isé. The other temple of Yoshida was a very fine one, and was also well-bosomed with trees. The approach to it was by a long straight-planted avenue, adorned with what they call stone-lamps. A fine fountain or tank occupied the court to which you were invited, or from which you were warned, by a furious-looking elaborate bronze dragon; the terrors inseparable from all religions being thus combined with its softer poetry. On one side, a white wooden horse in a separate box stood peering through an iron grating, on going to look at which I found him buried up to his knees and hocks in horseshoes made of straw, to be tied upon the hoofs. Fortunate for him, I thought it, that he was not bound to work and wear them. But I had to change my mind about these shoes in this regard. Here, however, they were only a Japanese form of the "Gift to the Altar."

On the morning of the 12th of May we were to start on our journey to Kofu and were to ascend a very steep mountain side; and here the jinrikishas came to a halt. We were to take ponies, and when I came out to observe the arrangements made, what was my astonishment to find all the nags' hoofs cobbled with those very same straw shoes. Nothing at first would induce me to mount, but I presently was persuaded by my guide to do so, on his authority that the horses could go in nothing else. He was to have something also, though he manfully protested; but I made him take a Cango or Japanese net upon a straight pole, with a carrier before and behind. Thus I could effect a change from time to time, and walk on foot besides. All went slow, but went well; the horse did not trip at all. We mounted very high and very steeply, and eventually descended to a place called Kuloyoma, eye-feasting, as usual, on the foliage. I wonder how many species of maple Japan can count? At this last place I resigned the straw hoofings and entered a horse-car, which at first nearly jolted my lunch out of me, but by-and-by got better because the road got flatter and uglier, till at last we came to ugly

Kofu. Here I found we were to sleep ; but I found also that I was still ten miles from our starting-point on the river—Kajica-zawa—whither we were to go in the morning. This plan I at once abjured, deciding to get to the battlefield at once. A new horse was therefore found, and after driving over a spread of ugly rice grounds, I reached the starting station, and sat down very comfortably in the boat-tea-house, ready for a start in the morning.

But there was a first and an immediate second question to be asked. First, what is the state of the river? for if the rains have filled it above a certain mark the boatmen are forbidden to go. Secondly, is there a boat? for once down stream, many days are requisite for crawling and fighting up again, and many days sometimes elapse between the last departure and the first return. Happily for me both questions could be answered satisfactorily. The river, though high, and though still rising, was still one foot below the forbidden mark, and happily there were still two boats at hand. So I slept in confidence, and prayed for fine weather in the morning, which therefore, for my audacity, came with pouring rain. One day lost was not of much account ; but of course I trembled for the rising of the river, particularly as the wet continued till the afternoon. I then walked out in the mud to look about, and was much struck by the abruptness of the change of scenery at Kajica-zawa. It is most remarkable. It is from a dead flat above stream to this very spot, when the river at once enters lofty green and wooded banks on both sides.

The morning of the 14th came with smiling sunshine, and at an early hour the boatmen came with smiling faces, and my guide, smiling also, to tell me that the river was still several inches below the forbidden mark, and that the sooner we were off the better; in which suggestion I heartily concurred. So exactly at seven we were in the boat with all our belongings and provisions and under the guardianship of three men and a boy.

The moment we began to move the river scenery began to charm, and from beginning to end I confess to have been enchanted. The time generally occupied in the descent was given as about eight hours, but as the water was high and the current strong we occupied only seven. During all this period I do not remember even one five minutes' space of flagging interest. The banks were mountainous throughout on both sides, but far from being monotonously so. They were green and folding and refolding in every variety, with constant perspectives of lateral valleys, which, as we looked upon them in passing, might seem as if of Rasselas. Villages were visible on high from time to time, and waving spreads of wheat, but principally of barley, sloped towards the river and swept from one's memory at the moment the dead, foul cultivation of the rice. Nor are hanging forests of Japanese foliage to be forgotten. Something of the general effect produced upon one must of course be attributed to the first time; something to the continuous movement, and much perhaps to the bright state of excitement in which the mind was kept by the constant succession of rapids, of which warning was from time to time given by the beating of a long oar against the side of the boat. The men knew well what they were about and that was enough. We were only somewhat splashed once or twice.

What are these rapids? They differ from those on the Tokio river in character, and in size of course immensely. They seem to be formed by vast promontories of boulders stretching out into the sloping river—how formed I cannot say—and occupying some four-fifths of the stream. The water therefore rushes with impetuosity through the remaining opening, running up to it along the upper side of the promontory. The art in navigation thus seems to consist in getting your boat well placed in this side current, but not too near the promontory, so that it is carried up to the opening just as if its nose was in a moment going belt against the rocky bank. But at that exact moment it comes in contact with, and is caught by the down rush, which, forbidding the seemingly inevitable contact, swings its nose down with a sort of unconscious vehemence, and carries it into the next space of comparatively smooth water. These spreads are sometimes very smooth and seem very lovely lakes. Do not content yourself with the front perspective only; continually look back and look round; you will find you are in a panorama of beauty.

At last all is over, and you emerge in an open country on a canal, and a railway station, Iwabuchi by name. This we did, but by my guide's advice I went an hour down the line in order to get a good hotel at Shidzuoca. Here I visited a fine but unpoetically placed temple, and afterwards discussed an across-country journey to the other river. But having deliberated for a while, wiser counsels prevailed. I was sufficiently charged with memories of Fujikawa, and resolved to return direct to Yokohama. This I did by the morning train of the 15th of May, falling in (not out) with Mr. and Mrs. Brooke at one of the short stations. Thus, including the deviation, which to some whom I know I would almost recommend, the seventh day found me at "The Grand" again.

It was on my return to Yoko that I decided about leaving Japan in consequence of a letter I had received, that opened me a chance of a visit to Peking. But I had now determined to see the Tenriugawa river on my way down to Kobe, and therefore I arranged to leave Yoko on the morning of the 22nd of May. Bidding good-bye to my friends, therefore, I sent my own servant on to Kobe direct, and started with Sosuke Yamamota by the 9.15 morning train to Tokio, in order to take the train from the Yueno station to Takasaki, and to continue thence by jinrikisha to Ikao. This I did, arriving late at Ikao—just too late to join a dinner-table—after having passed through the usual style of Japanese scenery among the mountains.

At a quarter to seven on the following morning I started to the voice of the cuckoo, and was accompanied from time to time during the day by a little bird, always too shy to be seen, but which I was told was of a plain brown; it would sing just one or two notes only, but those one or two of the nightingale. "Everybody" knew it, but nobody knew its name. The whole of the road was varied and striking: hill, valley, barley, foliage and mountain, with a peep at just the distant snow top of Fuji Yama to our left, standing out clean against the spotless sky. But finer scenery remains; for after you have descended to a very picturesque lake, and mounted again to a spot called Tenjin Toge, you stand before a beautiful surprise view of vast extent, and in the distance you behold the strange feature of perfectly serrated ridges perfectly covered with bright green grass. Snow tops back the picture. Here is a small structure erected to the God Tenji, and here I rested at the tea-house for a while to gaze and to sip and to gaze again.

As Asama Yama is now the only active volcano in Japan I must not of course omit noting that I saw him smoking, and as every little incident helps in a long march I must mention also a most singular recumbent profile marked out on one of the green hills, just before reaching the lake I had passed by. As it is not like the Duke of Wellington or Washington I don't mind calling attention to it. The small point is that besides the remarkably regular features, a most curious effect of a perfect eyebrow is produced by a large clump of bushes rising exactly in the proper place.

The peculiar charm of this day's march began at the Tenjin Toge. We were to descend the long wooded gorge, which increased in beauty as we went. The trees were fine and the underwood was fine, and here was a special beauty, in that every now and then vast blushes were thrown over the undergrowth by the copious spreads of the wild pink azalea. Then we came to the bottom where another gorge joined in and brought a stream, and where a huge, lofty, dark-coloured, integral panel-rock stood staring among the trees. The whole might have served for an imagined scene worthy of Midsummer Night's Dream. Shaking off enchantment I began to rise again, but still in depths of hanging forest, where amidst other huge integral panel-rocks, huge cedars, and a clear and rushing stream, I came upon the Temple of Haruna. So closely does all this scenery hover round it that some of its pillars may be at first confounded with the trees. The building itself will not for a moment compare with Nikko, but the position is far more romantic, and the care that has been, as usual, bestowed upon the curves of the roofings is eminently effective here. My guide had to pull me away that we might arrive at the Shi-shi-a tea-house at Mioge before night overtook us.

The next day was very fine, and the morning was devoted to a journey to the two temples on the high ridge, bearing the strange names, Kurakake-yan and Boson Gon-gen. Passing across a large wooded and fantastical dell, you mount the other side towards one large dark tree at the top. When you get there, *circumspice!* There is fantastic beauty everywhere; here I now found that I was close upon those green serrated ridges that I had seen from far off. Walk all along, continually delighted; go through the large natural arch and look round; finally mount the

140 steps to the Boson Gon-gen; again mount the top of this if you please, and *circumspice* again. There is a downright confusion, far and wide, of green serrated ridges, round heads, valleys, ribbed and wrinkled hill sides: all these compose a picture the equal to which I do not believe Japan itself can show elsewhere, and when you feel quite sure you have gazed long enough, you can return.

As to the temple which lies high up on the face of an almost perpendicular rock close by the tea-house below, I certainly cared not to climb to it, particularly for what the red guide book promised me: the "magnificent view of the whole sweep of the plain extending to Tokio." What *can* be the beauty of the "whole sweep of a plain"? Such also was the love of a plain displayed in speaking of the Usui Pass, where you behold about as fine a hanging forest all the way through as is to be seen, I should say, in any part of the world; and here we read that "*although* the Pass is thickly wooded," views of the "extensive plain below" can be caught. This seems to me to be a strange perversion of the picture. Who wants to see a plain, instead of hanging forests abounding in every wealth of foliage?

After continuing the journey with all the variety of pony, cango, and foot, and just one hour's railway from Karuizawa to Tanaka, we passed over the Wada Toge, seeing a large lake and a temple by its shore. This was at a height of 2500 feet. By-and-by we came upon the Tenriugawa itself, and crossed a wilderness of boulders, where its tributary, the Otangiri, flows in, backed by the fine snow mountain, Comangataki. But this was not where I was to take boat. Various spots from time to time arrested attention and excited admiration, and finally, after sleeping three nights on the road, including one whole wet day passed in bed, the river-side tea-house at the starting point, Tokimata, was reached at 5 p.m. on Wednesday, the 28th of May. Here my aneroid marked 1300 feet.

The boatmen were of course immediately sent for, and the two necessary questions put. It was the last boat, the very last! The water was now practicable, but high. It had been very high, too high, of late for the passage, and all the other boats were still kept down below. An extra fee of $4 being demanded, $25 in all, I naturally closed the bargain, and settling that at eight o'clock in the morning we were to start, I dined and went to bed.

In the middle of the night, however, I was waked by the entrance of two men with a large Japanese paper lantern. What was this? but the voice of my guide immediately explained the intrusion. The head boatman was ill, and another must be sent for, and we could not leave before two o'clock in the afternoon, sleeping at Siraoka; so to sleep I went again, quite contented with my next morning's respite.

By two o'clock on the 29th the afternoon was fine and bright. The head boatman had come, Motero by name, and we made our start for Siraoka, which we were to reach at five. and many villagers gathered round to see us go. We were but a few minutes away before we felt the run of the stream. The river is again larger than the Fujikawa, and there are said to be thirty rapids in its course. The scenery, as before, began at once, but wilder and more rocky (as my guide had told me) than on the Fujikawa. Yet there was always foliage. How many races we passed before we reached Siraoka I know not, but I remember a great deal of rapping and rushing. The style of the rapids is exactly like that in the other river, and we swept along at no snail's pace to our night's sojourn, making an awful climb to the tea-house. I could not regret the interruption, for the evening's bird's-eye view of the reverse curve of the river below, winding between its lofty banks, was as fine as sunset could make it. At night (but this time before I went to bed) Motero came with my guide to ask leave to put two more hands on board for the morrow, without extra charge, as the stream was running very strong, and to this I naturally very readily assented.

This made six boatmen on board, and on the 30th we left our eyrie tea-house at something before six o'clock on a very fine morning. For about two hours and a half we were passing through what they call the "grands," and mighty noisy and mighty rude they all were, none so rude, however, as the Chona, which struck us with some sort of violence, sousing me and flinging me off my raised seat into the boat, and treating the guide who was behind in even a more unruly manner. As a result of this we had to pull up and bale out the water. At half-past eight our extra boatmen left us. From first to last the scenery came up to all expectation. Rocks appeared from time to time of romantic shape, not towering up into naked precipices, but only standing bodily out from the upper green and foliaged mountains. Nor was it without much surprise that I almost always saw them blushing with the wild pink azalea, not then knowing, what I afterwards learned, that that delicate plant grows in dry places, and that indeed its name has been given as indicating this disposition. Though the "grands" had passed, some few hours yet remained of beauty, in the same alternation of lakes and rapids, until at last all was over, and we emerged into mere flats, and found ourselves at the Hamamatsu Station on the railway.

Here I settled everything with my young guide, and gave him, as he deserved, an excellent certificate. He returned to Yoko, and I went down to Kobe. I went direct, not stopping at the lake Bivar, partly because the weather was unpropitious for that day, and partly, almost mainly, because I could not gather, either from photographs or report, that there was any specially characteristic scenery to be found there. I was very glad to have a railway to take me to Kobe, and I was very glad to have the Oriental to receive me when I got there. I had seen the Fujikawa, and the Tenriugawa, and I shall not readily forget either. No other river scenery that I ever saw, none that I have ever looked for, approach the beauty and the grandeur of these two most enchanting streams, and the noisy anger of the close and threatening waters emphasizes the excitement and romance of the adventure.

Indeed, besides these two rivers I had seen a great

deal of Japanese scenery and of the people as I passed through. At the tea-houses I always found everything very neat and clean, and indeed almost too much so, for the whole of the arrangements are drawing-room arrangements. You are supposed to enter spic and span at once and so to continue; on stepping on to the raised matted open ground floor, you must take off your shoes, or have them carefully brushed and wiped before you tread within, and this in the dryest and cleanest weather; and when you have mounted the ladder to go upstairs, you find only your trim sitting-room. A faint show of chair and table is being now introduced, but when the bed is brought in it consists of one or more good full mattresses on the ground. I always carried my own sheets and coverings, and was never at all inconvenienced. The female attendants are always extremely attentive and polite, with the pleasant peculiarity of Japanese manners. I do not call the girls pretty, but they are very picturesque. Their dark hair is singularly well arranged, and always looks sleek and glossy, standing out in perfect bows. But if you touch it, you find it hard, to which quality indeed it owes its admirable form. The cheeks look almost painted, and the teeth are good, unless, indeed, the married women's black ones. The poets talk of smiles disclosing pearls, but with the smile of the married Japanese you are more readily put in mind of an old coffin opening to show a corpse.

Where Japan most suffers by her European spoiling is in the change of the costume. The Japanese have no figures. But in cases where they have now to enter on active work, how can they do otherwise than dress accordingly? I found this same necessary change among the Arabs in Algeria some years ago. The difference is almost magical. At one tea-house a servant of the house answered my clapping of my hands, and I said I wanted my guide. Presently another person came. "No," I said, "my guide." To which he answered, "I am your guide," and so he was. He had dressed himself in Japanese, and I did not know him again.

That was why I declined a friendly offer to take me to a grand ball in Tokio given by the German Minister. I declined, saying, "You will find the room overcrowded and no costumes; all will be aping the European style." And so it proved, as I learned afterwards. Look at the people about the railways and in the post office, in short in every official position; and not only at them, but their wives and children also. Look at that woman coming along the station now, she is disguised in necessary disfigurement; and as to her little child she is leading by her side, he is a mere little waddling apple dumpling. But go out into the country, where of old no stranger dared go, and you can always find Japan enough, and see what of old none ever saw.

When I passed through Iida and stopped to refresh the men, the tea-house was besieged by the whole place, as it seemed, to see the stranger. Young and old, male and female, crowded round, and partly for air and partly for diversion, I amused myself by throwing coppers. As to children, they are always in the streets in numbers. The parents, I was told, always send them out ; but the European pocket-handkerchief does not come with them. As to the general character of the people socially, intellectually, morally and everything else, as I was only so many weeks in the country I ought of course to know everything, and as I don't, I therefore ought to write ; but what ? I had need to give very little room for testing honesty, nor did I find any dishonesty ; but I suppose the brain that is so undoubtedly ingenious in many convenient things, may very readily be ingenious in inconvenient also.

It would be scarcely fair to leave speaking of Japan without dedicating at all events one special paragraph to her one great mountain—Fuji no Yama, or Fuji Yama, or Fusi Yama. And when you mention a great mountain, the first next thought is the ascension of it. In my own case this was quite out of the question, because I was in Japan out of the season for such an expedition. But, independently of this point, I should not care to undertake it for two reasons. In the first place, the mountain, as a mountain pure and simple, is totally unpicturesque ; and in the second place, it is the only one great mountain ; so that, wholly unlike all other mountain ascents, where the higher you rise the more is surrounding grandeur developed, you would here behold nothing of that character, and would moreover dwarf every other formerly appreciated eminence that you had admired. Fuji Yama is a noble object when seen in towering combination with folding foreground and middle-distance scenery to dress his snow-white head; but seen bare and alone he is wholly destitute of the picturesque, though he still may assert the wonderful. In this opinion I think many must concur, and a concurrent one of real value I can claim in that of my friend Mr. John Varley, the artist; alluding to whom, I cannot but mention his Japanese and Chinese paintings lately exhibited in New Bond Street. How he can have managed, by the way, to paint all those 213 pictures in nine months may be still more puzzling to artists than it is to me; but I specially mention them to note how he has in Japan, as he did in Egypt, caught with peculiar felicity the real atmosphere of the country. I speak of Egypt because there are now hanging before me two of his water-colours which continually recall old scenes; my joke with him being that he will never again paint an Arabian desert like the one he painted for me.

In now quitting Japan, I was to pass again through the Inland Sea, and, on information received, I determined to take my passage back to Shanghai by a boat of the Nippon Usen Kaisha, or "Japan Mail Steam Ship Company"; because that company run their boats not only through the best part of the sea, but so arrange their hours as to show everything by daylight. Accordingly I took my cabin in the *Saikio Maru*, Captain Conner, which was to sail on the morning of Friday, the 6th of June. But in consequence of some delay at Yokohama we could not get away till the afternoon. When I went down the first question I asked was whether this change altered the chance of seeing the scenery. "I am sorry to say," was the reply, "we shall this time go through the best part of it in the dark." Was I to be baulked again? Could anything be more provoking? What was to be done, but get on board and go? And this I did, revelling discontentedly in the finest cabin I ever slept in. These boats are really splendid.

A cure, however, came where I had least expected it. The afternoon and night were miserably wet, and this fact, which in general is a curse, for me was now a blessing, for it was succeeded by a heavy fog at sea; and in consequence of this fog we had to cast anchor and wait some hours before it all cleared off. By this happy interruption we were thrown back in time again, so that we did not reach the "best part" till very early dawn instead of getting through in the dark. At five o'clock, therefore, I was on deck and witnessed all the choicest pictures. Not only so, but I had the benefit of the growing light and the early morning ray. Nothing could be more beautiful to behold. There was lake scenery of the finest kind, and you looked through and through some of the small islands on to others. On shore there were waving high-pitched fields of ripe barley, villages and clustering forests, and the soil and the rocks were russet against the blue water. Then there was the early hour and the horizontal sunbeam. O ye, who love the landscape charms that Nature has to show, worship the morning and the evening in their rays and shadows, and leave the garish noon to worship its own self.

So we came through the Inland Sea this time; and by touching at Shimonosaki and also at Nagasaki we enjoyed what the French steamer *Yang Tse* had given us no chance of beholding. On Tuesday, the 10th, the yellow waters, yellow enough to pass for the Yellow Sea, proved we were approaching Woosung and the Whangpoo, and in the evening I was at the Astor House again.

XXVII.

I HAD now two grand excursions in view. One that I had long thought of, and for which Mr. Needham Wilson had sharpened my desire, was to mount the Yang-tse-kiang and see the Chinese Gorges commencing above Ichang; this same station lying a thousand miles (or, strictly speaking, 966) above Shanghai. The other excursion was a highly interesting one; viz., to Peking, the name of which city, as well as that of Nanking, I steadfastly refuse to deform by robbing it of its legitimate G. Thus indeed do all educated Englishmen in China spell it; the Chinese word Pih-king signifying Northern Capital, as Nan-king means the Southern.

This latter adventure I had not calculated on when I left London, nor had I thought of it until at Singapore, where I had received a letter from my friend, Mr. Stephen Busk, enclosing an introduction to Sir Robert Hart from my friend, Mr. Gerard Loder, the member for Brighton. The letter, however, awakened all my curiosity of travel, and I forthwith enclosed it to Sir Robert, waiting his reply. This came in due course, inviting me to come and stay with him. But, as the season at Peking is not to be played with, he took care to caution me not to appear before the middle of September. I had therefore plenty of time on hand so far as Peking was concerned. Then what of the gorges? Here, also, it was too soon to think of such a journey, for though the steamers go to Ichang in June, it is quite impossible for small boats to resist the enormous flow of water that pours down the river in that month. And to get to the upper end of the gorges you must go up stream; you cannot go by land, and then come down as you can in Japan. All this Captain Holmes explained to me, who came in while I was lunching with Mr. and Mrs. Robert Little, and I naturally acted on his advice to defer the attempt till October. Nothing could have been more opportune than this delay, thus forced on me, as time will show. But what was to be done meanwhile? The Club at Shanghai was pleasant enough, and my hotel was pleasant enough, but to remain lounging in Shanghai, waiting so long, was impossible. Besides which, cholera had begun to appear, so I determined to gratify an old schoolboy curiosity, of somewhat less than a hundred years ago, and get a sight of the Island of Formosa; the name of which had always excited my imagination. The port for Formosa is Amoy, where a large trade with the island goes on; and accordingly I took a cabin, but only to Foochow to begin with, on the chance of seeing certain beautiful river scenery there, on my way.

The firm of Butterfield and Swire were again my friends, and after dining with Mr. and Mrs. Bois, he was good enough to come and see me into the launch the next night for their steamer, the *Menelaus*, Captain Nelson, "blue funnel." He also gave me a letter to Mr. Martin of their firm, which eventually bore fruits of happy advantage in New Zealand.

We arrived at Foochow, the beautiful approach to which surpasses that of Amoy, on the 16th of June, and I immediately called on Mr. Martin, who introduced me at once to Mr. Pimm, to whom Mr. Graham, of the Nippon Usen Kaisha, an old fellow-passenger, had given me a letter; for Mr. Pimm was the authority for the river excursion. But I was out of season here: the weather was far too hot, and so was business. The fact is, if you are to do everything you must waste a great deal of time, and if the one season suits two places together, the seeing both must involve twelve months. All you can do is to do all you can. "Come back in October," they said, but in October I was in the gorges. So with Mr. Martin's help, I took my cabin to Amoy, and, most happily for me, took his future address at Melbourne, whither he was on the point of departing. The short amusement of Foochow, therefore, was to lunch with Mr. Martin, and to marvel at the rapidity of the process of the tea-tasting, for the spoon is run through a dozen samples in a shorter time than an uninitiated person would require to fully analyze one. That same evening I sailed in the Douglas S.S. Co. *Haitan*, Captain Ashton, for Amoy, arriving on the morning of the 18th.

Here I called with my letter upon Mr. C. S. Powell, and declared my intention of going to Formosa. But here there was an interruption again, for what with holidays and some irregularity in the boats, I was likely to lose several days doing nothing. So I sat down to lunch gloomily. "This is vexatious," I said, "for I have to dovetail all my movements. Are you sure there is no boat going? There's a blue peter flying now." "Oh! that's nothing; that's going to Manila." "To Manila? How far is that?" "Two and a half days or three." "Then why should I not go there and come back to fill up time?" "That you can do if there's time to get passport and ticket too." So I did not delay, but sped to the Spanish Consul for my passport. I found him rather out of sorts about it, as I was so late, and fearing that he might refuse altogether, I introduced a word or two of Spanish. This saved me. The clouds cleared off and I went on board the China and Manila S.S. Company's *Diamante*, Captain Taylor. We came out by a different route from the one we entered by. This depended on the tide. And it may well be so, for so remarkable an exhibition of a rocky entrance I have never anywhere else seen. To the view it is complicated in the extreme, but the passage seems clear. Accordingly, we steamed all round, as the expression was, and went out to sea. Between four and five on the 21st of June we were at Manila. The fine mountainous and wooded island of Luson looked well as we approached it in the evening sun, but the landing was flat. The town itself seemed all more or less littery, and the hotel with its dinner table was very much so. But on the following morning I found Mr. Wood at the club, two miles off, at San Miguel, where he gave me a resting place. In the evening we drove to the Praia of Lunetta. It was on a Sunday, and the picture was thoroughly Spanish, both as to crowds and colouring. Two military bands were in full play at different points, and carriages and horses of all kinds and degrees were moving to and fro. On the following day Mr. Wood drove me through the town, and we visited the immense cigar manufactory, also the ruins of the old residence of the Governor, destroyed by the earthquake of 1863, and suggesting in ruin, I am sure, a far higher character and greater volume of architecture than when perfect it could have displayed. Then we took a turn in the switchback railway—montañas Russas—going home to dinner at the club.

It was now Tuesday, the 24th, and the return boat was to leave on the 30th. It was therefore proposed that I might visit the lakes and the river beyond, in company with Mr. Wood's cousin, Mr. R. Wood. This we did, but the weather was not propitious, nor, if it had been so, do I fancy I should have found anything to justify what was represented to me on board. The scene painter always exaggerates. The narrow river, so far as we could ascend it, was charming, with its thickly clothed perpendicular mountainous banks, from the heights of which monkeys are accused of throwing stones down upon boats. But our course was very short indeed, and even so, the boatman had to get out several times. It was a bit of a scramble from first to last, but it was an excursion for both of us, and—was in the island of Luson.

I now learned, to my surprise and disappointment,

that we could not return to Amoy direct, but must touch at Hongkong on our way thither. This was the trading course, and the steamers are of course trading steamers. It was not therefore till the 8th of July that I found myself again at Amoy, and bid good-bye to Captain Cobban and the *Zafiro*. Mr. Powell was ready to receive me, and sent his gig to take me across the water to the island of Koolangsoo, where he was living in a fine airy house on the borders of one of the sweetest bays I ever saw. And there I enjoyed his hospitality until Saturday, the 12th, when he took me on board the *Formosa*, Captain Hall, ready to go to Formosa.

The passage was not long nor violent. At early morning on the following day we sighted the high range of mountains, with snow upon the highest, that form the backbone of the island, and making for the land direct, ran up the pleasant coast, mountain and vale in view, for some forty miles to Hobie, Tamsui. Thence I was to find my way to Mr. Best, Mr. Powell's partner, at the town of Twatutia, and this lay some two hours by steam launch up the wide and winding river Tamsui, adorned on both sides with cultivated slopes, varied with green folding mountains. The launch was ready, and the captain accompanied us. Twatutia itself is flat and ugly; one would not expect a spic-and-span city in those districts, nor is it found. But Mr. Best's welcome was very pleasant.

There is a railway even here, but it is still quite in its infancy. It runs through rice fields, crossing the river with a handsome wooden bridge. Of rice grounds there is a vast extent, Formosa rice being of excellent quality. This fact points more to fertility than beauty. To this must be added the cultivation of a special kind of tea, nearly the whole produce of which goes to San Francisco. The Latin-sounding name was given by the Portuguese, and the word is really Portuguese. The original name of the island is Tai Wan, which means "terraced beaches" or "terraced bays," and of these we saw several on our passage up the coast. There is also a town of that name.

Mr. Best took me a journey to see the savages, as they are called. They come down to a village called Kutchu, out of the range of mountains, where they live in clans in almost pathless forests. They are very friendly towards Europeans, but are deadly foes of the Chinese. Indced it is said that the price for a daughter in marriage is so many Chinese heads. We made a long day of our excursion in chairs; but I found the bamboo poles (as I had been warned) very stiff and jerky. Our point was Sintiam, where we breakfasted, close to a missionary chapel, and the whole of this course was through rice fields of the usual mud and slush. There we crossed the river in a ferry boat, and mounting a high crest on our way we came down on the other side, and finally reached Kutchu. But we were most unfortunate as regards the savages, for only one appeared, and he was not quite taken as a thoroughbred, except by the fact that he did not understand money. Very savage indeed! In returning home we came down the river through some gentle rapids, and the scenery was fair. From the twisting of the stream it took us two hours to get to Sintiam, and thence we repeated the stiff bamboos till home.

It was well for us that we thus chose our day, for the next would have been quite impossible, and must have made many succeeding ones equally so. One or two of the men had talked suspiciously of the sky, and in truth we were soon really assailed by a typhoon. All night long there was a furious pour of rain, and we got out of bed in the morning with a high wind added, to attend us in our toilet. Presently Mr. Best came into my room to say that his barometer had suddenly fallen alarmingly; and very soon afterwards the real war began. Still the glass fell, and still the storm increased. It was a real typhoon, but we fortunately were on shore, and were not near the centre, nor did this move at all near us; that was Mr. Best's experienced report. But rain and wind were eccentrically mad enough; the whole place was rushing with water; trees were torn and twisted and the house quivered. At length the glass rebounded; "now the worst is passed," said Mr. Best; "the glass never goes back again." And so, in effect, it proved; for all at length grew calmer by degrees, and night was tranquil.

Before leaving I had the pleasure of meeting Mr. Wilson, the engineer of the railway, at dinner; and also of dining and lunching with Mr. Hutchison, formerly resident in Korea, who gave me valuable letters for that somewhat remote country, whither I was going. And on the morning of the 21st of July I left Twatutia by the steam launch to join the *Hailoong*, Captain Goddard, for Amoy again. The last event I witnessed at Twatutia was not felicitous. We had had wind and rain, now we had fire. Just as I was leaving the cry was raised, and in the distance there arose a wide and almost quite sudden mass of pure flames. They shone forth furiously, though the air was bright enough to deaden many a glare; and this was the distressing feature of the catastrophe; the conflagration had taken place amidst the mere thatched bandbox dwellings of the crowded poor, and the greedy flames must surely have swallowed life.

Our passage to Amoy was uneventful. We rounded the island of Koulangsoo about noon on the 23rd of July, and after again enjoying all the strange rocky scenery of the bay, I found myself domiciled once more with Mr. Powell in his charming home. Here there was interchange of hospitalities, and information as to future plans obtained; and I remember with pleasure, besides my good host, Mr. Cass, Mr. Leyburn, Mr. Bruce, and Mr. Gettens. I was to have gone by the Shanghai steamer, but at the last moment was advised to change for the Canadian Pacific's larger vessel, the *Parthia*. The obvious advantage in doing this was the getting a more commodious passage; but the latent disadvantage was, that when we came to Woosung it was found we were drawing too deep to pass the bar. Meanwhile, my discarded humbler coaster had gallantly steamed up unhindered; and it was only at night that the steam launch took me on board, from my prouder, to sup and to go to bed at the Astor House on the 23rd of July.

XXVIII.

As I was now at Shanghai again and quite at the end of July, I began to think seriously of my intended visit to Peking; and as a first step called on Mr. Graham at the Nippon Usen Kaisha to consult him. The course open to me was to go to Nagasaki, and there wait a day or two, and take their boat to Chemulpo, Korea. By the best rough calculation I could make I found I ought to leave Shanghai on the 9th of August. Taking into account Nagasaki, Korea, and Tientsin, I judged that I should arrive in Peking within the first fortnight of September, which would fairly square with Sir Robert Hart's advice; and therefore I followed Mr. Graham's suggestion, and took the ticket.

During my remaining days at Shanghai I had the honour of calling on our Consul-General, Mr. Hughes, and lunching with him and Mrs. Hughes on the following day, where I met General Jones, the American Consul at Chin-Kiang, the first station on the river, who recalled a good deal of what I had seen and heard in Mexico, where he had resided, including the fate of General Lopez. Having also called on Mr. and Mrs. Marshall, I lunched with them and obtained a valuable letter of introduction to Mr. Walter Hillier, our Consul-General at Séoul.

Then, again, the same intercourse occurred with Mr. Commissioner Bredon, Sir Robert Hart's brother-in-law, who also sped me on my way. So bidding all good-bye, till my return to ascend the mighty river, I went on board, as I was bid, on Friday night, the 8th of August, and found to my satisfaction that I was to be with Captain Conner again sailing on the *Saikio Maru.* It so happened, however, that this was some holiday time, and certain return-ticket folk were on board; and as we were not to sail till early morning, the captain was not to be on board till then. The consequence was that during the night the usual form of English holiday-making among a certain class was kept up, and under their auspices the *Saikio Maru* became a first-rate specimen of a night pot-house.

We had a glittering sea passage all the way to Nagasaki, during which Captain Conner told me, what out of gratitude to fate I cannot but record, that two friends of his had gone all the way to Tokimata for a passage down the Tenriugawa, and had been obliged to return disappointed. Truly they who would make that excursion ought to pave the way beforehand. In this case the rain was the enemy; the river would have been too high for too long a time to wait. Remember the boats also.

The only decent hotel at Nagasaki is the Belle Vue, which is very well conducted and beautifully situated on a well clothed eminence. The bad position of the other, to say no more of it, is quite against it. I changed from this to the former, and will at all events give the gentle landlord credit for Christian candour when he growled out, "You are welcome to go if you choose."

I had two days at Nagasaki—one wet and one fine. On the latter I made one of the short excursions there with a young American, whose father had married a Japanese lady; and if I were ever to go to Japan again, I should confine myself to the Inland Sea as far as Kobe and to Nagasaki. The undoubtedly attractive scenery in these quarters might well satisfy many. Kioto, and the river there, might be added, and much of Japanese special scenery thus be realized.

The *Owari Maru*, Captain Jones, was to arrive that evening, and sail on the 14th, at 8 o'clock in the morning for Chemulpo, Korea, for which port I was to take my ticket, arranging one for Tientsin afterwards. All therefore was put in order with Mr. Duus, the Agent, and on a very fine morning I left the charming Belle Vue Hotel, and went on board with this quite new country now in view, thus commencing an excursion which formed one of the most pleasing chapters, and certainly the most novel, in all my varied wanderings. Captain Jones was a genial captain; in former times that might have required a note or two of admiration, but instead of putting any at all, I will add the same character to the weather.

Over this line of ocean there is much to engage the eye; much, in short, that is far more pleasant to the passenger than to the navigator. However picturesque a rock may be, the captain hates it, nor is the passenger often fond of it, unless it be picturesque and his captain be a good one. And what of the fogs that far too often hang about these regions? I well remember my crossing one fine morning, now many years ago, from Holyhead to Dublin. On approaching Dublin a glorious bank of cloud, with full sunshine making a very striking picture of it, lay upon the ocean far before us. "What a splendid sight!" in my ignorance I exclaimed. "Splendid!" cried the captain, half in pity, but with natural irritation, "if you knew a little more you'd know it's about the *blessedest* ugliest sight a man could see." And on entering it so it proved. A dreary mass of fog and the howling fog-bell echoing through it from the pier welcomed us into Dublin Bay.

But for us, on our way to Korea, the fogs were absent, and the captain joyous; nor was he angry with me for admiring his varied and variegated enemies. We touched at pretty Fukie, on the Gotto Island, all of which I appreciated from on board, in the perspective, as it is often best to do. Then through green rocks we came at night to Itsuhára, on the Island of Tsushima. On Friday, the 15th of August, we sailed to Fusan; and on Saturday, the 16th, we were engaged all day long in taking in cargo. But what sort of cargo? Well, I have had my wonder excited in Norway by downright cairns of dried fish. But in this respect Norway must yield to Fusan here. The bundles were a sight to see; and the nose was not much less astonished than the eyes. Till 9 p.m. we were thus employed, and then we sailed for the port of Chemulpo, *my* rocky friends, and the remarkable "Two Mountain Island" conspicuously so, adorning our course through what I might call a Ko ean archipelago. On Monday, the 18th of August, about 3 p.m., we arrived at Chemulpo. Some time before so doing Captain Jones had pointed out to me the naked shining roofs upon a slope; and the general outline of the land gave pleasant evidence that the country was hilly, and indeed mountainous. Korea is, for Europeans, a very young country, and the sight could not be expected to astonish. The tide was low when we arrived; it recedes extensively at Chemulpo; and moreover it was the moment of spring tide. We anchored at some little distance from the shore, and Mr. and Mrs. Hulbert of Séoul kindly proposed to me to share their sampan to get to land. So with the usual mingling of regret and satisfaction I bid a "sans adieux" to Captain Jones.

Scrambling out of the sampan, I was recommended to a two-storied red-brick house, standing with a sort of naked tyrannical appearance among the lesser subject surroundings, on entering which I found the inside looking about as naked as the out.

The name of the proprietor is portentous. He is a Japanese, and calls himself and his hotel by the name of the great Buddha at Kamakura—Diabotzu! But this had not saved him from mortal infirmities. He was ill in bed, and the sons and boys were the supposed directors. Which was which I did not know, and I am not quite sure that they did.

In this state of confusion I consulted my letters of introduction, and went to call on Mr. Townsend, who received me very kindly and told me where I could find the Consul-General, Mr. Hillier, for whom (as I have said) I had brought a letter from Mr. Marshall of Shanghai, the Director of Public Works. In a very pleasant interview with this gentleman he suggested that we should go together to Séoul the next day on horseback, and on my showing him a letter for Mr. Schœnicke, Acting Chief Commissioner of Customs in that city, given me by Mr. Hutchison at Formosa, he very kindly telegraphed to that gentleman that I had arrived.

Having managed to get through the night at the hotel, the morning brought Mr. Hillier and his two ponies, and I mounted a white one. But the other would not let Mr. Hillier mount, and after a long fight and a long walk, and several ineffectual attempts to enforce obedience, we were obliged to return. I am particular about this because of the subsequent amusing incident that it gave rise to.

On getting back to the hotel, Mr. Hillier suggested that I should at once order a chair, but that I should not start unless I could get away well before eleven o'clock, or I might find the city gates shut at Séoul. This I made the hotel non-directory understand, and at twenty minutes to eleven we started. The men jogged along very merrily through the long street until they came to a turning point; and then they suddenly set down the chair and began to chatter at me: a tolerably perplexing situation. Only with gestures could I answer them, which they contemptuously disregarded, and finally set themselves down in a group upon some boulders. On this, I got out of the chair and began to walk back to the hotel, when I was met by the proprietor of a hotel on the road, an Austrian, whose name I regret I cannot recall, who very kindly offered to speak to the men, as he saw I was in difficulties with them. So we went back, and as far as he could make things out, their rebellion had arisen because they had not been paid half their money at the hotel. "But I knew nothing of these rules," I said, "and my money is with my servant on ahead." My friend in need then offered to advance the required sum, but time had been lost, the gates might be shut, and the men were a doubtful lot, so that I relinquished the journey and ordered them back to the hotel.

On arriving there I called the "people" to account, and one of them went to upbraid the men, but on coming back told me another story—that the men found the hotel chair too heavy, and would not carry it. This decided me to dismiss them altogether, which I did in a sufficiently emphatic manner, notwithstanding their evident desire to make terms. To Mr. Hillier I therefore again had recourse, who at once undertook that his "boy" should set all things in order for me for the next day; and after dining with him and getting through the night as best I could, he and I, he on his white pony and I with excellent coolies and a good chair, found our way on the 20th of August to Séoul.

Mr. Johnston, the Acting Commissioner of Customs at Chemulpo, had paid me a very friendly call on hearing of my misadventure, offered me any assistance I might require, and pledged me, on my return from Séoul, not to come merely the day before the boat for Tientsin sailed, but to give Mrs. Johnston and himself the pleasure of entertaining me for a few nights—an invitation afterwards confirmed by Mrs. Johnston, who jocosely and wittily thanked me for having "given them something to talk about!" My journey to the capital—the word Séoul, I am told, signifies capital—represents the extent of my incursion into Korea. The distance from point to point is about twenty-six English miles, and the coolies, two sets of four each, accomplished the course in about eight hours to the banks of the river Han, including a stoppage of nearly an hour at a rough resting-place, called "Horikol," some sixteen miles from Chemulpo. These coolies were manly, active fellows, and very willing. They walked very smoothly, and with short steps; the carrying rods were elastic, and in this respect I was much more at ease than in the dancing and jerking chairs in which I rode in Formosa. On approaching this river, the way, at this time of year, lies over a wide and desolate plain of sand, the whole of which must be covered in the rainy season. The river itself is ferried over by a broad, rough boat to a very ragged wall on the opposite side, and when you land and are carried onwards you realize what sort of place you are in. The first town is called Mapu, and I can best describe my first impressions of it by saying that it represented to me a crowd of badly-built and badly-thatched tumble-down cow-houses, with very little more than cow-paths to walk through upon, and these adorned or unadorned with the dreariest of open shops and stalls, and further still with petty cesspools.

Passing on and through, the capital lies between three and four miles further, and in its general aspect shows very little better than Mapu on first appearance. I seemed to be carried through something like a city conjured up in a nightmare, until at last, in greatest wonder where Mr. Schœnicke could have found a dwelling, I was suddenly turned into his compound, and a host, full of the sunshine of hospitality and welcome, stood at his door to receive me.

Once within the precincts of his dwelling, I felt separated from the city; and it soon became evident that, happily for all the Europeans officially occupied in Séoul, all their compounds are grouped together. The ground is very uneven; some houses stand higher than others. Mr. Schœnicke's is rather lower than some others, but very picturesque. A fitting dwelling has been designed by Mr. Marshall, and is now in course of construction, for Mr. Consul-General Hillier, in an excellent position, and Mr. Waeber, the Russian Chargé d'Affaires, with whom and his hospitality I had the opportunity of making a very pleasant acquaintance, is also building for himself a house worthy of his office. Well indeed do gentlemen occupying these positions in Séoul require every fitting comfort in existence that can be afforded them.

The position of Séoul is peculiar. It is not many feet above the level of the sea in any part of it. Its surface is very irregular, but it is chiefly in a hollow, and is surrounded by peculiarly arid serrated ridges, some nearer than others. From one of these, when the weather is not too hot to make the excursion, I am told a most effective view of the city can be obtained: and it must be a curious view. During my stay my thermometer stood too high for the attempt in question, the summer having tediously lingered.

While in Séoul, and seeing that my host was busily occupied in his duties, Mr. Stripling, to whom I had a letter of introduction, kindly called and showed me over what was to be seen. Among other things are two old palaces; and Colonel Cummins afterwards took me to the outside of the one occupied by his Majesty, showing me also the Great Bell, and the great Regent Street of Séoul. On my return with Mr. Stripling, we mounted over uneven ground to the walls of the city. These encompass a far wider space than is really populated, and the following of their wandering course up and down the various heights and hollows offers an attractive pursuit for the stranger's eye.

While I must confess to have been struck with the utterly ragged appearance of almost everything about me, I must not forget to mention another sight that also struck me at one of the old palaces. I refer to a large plantation of mulberry trees. They were too healthy and luxuriant to escape my immediate notice, and the natural question arose as to the cultivation of the worm and the production of silk. The attempt had, it appears, been made, but the result, from certain causes, was rather more akin to the state of the city than to the luxuriance of the trees. Surely the matter cannot rest here. Other signs of fertility were visible in other spots, and I must mention the garden belonging to Judge Denny's house, where

Mrs. Denny appears to be able to make everything of fruit and flower grow and give.

The soil of Korea, indeed, has the character of remarkable fertility. I have said that my invasion of the island extended only to the capital. But even over that short space I was continually surprised by the luxuriance of the crops. Wherever the earth had been appealed to it had responded generously, and produce was abounding. Among other species appears a bean, cultivated very extensively, and exported very largely to Japan, being used (as I was informed) as a manure, and also for its oil. The people, though of course very backward, appear to be strong and active, and ought to be able, by-and-by, to take a far more prominent position than they at present either can or would be permitted to occupy.

As regards the climate, it is reported as excellent. The road from Chemulpo develops largely the general character of the country. It is undulating throughout, with a surrounding prospect of hills, and even mountains, the serrated ridges in the neighbourhood of Séoul being visible almost from the beginning of the journey. There is little or no timber in the districts I speak of, but large forests are found in the north, and much mineral wealth is said to exist. Fertility and climate, those two vital gifts, may fairly be attributed to Korea. Everything (so to speak) will grow; and I am told that, as a general rule, only two summer months in the year are oppressive. Nor is the cold of the winter more than may be borne with health, provided always that people have something better than cow-houses to live in.

On the 28th of August I bade adieu to my most pleasant host, and started for Chemulpo. My journey throughout was prosperously made, coolies and all having been set under command with Mr. Schœnicke's usual kindness and consideration, and again I appreciated the healthy undulations and the smiling fertility around me that had attracted my attention on my journey upwards.

Happy man! Scarcely having relinquished hospitality in Séoul, I was regaled with it immediately on my arrival in Chemulpo; and my bearers, on arriving at the Buddha Temple, were met with orders to carry me up at once to the Eagle Nest of Mr. and Mrs. Johnston, where, in their perfect little guest-house, I enjoyed society, comfort, and repose till my departure for Tientsin. This was to take place at six o'clock on Tuesday morning, the 2nd of September, by the *Tsuruga*, Captain Thomsen, for which I arranged a new ticket, as agreed. Meanwhile I called on Mr. H. T. Stancliff, the paymaster on board the United States s.s. *Swatura*, whom I was to visit at Chefoo, two of the officers, Lieutenants Perkins and Reynolds, afterwards dining with Mr. and Mrs. Johnston. But on the 31st a great change of weather took place, and we were hindered from lunching with Captain Tisdale, of H.M.S. *Linnet*. All such passing events are uneventful in Pall Mall, but if you go to Chemulpo you will find they give you "something to talk about." Finally (for one more) we sat down to a cheerful dinner on the evening of the 1st of September, at which, to my great subsequent advantage, I made the acquaintance of Mr. Michie, the proprietor of *The*

Chinese Times at Tientsin, and found he was to be a fellow-passenger on board. After dinner and talk, on board we all went; and the usual parting sentiments were abundantly interchanged. So farewell, Korea! with the fullest meaning of that word. Nature has done much for you among your neighbours, and Man must not be permitted to undo you. And you, commercial England, behave well to Korea; for her trade with you in necessary articles is already comparatively large, and is increasing yearly; your position is good, so take good care of it, and your Consul-General, Mr. Hillier, will take good care of you.

And finally, you, my two good hosts, farewell to you! I have many thanks to pay to you, but happily no Customs duties; but were it otherwise, to none would I pay them so cheerfully as to Mr. Schœnicke and Mr. Johnston.

XXIX.

We had a most propitious passage on board the *Tsuruga* to Tongku. Our weather was as genial as our good captain—Thomsen; which is saying much. On Wednesday, the 3rd of September, we stood off Chefoo, at early morning, the shore view looking very inviting; but no time was given to land, and I could only hail Mr. Stancliff in his boat. Steaming on again for a few hours' voyage, we breasted the now historical Taku Forts. As a rule, I take no special interest in forts, in visiting which my mouth is generally wider open than my eyes; but here, in full view of Taku, I could not but bestow a special gaze upon them, for I had received a letter from my intimate friend in London, Surgeon Lieut.-Colonel Dr. Lewins (who had been engaged in the Chinese war of 1860–61), in which he wrote, "Think of me at the Taku Forts, if your enterprising steps lead you in that direction." I was happy in the reflection that the forts were tranquil, and that he was safe in London.

My friend was surgeon in charge of the *Mauritius*, hospital ship, at the taking of these formidable forts. We had more than once conversed upon the subject, nor can I refrain from here noting down some interesting and important particulars of that operation, as recounted to me by him, while I seem to have Taku now standing before me.

In the year previous to the war I speak of, these forts had successfully resisted Admiral Hope's determined attack, and Dr. Lewins has always attributed their capture in the war of 1860-61 to the genius of the late Lord Napier of Magdala, who, as Dr. Lewins thinks, was the first engineer or artillery officer who ever commanded a division of the British army. The then Commander-in-Chief was a cavalry officer, Sir Hope Grant, whose qualifications for the special art of siege operations might naturally be doubtful; nor was the French general, Montauban, at all superior to him in this respect. The original intention was that the English army should attack the Northern Forts, and the French the Southern; tactics which Dr. Lewins thinks would have caused great slaughter, without being very well calculated to succeed. But Lord Napier at once sagaciously detected the weak point in the Chinese position, and attacked the 3rd Fort from the sea, in which there was a raised mound where guns could be placed for raking the whole range of the defence. The attempt entirely succeeded, and this fort was captured at the cost to the English of 200 killed and wounded, and to the French about the same. Nor would this loss have been so great had not the French, out of mere bravado, proceeded to escalade before the Tartar force was completely crushed, thus obliging the English to follow them into quite useless destruction. Dr. Lewins particularly mentions it was on this memorable occasion that, under the command of Captain Barry, a battery of

Armstrong breech-loading guns were for the first time brought into play; and (says the doctor) it was dreadful to witness their terrible efficiency. Not a single Tartar escaped death, for all refused quarter or surrender to the very last; those who had not been shattered by the Armstrongs perishing by the bayonet. Here, I may observe, is another example of these people's indifference to life. "Moreover, even those recruited by us for the Transport Corps, and treated among the wounded on board the *Bentinck*, preferred death to surgical treatment, and it was a constant source of anxiety to the officials to prevent their committing suicide in order to avoid the alternative."

We sailed as nearly up to the railway-station of Tongku as the tide would admit of, and, when we anchored, our good captain immediately placed his gig at our disposal, and we bid him a hearty farewell. Being kindly hailed by the Engineer of the line in the usual form, we left by the 9.42 morning train for Tientsin, where we arrived at 11.8 o'clock. This railway was a real blessing, and certainly it has not invaded and wounded any very delightful scenery. At best, the whole surrounding lands are flat, but as we saw them on the 4th of September—oh, what a desolation of outspread waters! In this respect there must have been novelty for all of us, and, to a certain extent, to the poor inhabitants, for I believe the floods of 1890 were quite unusual. On arriving at Tientsin Mr. Michie was good enough to take me to the hotel, and a certain guide presenting himself, he forthwith recommended him to me—Ngan Chii Shing—a heartily opportune circumstance.

My first object was the Chief Commissioner's office to get my letters, where I had the pleasure of meeting Mr. Yorke, in the absence of Mr. Detring; and here, to my agreeable surprise, I found among them a long letter from Sir Robert Hart, full of suggestions as to my course to Peking. Mr. Yorke was kind enough to recommend to me one Hu Yung-an, for ponies, who served me well: these I had been recommended to bring up with me, for none are to be had at Peking. Thus I was prepared so far for a start; and it was decided that my journey must be by the river Peiho. A conference with Mr. Ritter, of the Astor Hotel, put me in the way of securing all the provisions I should require for my river journey to Tungchow, and my guide undertook to find the necessary house-boat. I am not at all sure I should have chosen any other mode of travelling here, but fortunately no room to doubt and choose was left, for though the ponies could be led in some fashion to meet me at Tungchow, to ride there was impossible on account of the floods. An afternoon's visit to inspect the chosen house-boat was *pro formâ* only, for all the boats were alike. The system of their structure reminded me of the one I had floated about in while touring in Kashmir; but the details here are far superior. Here there is wooden framework; there you are simply covered in with matting, above and around, and are never free from draughts of wind at night, and, the boats being smaller, it is always necessary to have a second one for cooking. But they do their best among the very poor workers in Kashmir with their scanty means.

Solids and liquids and ice being on board, and the British Consul having furnished me with the indispensable passport, all was now in order, and I started for Peking at eleven o'clock on the morning of the 5th of September, wondering what sort of a city I was to see, and feeling sure it must be very unlike Tientsin, through the narrow bizarre bazaars of which I was carried in a chair to meet my boat at "The Bridge." I had my guide and my Indian servant with me, and both proved essential throughout. One great help I also had at Mr. Michie's hands—a full large bundle of the latest London *Times*, to read and digest in case of monotony on my river journey. For some considerable distance up stream I was surprised to observe the close and varied number of sampans crowding both sides of the Peiho. Later on these disappeared, but the breast of the stream was always adorned, and sometimes clogged, with rice boats and their rectangular crumpled sails shining in the sun. The shores gradually became naked, and of course merely flat and muddy, and twice I was surprised by a heavy splash on board, produced by a fall of earth from a dry, low bank into the water, in feeble imitation of grander catastrophes.

On the evening of the 6th we came to the village of Ho-hsi-wu, which my guide told me was just half way on the journey; and we passed onwards under its group of trees on the flat shore to our night anchorage higher up stream, at eight o'clock.

The 7th was chiefly remarkable for the complete

regiment of rice boats we passed with their sails glittering in the sun; they lent life to the scene, but their charm was a charming bore sometimes, and especially so were some very huge boats belonging to the Emperor. But we managed to pass through them without entangling our lines or being imperiously crushed. Nor were these the only troubles on the way. I must add the impalpable dust from the banks, reminding me of the Nile; and especially the sun. Wind about as we would—and the Peiho certainly does wind—our main direction always brought us sun, direct or by reflection;

> Sun, sun, sun,
>   Wherever we wound or turned;
> From sky to water, and water to sky,
>   Both of 'em blinded and burned.

As to the river's windings, it reminded me of the Jhelum in Kashmir, both flow through dead flat banks; and here again I noted that the flatter the territory the more winding and devious is the stream, as if it were without a guide and did not know whither it was going; meeting with no troubles to control it. I am told that while the distance from Tientsin to Tungchow by land measures eighty miles, that by water measures 120, or just half as much again. However, all here was new, though small annoyances themselves are very rarely so; and at eight o'clock at night we anchored.

The 8th was to show me my last half day on the river, and at very early morning I was waked by a loud Buddha gong. Yes, we may object to this; but what of the wild howlings of our Salvation Army at home? Are the gods so fond of discord? Where is St. Cecilia? Has she no throne in heaven? or has she turned enemy to harmony? The Buddhists are the more tolerable by far. Their bells are sonorous.

At about noon or a little after we landed among a crowd of boats, thus making the river journey in three whole days and an hour—or seventy-three hours altogether. The stream was strong against us, and the men worked well throughout, stopping for a certain number of hours each night, and feeding on their rice at intervals. My own cook, Ngan Chii Shing and my Indian servant kept me supplied with everything, and were most attentive.

On landing, my first question of course was, "Where are my ponies?" "There," said my guide, "there;" but before I could catch sight of them a letter was put into my hand, being another explicit one from Sir Robert Hart, who had very considerately sent down a chair and two carts to meet me, in case my ponies should not have arrived. Nothing could have been more welcome to me; and as the sun was very hot I availed myself of the covered chair, and sent up the ponies with the mafoo, and my guide and servant with the carts.

Sir Robert Hart had warned me in his letter that the gates of the city closed at half-past six in the evening, and that I must by no means start one minute later than 2 p.m. or I should run the danger of being shut out, and have to pass the night in whatever miserable Chinese *hotel* the chair coolies might take me to. The journey was to occupy five hours, and the coolies were to have an opportunity of stopping two or three times for tea and tobacco.

We started in good time. They had their instructions, and I consigned myself to their care like a bag of merchandise. As was to be expected they carried me well and faithfully ; and in very good time before the forbidding hour I found myself close under the vast perspective of the imposing thirty feet high dark walls of the Capital of the North, Peking. There was a certain majesty in this towering outside aspect in the evening, as there was also something of imagined awe as I was carried through the dark depth of the Tung-pien-mên, or Eastern Gate, into the Chinese city, the first of the three that you come to. But immediately on emerging, there was a striking and entertaining change. A medley, as it seemed, of streets and houses, and carts, and flat yellow faces in various costumes suddenly took possession of my eyes, and in the midst of all my coolies set me down to take their five minutes' rest. It was most amusing. Had I been a monster as rare as some of their peculiarly impossible statues, I could not have been more intensely gazed at. It was *monstrari digito* with a vengeance, though not in the Horatian sense, and astonishment commanded silence. The crowd at last became so great that my coolies hurried themselves to move on. Through this part of the Chinese city I passed to another gate, an inner one opening into the Tartar City, and called Ha-ta-mên ; though why we spell Tartar with the middle "*r*," I do not know. The word is Tatar. I was not set down again, and indeed soon found myself carried over a large open space under the wall. But I confess to have kept asking myself the question, "Where on earth, among all these strange streets, and openings and dwellings and people, can Sir Robert Hart be living?"

XXX.

At last, however, encountering crowds again, we arrived at T'ai Ch'e Ch'ang—where stands his walled domain,—and entering in, I found myself surprisingly separated from all associations with the city, and in the presence of Hay-Ta-Yin, Sir Robert Hart's self. A spacious house, surrounded by a well-planted garden with lawns and trees, was before me, and a genial welcome, uncompromised by the title, greeted me on entering. Sir Robert was at home, and the rest of the evening before dinner time was pleasantly filled up by a quiet walk under the trees and over the lawns, not huge but ample; and scarcely less influenced by the general aspect of the ground than by the easy hospitality of my host, I fairly felt myself "at home" at once.

I must confess I was particularly taken, during our conversational stroll, with the garden; not only flowering shrubs and lawns, but quiet avenues of trees being included; and the owner had planted them all. That surprised me, for their growth was notable; and being passionately fond of trees, their screen and shade were charming to me.

Nothing could be more comfortable and independent than the arrangements made for my sojourn. My rooms were on one side of the hall, the house being built in spacious English style, and there and thence I had free dwelling and exit just as I pleased. Every morning came my coffee with an abundance of grapes, for which Peking is at this season so deservedly famed, and of these grapes it is worth while observing that the Chinese have some secret method of preserving their freshness all through the winter. The fruit is particularly fine, and well worth their ingenuity. Sir Robert was engaged all day till five on the opposite side, free from interference; luncheon only intervened, and dinner and conversation closed up the evening.

On the following day, the 9th, I was of course to call upon our Minister, Sir John Walsham, which I had much personal pleasure in doing, for I had made his acquaintance some years ago in Madrid, as the eldest son of his late worthy father, whom I had known very well indeed. I found his Excellency living in a very handsome temple, with all dignified approaches, now converted into a Legation, and I sat for a long time conversing with him. This dwelling in temples, particularly in the hills, when vacation comes on, is notable. It was vacation time when I visited Peking, but Sir John was at the Legation, and, fortunately for me, Sir Robert Hart never takes a holiday.

It was now the 9th of September, and I had to consider the realization of one great object of my coming to Peking, besides that of enjoying the society of my distinguished host and making myself acquainted with the great city, its crowded streets and alleys, and its large open spaces, unoccupied. That great object was to see the great historical

Wall, and the now forlorn tombs of the Ming Dynasty; and as I had yet to visit the gorges of the Yangtse Kyang, and to take care not to be too late again for the temples in Cambodia, it was necessary not to loiter, though there was no occasion for hurry. Sir Robert had at once made me acquainted with his Private Secretary, Mr. Ludlow, who naturally speaks Chinese well, and under his guidance I had made that one generally necessary visit, viz. to the Bank, or what was as good as a bank, for foreign establishments under that name are not permitted in Peking. Then it must enter into my head: "I wonder whether I dare ask for Mr. Ludlow as my companion for the journey?" I made bold, and did ask, and behold, taking into consideration the utter loneliness I should suffer and the necessary incompleteness and discomfort of my journey in consequence, the request was most considerately granted. So preparations were forthwith set on foot for a start on the morning of Friday, the 12th, and leave of absence was accorded until the following Tuesday, just five days. Meanwhile, on the intermediate Tuesday, Wednesday, and Thursday, Mr. Ludlow made it more apparent to me than ever how much I depended on him, by riding with me through almost every part of Peking, over paved streets, and dusty streets, and crowded streets; among carts with dangerously projecting axle-trees, and other carts with dangerously projecting corners of awnings; between ugly booths, and stalls, that were hiding better shops; and chairs, and handsome mules, and even barrows. It is almost impossible to believe that Canton and Peking can belong to the same nation, so utterly different are the two. As regards the plan of the whole of Peking, I made every effort to obtain a copy of a small pamphlet containing one, with a quantity of other useful information, but in vain.

The whole city, as Peking, is built on a vast flat, sandy plain, between the river Peiho and its affluent, the Hoen-ho; and it consists of three walled cities. The Chinese city is a rectangular parallelogram running one way in length. The Tartar city is such another; longer and almost as broad, joining at right angles, and making a sort of very broad some and the Imperial city is walled up within the Tartar city. The outside walls cover, I understood, some twenty miles. The Chinese city is said to contain nine square miles, is thickly populated by the Chinese, and is the seat of general business. The Tartar city is not so thickly populated. It contains fourteen square miles, and contains also the forbidden Imperial city. The whole is flat and sandy, dusty enough, and a great deal too much so when the wind blows. The main streets are straight, and a curious raggedness is given to the scene by the arrangement of them. There is a raised dusty causeway (as we call it) in the middle, on each side of which there is a lower dusty breadth, and then come the real shops. These are in many cases coloured and showy, particularly the tea-shops; but between these and the raised street ragged and paltry places of active business are built, materially hiding the others. These, they say, are removed when the

Emperor comes out; but there was no sign of this Imperial movement during my short sojourn.

In the Chinese city, crowded with life and movement, I remember to have been conducted up the Long Street, the Curio Street, where I made no purchases whatever (the street being Curio enough itself), and the Lamp Street. Now and then a mandarin in his official chair and with his retinue will be met with; and everyone gives way to the palanquin. In short, the glory of these streets is their colour and confusion, and I rather delight in courting confusion of recollection. Some strange things I saw in the Chinese city, some in the Tartar city, nothing beyond something of the outsides of the Imperial city. But I should here mention one famous temple of which a certain uncertain view used to be obtained; it has, however, been totally destoyed by fire. I mean the one illustrated at page 690 of Fergusson, and called by the two singularly contrary names, so far as the Christian ear is affected, of the "Temple of Heaven," or of "the Great Dragon." But the great dragon is, we should remember, the symbol of the Chinese nation, intended, of course, to strike terror; as also it is in the Apocalypse, but in a different sense. The Tartar city is the residence of all the Legations and of all foreigners. Many Manchus reside there, and if you meet a woman astride on horseback she is a Tartar and never a Chinese. Look at those mules, now and then. Where else can you find any such truly handsome animals? I had almost said any approach to them. We used to boast of our mules in Brazil, but they would be literally nowhere here. I am afraid to say what some of the best saddle-mules are worth; but I believe you may add an *s* to hundred; and if I have said, "Look at the mules," I may now add, "Listen to the donkeys!" I may safely say that Peking brayings appeared to me to create a new sensation. Always bear in mind—crowds.

In one of our daily rides we met a very singular procession. There was a good nosegay of variegated costume and there was a carrying on high of certain large gilded or golden boxes of a certain size. What on earth are these? The procession is a marriage procession, and those boxes contain geese. Boxes of this historical bird are carried as a present to the bride, but they are only hired for the purpose, and having been presented, are taken away again and serve for a new occasion. I know not whether they intimate future happiness in marriage, or are intended to signify that the married are geese if they expect it; but, strangely enough, they serve opposite purposes, for, having paid their respects to marriage, they are equally carried to funerals. Geese, I was told, are not eaten in Peking. Ducks, I know, are, and considering what these birds must feed on, I cannot think them wholesome. If you see beef in a butcher's shop, you may be sure he is a Muhammadan. The Chinese do not eat beef and mutton, but pork *ad libitum*, and veal. They are known to eat a good many odd things. In the Chinese city I certainly saw laid out in admirable symmetry dead rats upon a stall, in fair number, their tails being as carefully arranged as though they had been those of Chinese themselves.

A highly interesting and impressive scene presented itself one morning when we mounted to the top of the thirty-feet city walls, and walked along a considerable space of its many surrounding miles. The width of these walls at the base is called twenty or twenty-five feet, but they taper inside; and the top is given as only twelve or fourteen feet. It looked more to me. The construction consists of two outsides to protect a mass of stuff thrown in between. The labour of it all may be contemplated. Shrubs and brambles were growing on each side of us as we walked along, and it was easy to imagine ourselves upon a country road. We enjoyed a fine view of the city below us, which was thickly dressed with trees, reminding me in this respect of Bangkok in its far lesser scale. Again, on another part of the Wall we saw the extraordinarily well preserved instruments of the old Observatory, all for many a year exposed to the air, and yet presenting perfect surfaces.

The material was bronze; the various scientific instruments were elaborately ornamented, the Imperial Chinese Dragon figuring with his *five* claws. These instruments were constructed in 1674 by order of the then Emperor, Khanghi, under the direction of the Jesuit Father, F. Verbiest; and the large azimuth was presented to that Emperor by Louis XIV. Note, therefore, the quality of both material and climate.

Religious liberty must to a certain extent be recognized in Peking, because I saw a Roman Catholic Cathedral and a Mosque. I was also shown an Examination Hall, as in Canton. Here, as there, there is said to be great competition for degrees. The chance of later promotion is thought to be well worth contending for. Intellect and literary capacity are much esteemed; but the ranking of the successful, as explained to me, seemed singular. Three degrees of "Doctor" are conferred in groups of hundreds. To the first class hundred are granted Sinecures, to the second class *quasi* sinecures, and to the third class offices of generally useful service. So thus it would seem that learning in the shape of scholastic acquirements is considered to exist in inverse proportion with usefulness; in other words, the less of the scholar, the more of common sense. What, then, if all the world were scholars? where would the world look for common sense? Not among the too erudite, entangling and inventing.

Thus were my three days passed in Peking; and on the evening of the 11th, the eve of our departure to the Great Wall, Sir Robert Hart showed me his beautiful phonographic instrument, in experimenting on which and viewing certain mechanical contrivances I passed more than an hour of entertainment and surprise. Then came the morning of our departure, for which all preparations had been carefully made with the assistance of Mr. Taillen and his store; the sumpter animals and baggage being looked after by proper authorities, whom Mr. Michie's recommended guide actively assisted.

XXXI.

ACCORDINGLY, on the morning of the 12th, I was called at five o'clock, the weather being very fresh and fine. At 6.30 my guide, Ngan Chii Shing, and my Indian servant, Bana, left with the coolies, mules, and cargoes, and at 7 a.m. Mr. Ludlow and I followed with the mafoo on our three ponies, leaving Peking by the An-ting-men Gate. My guide had made out his programme for four days, but Mr. Ludlow greatly improved upon it, and marked out five. The great point gained by this arrangement was that we were not simply to get to the Wall in the middle of the day and leave it again after only an hour or two's stay, but we were to go through it, and sleep, and return through it the next morning; and we were also to make a round on our return. We lunched at Ching Ho (or Clear River) and slept at Ch'ang-p'ing Chou (familiarly called "Jumping Joe"), and as the ground was fair for riding, we covered twenty-four miles quickly; visiting the Yellow Temple, with its curious white monument, at a short distance from Peking, an illustration of which is given in Fergusson. I know not that I was particularly struck with any feature of the country in this ride, except it was with the splendid crops of what we call buckwheat (buchweisen); not even in Germany had I ever seen such splendid spreads of it.

The next day, the 13th, was to be the day for visiting the Ming Tombs, and after passing a very comfortable night (in our own beddings, by-the-by) at a rather rough but fairly convenient hotel, we diverged towards the north to visit these tombs. The scene is most striking. The large valley round which they are placed is quite flat, and is encircled by a vast and varied range of green mountains, curiously folding one behind another, and presenting a ribbed and wrinkled appearance. The first object met with is a large white marble gateway: the first. The second is called the Red Gateway. Then appears a large stone tablet, with a huge tortoise, and this is surrounded by four pillars; and from this point there begins the much-renowned, and very strange, long avenue of stone animals; and not of natural animals only, but of fabulous animals; and fairly, may I also add, of fabulous men. All these objects (including camels among the number) are of gigantic size. I believe they extend altogether for a mile, and they astonished our own animals even a good deal more than they did ourselves—a certain sort of sarcasm being thus expressed towards these intended tragical and impressive productions. This, I thought, was particularly expressed by my pony's terrified objection to face one majestic interpretation of a horse, which he viewed with terror instead of fraternity.

At various distances round the very extensive ridge of the mountains there are thirteen tombs constructed; but you may well look for the tombs. They are all more or less elaborate buildings with courtyards, and are surrounded by a screen of trees planted for their protection. We visited (I may say travelled over) the chief tomb, called that of "Yung-lo," among other features of which was a large hall supported by several very lofty wooden trunks or pillars, said to have been sent from Burmah, and reminding me of some even loftier trunks which supported one of the halls of the late King Thebaw's Palace at Mandalay. The hall of this Ming Tomb is said to be seventy yards long by thirty deep. The whole encircled space forms a complete domain, and from the highest point of the buildings a fine view of the amphitheatre of the green mountains is obtained, these, taken far and near, appearing to entirely encircle the enormous flat valley. The thirteen funeral processions of Imperial burials, as they severally took place across this vast solitary space, must have offered an imposing scene and attracted thousands of admiring followers; but now mere gaunt, unheeded ruin stares; for at the funeral of the thirteenth emperor, Wan-lie, almost three hundred years ago, the Ming Dynasty itself was the companion of his corpse to that yonder thirteenth tomb, and was buried with it.

And now for Nankou, a town at the foot of the Pass that is to lead us to the Great Wall. Bearing off to our right in a south-westerly direction, we reached Nankou for tiffin, and after tiffin we set out for the Pass. The walls round Nankou gave us some small notion of the great structure we were about to visit, clambering about the surrounding most uneven ground; but our attention was soon called to the Pass itself, presenting (as it does) the great high road to Mongolia, Kashgar, and Siberia. The general aspect of the highest mountain on each side is by no means so savage as has been presented in certain prints. The rocks are almost always covered with grass, and in the light and shade of the afternoon presented often a velvety appearance. The road (as may be supposed) is generally rough indeed, but in many parts it has been repaired. In many, however, repair is quite impossible: torrential streams have torn it all to pieces. This feature, nevertheless, is not predominant, and we made our way very fairly so as to arrive at the Wall itself some easy time before sunset. Long before reaching this point, however, we caught sight of the great animal coming headlong down an apparently vertical side of a big mountain in the distance straight before us; but we were not yet to get through the archway. I thought we should never do so. The windings of the road towards the upper end appeared to me interminable; at last, however, behold the longed-for goal. The wandering, pitching, clambering line stood close before us; and here, by the irony of history, was seen that vast structure which was erected in order to keep out that race—the Eastern or Mantchou Tartars—one of whom now occupies the Imperial Throne of China. We of course dismounted and climbed on to the serpentine monster. The evening light and shade lent great effect to the surrounding scene, and as Cha-tao, where we were to sleep, lay only one mile below us and beyond us, we were quite at liberty, as regards time, to examine and survey. We therefore wandered and pondered at our leisure, and walked on the top up the declivity to our left for some little distance until brought to by a huge and ruinous fall of the structure, which made farther passage impossible. This stupendous structure, said to have been completed some 200 years B.C., appears to be composed, as the walls of Peking, of a huge mound of earth in the middle, built in and supported on both sides by walls of mixed brick and stone. It begins with a mass of stone at the sea side, and runs over hill and dale some 1500 miles, varying in height all through; and at short intervals it is fortified with large square towers, perhaps thirty feet high. Where we saw it the Wall itself might be twenty feet high, or perhaps something more, and its width at the top perhaps fifteen feet. You cannot see any great length of it at one time because of the great and sudden irregularities of the ground. It shoots down upon you, runs by you, mounts and disappears, and then gives you a parting glimpse on a yet more distant apex. When we had gazed enough we came down to the comfortable reality of our saddles; into these we mounted and found our way with easy descent to Cha-tao, only one mile away, where our servants had prepared for us our dinner and beds, and where, after a toughish journey of some twenty-eight miles, we enjoyed our champagne and bed. But if you want the real benefit of champagne after fatigue, drink some immediately on coming in, and don't wait for mere dinner sippings, which may come afterwards.

The next day, the 14th, was to be a long one; no less than thirty-three miles; through the Pass again, *viâ* Nankou, to the temple, Ta Chiao-ssŭ; and my companion considerately suggested to me that I should take a mule litter over the Pass, at all events, instead of quixotically riding as I had come. I wavered a little, and, on beholding the litter, absolutely revolted. But presently an open chair appeared, not very elegant or luxurious, but open; and my rebellious spirit bowed; I accepted the considerate suggestion. I never made a more judicious submission, for, starting early, we had the benefit of the light and shade of the still low sun, and the surpassing freshness of the morning air to sharpen the perceptions. The road gradually ascended to the Wall, which thus we saw for the second time; and though it is often said with truth that a first sight is the most impressive, yet it was not so in this case, for I must give my verdict in favour of the second. The whole scene remains imprinted on my memory, and I should always say: "If you wish to see this section of the Wall to the best effect, pass through it from below." I did not climb again, nor was my companion yet up with me; but I was set down for a short time to inwardly digest; and it is just possible that my now certain comfort of being carried over rattling stones and rocks on men's shoulders, without the jar of the jerking hoof, insensibly elevated my feelings into that generous appreciation of all around which we can so generously give way to when, for the moment, our restless uneasiness is completely satisfied.

Just as I had found the approach to the Wall from the outside afford the most effective aspect, so

I found the descent of the Pass much more effective than the ascent, and, seated in my chair, I had the greater opportunity of enjoying the lights and shades of morning. But one most impressive feature I must not omit to mention most particularly—the enormous and continuous flow of hairy, two-humped camels on their long way through to Kashgar, Mongolia, and Russia, laden heavily with tea. Add to these as many more coming in, and thousands of white sheep, with black heads and faces, also being driven inwards from the north. As on the river with the rice-laden boats, so in the Pass with the animals and the tea-laden camels. On arriving at a toll station we asked what was the number of camels daily passing through during the season. The answer was remarkable: "From eight to nine hundred daily on the average; but this morning I have already checked off two thousand." Yesterday had already astonished us in this respect, but this morning astounded us. There was something wild and exciting in the sight of these camels: in that they were going on a far, far journey, and that the tea they were carrying had come all the way from Hankow. The camels themselves also vividly recalled to my mind those troops of them, though not so numerous as these, which I had met with in the wild Khyber Pass on their road to Cabul.

At Nankou we took our tiffin and rest, and started off for the Ta-chiao Temple on our homeward road. And here we enjoyed the occupation of the rooms lately left by his Excellency Herr von Brandt, the German Minister, and also some remarkably fine specimens of the always abundant grapes, and some splendid water. But when I speak of grapes, do not let me forget the fruit called Persimmon, about the size of a small plum, and in consistency and flavour not very unlike the gooseberry; a most refreshing aid in travelling. What I did not so much enjoy was the deep-toned midnight Buddhist bell. But if you will seek shelter in religious precincts, you must conform to religious proceedings.

Our thirty-three miles being thus accomplished, we woke up on our fourth day, the 15th of the month, to find our way to Wo-fu-ssu, or the "Sleeping Buddha" Temple. This proved to be a day of twenty-three miles, but it was a very varied one among temples, and hard in performance, involving a climb on foot over a rocky mountain. My companion had suggested a round by the Western Hills and to sleep at the Ta-pei-ssu, but we thought it better to curtail this round and pass the night at Wo-fu-ssu, visiting the Pi-yün-ssu, and returning. To this arrangement the priests invited us in something very like a hospitable tone. Suddenly, however, but not until all our goods and chattels were spread forth and the beds laid, we were informed that for their thus proffered night's repose they would expect us to pay the modest sum of $20. To this Mr. Ludlow, in very quiet but decided Chinese, flatly objected. Whereupon the demand suddenly and precipitously tumbled down to $7, a still exorbitant sum. We would have paid $5, or just double what we had hitherto paid, but this was declined. So we lunched, paying a mere nominal occupation sum, and got into our saddles. Then, while our men were beginning to pack, came the message, but all too late, that the priests would be content with the proffered $5. They did not get more than one quarter of that sum; and thus, while attempting to be very wide awake while Buddha was asleep, they proved themselves to be even more asleep than he. In this escape, our guide, Ngan Chii Shing, was eminently useful.

This reclining Buddha (either of metal or ivory) measures some thirty-six feet in length; but the one I saw in Siam (though not of either material) measured 126 feet, lying with bended knees. Both were surrounded with (perhaps) thousands of baby Buddhas, the personal offerings of pilgrims: but while those in Siam were placed in niches in the wall, these were on open shelves.

Our next halt, at a short distance, was at the extraordinary and picturesquely situated temple, Pi-yün-ssu. A pagoda of fine white marble, but of curious design, forms the chief architectural feature. But the marvellous contents of the temple consist first in the large hall containing no less than 500 gilded wise men, perhaps a little larger than life. All are in different attitudes, apparently of recognition of the visitor; and of the thousand hands perhaps no two are in the same position. They reminded me of the corresponding sight at Canton. Five hundred is a large number to call wise, and it must be confessed that there are not many outward signs of wisdom among the faces of the multitude. Then, in other parts, are thousands of other smaller figures; representation of hell and hell torments, of course from which some slight hints might perhaps be taken even by those who are said to be appointed below to plague almost every mortal that was ever born. Pass on, and you come to those who are enjoying happiness in another quarter. In short, from first to last the whole place seems to be alive with lifeless figures of all sorts and sizes.

It was now time to leave for the Ta-pei-ssu on the Western Hills, and for this spot our road lay across rather rough country. These Western Hills (as they are called) contain eight temples dotted on the hill-side at various intervals, and it is here that the various Legations are in the habit of retiring during the hot season. Some of them are perched high indeed, and if our road was rough, so indeed did I find the steep paved approach even to our destination, which was by no means the highest. But in the season these rough paths are thought nothing of, and the communications are carried on between the temples with frequency and activity; contrasting strangely, as may be supposed, with the abandoned and snowy desolation of the winter. We reached Ta-pei-ssu at evening, and thus completed our fourth day and our additional twenty-three miles.

Now came our fifth and last day, the 16th of the month. Our road to Peking would have been short and easy if followed direct, but we considered it quite worth while to take a round by the Summer Palace and the Bell Temple, or Ta-chung-ssu. At the former great repairs are going on, and much building also in the close neighbourhood. For the present, the Summer Residence, which was burned in 1860-61, presents no very inviting aspect for residence. The situation is striking. The enclosed domain with all the attendant buildings occupies a large cone or mound, which stands out singly on the plain.

We lunched at the Bell Temple in a remarkably pleasing quadrangle, and saw the greatest hanging bell in the world, covered with sacred writing inside and out. I say the greatest hanging bell, but the bell which I saw at Moscow is larger still, being the largest in the world. This, however, is not a hanging bell; it fell in the great fire, and remains where it fell.

And now for Peking again, after a most successful, interesting, and pleasant journey, occupying just five days, during which, with this day's seventeen miles, we had ridden 125 miles. The great walls looked majestic, and now hospitable, as we approached them, and we entered by the Tê Sheng Men.

Instead, however, of riding direct to our destination at Sir Robert Hart's, Mr. Ludlow added further to my knowledge of the city by taking me round by the Drum Tower, Coal Hill, and the Palace Ground and moat; and thus at last, still under the guidance of my indispensable companion, I came again to the hospitable roof under which I have passed so many interesting hours of perfect liberty and repose. A quiet dinner and a long quiet evening of conversation offered a very pleasant close of my five days of lively interest, and, to a certain extent, of bodily fatigue; but after a good night's rest, and my coffee and grapes, all symptoms of the latter had disappeared, and left the former unalloyed.

The shadow of the day of departure now began to fall, and this was fixed for early morning on Sunday, the 21st of September. Meanwhile, Sir Robert had arranged a dinner party for me, although almost all the world were absent, and after dinner there was a vast amount of entertainment among all the company with the marvels of the phonograph. "What next will be invented?" has been a perpetual interrogatory, and I never forget a strange phrase used by an old home gardener when informed of some (to him) new horror, that "by-and-by we should be getting too cunnin' for God A'mighty." And there are certain of a higher rank, too, that labour under much the same misgiving.

On the Saturday afternoon we were regaled on the lawn with a band of music, conducted by a Portuguese bandmaster, whom I, of course, invited to a Portuguese conversation. This band is one especially belonging to Sir Robert, and is exclusively fostered by him. It plays every Saturday, and the lawn is an harmonious scene of social meeting.

That evening we had a trio dinner of adieu, Sir Robert, Mr. Ludlow, and I. The chair which Sir Robert had sent for from Tung Ching had arrived, my guide and servant had already departed, and late at night I gratefully bid my hospitable host good-bye. Nor can I better do so again on these pages than by transcribing the acrostic that I ventured to write in his Visitors' Book :—

High sound and phrase may greet the ear,
And surface forces show ;
Repose and intercourse are here—
The forces lie below.

Sunday morning came, and with it Mr. Ludlow to shake hands. At five minutes past six I was again alone upon the road, and at twenty minutes to eleven I was at Tung Ching.

Down the river is generally easier than up, and on the Pei-ho there was no exception to this rule. It cost me just four days to go up and one day and five hours, or twenty-nine hours in all, to come down. At five o'clock on the afternoon of the 23rd, I was at the bridge at Tientsin, and at half-past seven at the dinner-table with Mr. and Mrs. Detring, a pleasure that was repeated on the following day. At half-past four on the 25th the same kind Commissioner sent his steam-launch round to the Astor House Hotel, for which I leave the very best report, and thus I came on board the *Chungking*, Captain Hughes, for an early start next morning for Shanghai. There we arrived about noon on Michaelmas Day, and having left the Astor House at Tientsin, I resumed the Astor House at Shanghai.

XXXII.

It was now the moment for arranging my contemplated excursion up the Yang-tse-Kiang, before finally leaving Shanghai, and well it was for me that when I first spoke of doing so the swollen river cried "No." For now I came armed with a full recommendation from Sir Robert Hart to all his Commissioners at the various ports to take me under their protection; his letters, I should observe, having already gone before me, on my having expressed to him, while in Peking, my desire to see the gorges. I therefore called on Mr. Bredon, Sir Robert's brother-in-law, and Commissioner of Customs at Shanghai, who had forwarded the letters up the river, and again having recourse to Messrs. Butterfield and Swire, Mr. Bois furnished me with a ticket to leave by their S.S. *Peking*, Captain Batten, early on Wednesday, the 7th of October; and I was to be on board the night before. My first resting place was to be Hankow, the limit of the steamer's course of 598 miles; and Mr. Lay, the Commissioner there, had already written that he was expecting me.

After enjoying the hospitality of our Consul-General, Mr. Hughes and Mrs. Hughes, Mr. Bredon, Mr. Bois, and Mr. and Mrs. Robert Little, the night of the 7th of September found me on board, and 1 a.m. on the 8th found us in movement. As the day opened the enormous width and windings of the uncouth and unruly river became strikingly apparent, but the banks were all low and flat and totally uninteresting. Side creeks led up into the country, stretching for many miles. We stopped at Chinkiang about cargo at night, both going and coming, so that I had no opportunity of landing there. The next station was Wahu, and the next Kiukiang, but in both these cases I had to defer my visit till my return, and eventually we came to Hankow at about 11 a.m. on the 11th. Here Mr. Lay came on board, and I was escorted to his house, enjoying his and Mrs. Lay's hospitality till I could continue my journey to Ichang, where the excursion to the gorges begins. Every morning a regular report was made as to the inches which the river had sunk during the twenty-four hours: these two or three inches in so immense a body representing enormous masses of water.

There was some delay here from an accident to the continuing boat, the *Kiangtung*, and various contradictory reports kept me in doubt as to how I was to get on, until the night of the 15th, when Mr. Lay and Mr. Gardener, our Consul, took me on board the suddenly-appointed *Paohua*, Captain Lewis, at about half-past eleven, and we started soon afterwards. I cannot remember any scenery calling for special observation throughout these 370 miles. The general feature was flatness, with agriculture going on by help of the European-hating buffaloes, who even know the stranger by the smell. On the river itself, Sha-Sze attracted attention by the large assemblage of junks—some said a thousand—lying off the straggling town, which is about to threaten Ichang. We left almost immediately after arrival, for the protective laws would not allow our vessel, which was not Chinese, to take Chinese passengers.

We were late in arriving at Ichang in consequence of fogs, but found ourselves at the pontoon on the morning of the 19th, when the Count d'Arnoux, the Commissioner, came on board and took me to his temple, where I was introduced to the countess, and spent the day. To show how much is wanting still to develop these treaty ports, not only was this temple the only possible place of residence for the Commissioner, but it was scarcely large enough to hold even him. However, though the *Kiangtung* was not fit for steaming, she was good for sleeping, and the good Captain Yankowski, then very ill and since dead, granted me a bed. In the afternoon we walked out with Consul Fraser and Dr. Aldridge, and saw the site chosen by Mr. Marshall for the new residence he had designed; and a strange walk part of it was. An extensive old Chinese burial-ground consisted of nothing but huge mounds, each apparently containing perhaps a score of bodies, and on the other side was a large dead pool of water. In the distance beyond there rose a range of picturesque hills, and on one of them appeared a tower of peculiar origin. On the opposite side of the stream from Ichang, you must know, there is a very curious and regular line of successive pyramidal hills, very striking to the stranger's eye. But the inhabitants persuaded themselves that the largest, and therefore the most attractive of these was an evil—had an evil eye—to the town. So they did not attempt to lower it, or to pull it down, but built the tower I have mentioned to counteract its evil influence. More refined superstitions, however, might appear to the Ichangese quite as ridiculous as may this to ourselves who assume to be the enlightened.

I learned that the proper season for visiting Ichang, and therefore the gorges, is the month of April. All is then green, and flowers are spangled everywhere; nor is the river too high or too low. In this particular feature October corresponds, but it is brown and colourless, as I found it to be, instead of green and spangled.

The count, having received Sir Robert's letter, had very kindly at once set all things in order for me, and everything was in readiness for my start on the following day, the 20th. Sir Robert had suggested that the Count might possibly be my companion, but this being otherwise, he considerately found another in the person of Mr. Balharry, one of the staff, who happily was young, bright, and cheerful, and kept up life all through.

Our boat lay close below the steps, and for this night I slept on board at once. Mr. Balharry joined in the morning, and we crossed over to Shipa Island, waiting for our cook, who had gone to make purchases. At half-past eight on the 20th we began our excursion to the gorges. The scenery was pleasing until half-past eleven, when we turned suddenly to the left and entered the Ichang Gorge. This offered a very long perspective of mountainous banks blocked to the eye at the far end by a large massive group. The October want of colour was evident all round, the masses were rather uncouth than impressive, and sloped off raggedly. In particular, for the word "gorge" the river was too wide. Some one or two of the precipices might be called fine. At about 2 p.m. we came to the Pin-San-Pah Station, and continued till dusk as far as below the village of Lantoo.

Our modes of moving were various: there were long oars, there was the breeze, and there was the tracking of the men on the sloping, ragged sides with ropes. We had fifteen altogether. They fed, slept, and worked in the front, making noise enough, and the pulling in and out of the wet cord according to the tracking was not a little tiresome. Rice was their exclusive food, cooked by their own cook in front; rice, like corn to horses, or grass to cows. But we had a scene the very first evening. One of the men wanted to desert, and he was followed, seized, punished, and brought back to duty. In this small episode you might gather the style of Chinese punishment and of Chinese want of sensibility. It is impossible they can feel like other people. At home the exhibition would have represented "attempt to murder," but the man came back and forgot it all at once.

On the 21st we started at about six in the morning, and in very fine, fresh weather. The character of the scenery I have marked was increasing in bulk and variety, but coarse in kind, and the river always wide. At eight o'clock we breasted on our right what is called "The Needle of Heaven." It is a fine individual striking object, and is given as of 2000 feet in height. After passing this the scenery became tamer, and, indeed, I have marked tiresome; but a small incident aroused us. Our rope broke in tracking. We were not, however, carried down the stream; that was somehow managed; and on coming to a place called by the euphonious name of Huanglien Mien, an enormous purchase of new material was made, including some of alarming thickness. These ropes are of bamboo, which alone is capable of withstanding the friction and the snatching, as the men on shore track along the spreads of ugly rocks. At dusk we were at San-to-pin, and stopped for our second day.

On the 22nd we started at seven, and to-day we passed up the Tatung Rapid, but without particular feature, and several rather rushing corners gave us a little trouble; time lost, noise and wet ropes being unpleasant. But, in compensation, a good breeze sprang up afterwards, and we covered a good space.

It was about three o'clock in the afternoon of this day that we came in perspective sight of the entrance to the Lukan Gorge. This entrance is considered to present the finest scene on the river, and I quite concur in this opinion. As we approached it it looked really fine and mysterious, and it offers the only really first-class piece of scenery that I found on the river. The effect was also increased by two small white sails under the cliffs at the moment. I believe my companion would say the same. It is true that it lies rather at an angle as you approach it, the effect of which is that the river appears narrower than it really turns out to be when you come close up. But this may pass. What is quite disappointing is the gorge itself when entered, for the mountains fall away upon your left, the river's right, and let in a vast amount of breadth and light. The whole gorge, running into the Mittan Gorge, offers the best run of scenery, but it has been grossly exaggerated in some of the descriptions of it, justifiable only if written by persons who had seen but little else besides the rest of the river, or (say) Shanghai, of which it has been declared, almost too severely, that it has nothing higher than a mole-hill, unless it is a grave.

On our fourth day we started at six o'clock and came to the Shintan Rapid, and reached the Yatan Rapid, standing second in the crowd for the morning's haul; and on the next, or fifth day, we came in sight of Patan and a pagoda; and here we turned round. After the scenery of the Lukan and the Mittan, which I have mentioned, there was nothing worthy of special remark. In coming down, perhaps, some parts of the river looked more impressive than in going up, and that is all I can say. What did impress me was the quiet and imperceptible manner in which we were rapidly carried down to Ichang, and the quiet, contemptuous manner in which the stream completely turned our boat about among some harmless eddies. And what is that diminutive model of a boat with paraphernalia floating on the water, and looking like a nursery toy? It is there to float about and commemorate, so long as it will last, some fatal accident in the floods, and it represents a usual practice.

It was on the 25th, at noon, that we turned, and at

one on the 26th, after resting a whole night below the Lukan, and spending forty minutes at San Yu Tung, we were at Ichang. We could not have been more than twelve hours on the water. San Yu Tung is a natural cave turned into a temple, and with its rude centre rock looks like a rather clumsy chapter-house. On arriving, I immediately sought shelter at the former refuge, and in the afternoon we had a quiet sail upon the river, up to the entrance to the Ichang Gorge, and, viewed in this quiet manner, without the exaggerated fuss that had been made about it, it really looked important in proportion.

One more day and we dined with the Consul; on Monday night I bade farewell to my hospitable friends and went on board the *Kiangtung*. At two in the morning of the 28th, I was unconsciously moved off, and on the 29th, in a very fine morning, I was again shaking hands with Mr. and Mrs. Lay at Hankow. It was here that, on looking through some newspapers, I came upon a telegraphic paragraph from London, headed, "Death of a Man of Note." My friend of many years, and my colleague, not competitor, in translation, Captain Sir Richard Burton, had gone. Linked with some foes and with a thousand friends, this indefatigable author and explorer was, perhaps, too independent of public opinion to be conventionally popular and to be fairly recognized and rewarded. His papers showed that he was on the point of writing to me in answer to my letter on the subject of my visit to Macao; but the letter was never written: "*Flere et meminisse relictum est.*"

On the evening of the 30th we all dined with Mr.

and Mrs. Smith, and met Captain Shaw, of the *Gnankin*, with whom I was to sail that night for Shanghai, so that I was safe, and at half-past ten I went on board with him. This time I did not miss Kiukiang—"Nine Rivers"—and had the pleasure of enjoying some hours with M. de Bernière and his family, regretting not to have seen madame also. Everything looked gay, especially a splendid show of chrysanthemums, and I was sorry at not being able to make a longer stay. One little incident considerably amused me here. A Mr. Currie, in the Customs, was changing to Wufu, and as he was very popular, an enormous number of crackers were (*more populorum*) discharged as he came off; but a good lady on board, knowing nothing of all this, was highly indignant at the interruption, and we found her wanting to know "what all this *disgraceful* noise meant." So that, for want of knowing what was really going on, an affectionate farewell was condemned as disgraceful. There are corresponding cases in life of very much more consequence.

At Wahu it was again my lot to be very pleasantly entertained by Mr. and Mrs. Spinney, with a walk and a visit to the garden, which Mrs. Spinney took care to have dressed under her own special care. In China this is very important. The Chinese are excellent gardeners, but the unwholesome modes they pursue of manuring the ground are mischievous both to the air and to the vegetable as an edible. Passing Chinkiang again by night, I was at the Astor House, Shanghai, in the afternoon of the 2nd of November.

Thus ended my visit to the sc-called gorges. Gorges

they are not, for the river (as I have said) is always wide. I went about a thousand miles up to begin them, and taking my excursion altogether, as it was laid out for me, I would not on any account have missed it. That I was disappointed in the scenery is most true, chiefly from exaggerated reports in Shanghai and elsewhere, and by illustrations worked up in London from verbal boastings. Observe what I was told of the Lukan Gorge: that you entered a completely dark defile, and that only after proceeding some distance a vertical silver seam of light began to appear, and gradually expanded into day. When people grossly exaggerate scenery they do not seem to understand that they are misrepresenting just as much as if they were passing off silver for gold. If you ask me whether I would recommend you to go up a thousand miles of river simply and solely to see these "gorges," without such introductions as charmed and adorned my path, my unhesitating answer would be "No."

XXXIII.

THE one remaining Asiatic excursion I had now to make was that to the great temple of Nakhon Wat in Cambodia, and in order to accomplish this, for which I had waited one year, occupied as above, I must get down to Hongkong in time for the French boat that would touch at Saigon, sailing from Hongkong on the 20th of November. To Mr. Bois, therefore, I again appealed for a safe passage, who furnished me with a ticket by the *Menelaus* to sail on the 9th, and promised me the launch to go off in. This would still give me time to touch at Foochow in hopes of yet seeing the famous river, and I therefore telegraphed to say I was coming, and received for answer, "Come."

Bidding all friends good-bye, therefore, on the night of the 8th, I went on board to stop at Foochow, and passing out by Woosung, beheld a sight of twelve old-fashioned war-junks in a row. All was fair for some time, but presently the sea began to roll, or rather, perhaps, to make the *Menelaus* do so, and a bad night we had. But I was quite content to be tumbled about for the result that ensued, for the boisterous weather had filled the waters with their phosphoric propensity—whatever the cause may be—and when we slowed down at about two in the morning of the 10th, I looked out and saw what I had so longed wished to see, the spread of phosphoric light all over the ocean. It must not be understood, however, that there is one widespread sheet of this light, as I must admit I had conjectured from descriptions. It is only the breakers, or "white horses," that show the phosphorus. This is, of course, grand and astonishing enough, but not if you expect the other. Certainly, in our case, the wind being high and the sea very rough, the breakers were most abundant and the night scene was magical, extending to the very offing.

On the afternoon we arrived at the beautiful pagoda anchorage at Foochow, and I went to find Mr. Pim. He was absent, and Mr. Oswald had kindly replied, not wishing to disappoint me. But how many difficulties are in the way of doing easy things! If I went up the river I could not continue in the *Menelaus*, and if I did not continue in the *Menelaus* there would not be another boat to Hongkong in time to catch the Saigon steamer. So I had to give up the Foochow river entirely, and contented myself with the shorter excursion to Kushan, and its rocks, priests, and temples, which made up a very pleasant day on the 12th : and after being Mr. Oswald's guest until late that night, he insisted on accompanying me on board, to sail in the morning, giving me—an immense gift in China—two bottles of fresh milk from his own dairy, which I had visited and appreciated on shore, and also conceding me ten pounds of crack chop Pan Yong tea, a district 100 miles from Foochow.

We sailed at 8.45 on the morning of the 13th, touching at Swatow on the following day. The entrance is picturesque, but certainly not equal either to that of Foochow or Amoy. At four o'clock of the same afternoon we sailed for Hongkong, and when I left Swatow I took my final leave of China, the Empire of the Brother of the Sun and Moon. We were at Hongkong at nine the next morning, and the weather contributed to adorn the entrance, but the colours of earth and sky were now russet and blue, for the brown of winter had superseded the green of summer.

My first object at Hongkong was to secure a passage for myself and servant to Saigon by the French steamer, and this I did at once by the *Natal*, Captain Bretel, to sail on Thursday, the 20th. In the meantime I was honoured by a visit from Dr. L. P. Marques, and Senhor J. C. da Cunha of the Bibliotheca Lusitana de Hongkong, who generously hailed me as translator of their great national epic poem, "Os Lusiadas," by Luis de Camões, invited me to pay their club a visit, presented me with a handsome volume of views in Macao, and have since honoured me farther by electing me an honorary member of their Society, of which degree they have lately sent me an illuminated diploma. This patriotic body of Portuguese, though not numerous, cherish in connection with their colony at Macao the name and fame of an author whose presence has sanctified that scene, and of whom their nation is most justly proud. They conduct their club with energy, publish a Portuguese journal entitled *O Extremo Oriente*, and are ever alive to maintain their nationality. Macao, it will be remembered, was given to the Portuguese in 1586, by the then Emperor of China, in return for assistance afforded by them against pirates who had infested the coast.

We made a rapid passage to Saigon, arriving there at midnight of the 22nd. Consul Tremlett, whose acquaintance (as already mentioned) I had made in Yokohama, sent for me, and I was conducted to the "Hôtel de l'Univers," afterwards dining with him and his partner, Mr. Detmering, the brother of Mr. Detmering at Canton.

My ticket for Pnom Penh and beyond being secured in the *Phuoc Kien*, Captain Bouillet, which was to sail on the night of the 25th, I passed my intermediate two evenings in driving about with Mr. Tremlett. The French have made a good, decent town, and have, as usual, planted avenues of trees everywhere, but everything all round is as flat as a sheet of paper, and one cannot help wondering whatever induced them to take possession of the place. However, there they are, and they make the best of it, so far as outside show is concerned. The public gardens, or park, afford a very pleasing evening drive, and plenty of carriages are to be found there. The climate cannot but be depressing, and the soil produces large crops of very excellent rice. This refers to Cochin China, of which Saigon is the capital, and which the French have held absolutely since 1867; but they have other projects in view.

On getting on board the *Phuoc Kien*, I found two young Frenchmen were coming on the same excursion as myself: M. Laffont, of the India and China Bank, and M. Furiet, Aide-Commissaire de la Marine. They, like me, had made all their separate arrangements, but we became companions nevertheless all through, and so far as I myself was concerned, with great consequent advantage; nor have I reason to doubt that this feeling was mutual.

Our first night was certainly not pleasant. We had to make a round to get into the Mecon, on which Pnom Penh, the capital of Cambodia, is situated ; and although we came through some inner course to avoid the turbulent shallows, we rolled so far on our beam ends that our cabins were deluged with water. However, on the large river we were quite quiet. Nor was it likely that I should here fail to think of Camoens; for it was on the Mecon that he was nearly drowned, swimming to shore with one hand, while he held his poems in the other.

> And Mecon shall the drowning poetry
> Receive upon its breast, benign and bland,
> Coming from shipwreck and from misery,
> 'Scaped from the stormy shallows to the land ;
> From famines, dangers great, when there shall be
> Enforced with harshness the unjust command
> On him for whom his loved harmonious lyre
> Shall more of fame than happiness acquire.
>
> *Lusiads*, Cant. X., St. cxxviii.

Our course up the river, larger than the Pei-ho, but not so large as the Yang-tse-Kiang, was calm and uneventful, and we arrived at Pnom Penh on the 27th. Here I had to pass the afternoon and night, save that I paid a visit to Mr. Meyer with a letter from Mr. Tremlett about a guide. The person intended was ill, and sent his son, and he embarked accordingly in the morning. As for the night, I think it was the noisiest I ever passed—cargo and cries till very sunrise.

Here we left the Mecon, and turning to the north-west, made up another river flowing from the Tale Sab Lake, some short distance from which Siem Riep lies. This stream showed remarkable masses of thick creeping plants which entirely covered the riverside trees like canopies, and the woods were peopled by flocks of white birds of a very elegant form, called here *aigrettes*. They are killed for their feathers; but my young French friends were pretty active with their guns without a hope of any such profit from them. They flew in circles far and near about the steamer, and into the solitary forest again, generally choosing a dead tree to settle on, and looking in the short distance like a profusion of large white blossoms growing on the barren branches.

At last the steamer anchored at the head of the lake, and we all three, with my servant and guide, disembarked in a large sampan. Presently we came to a sort of custom-house, where we had to find small boats to go up the creek, and very luckily they were found; but this is a sort of venture, and should there be half a dozen passengers, notice should be sent beforehand. We punted and pushed up the narrow creek till we came to an uncouth village, where carts and buffaloes had to be found, as the creek failed us. The Frenchmen's equipage was there, and so was a chance cart for me; but all the buffaloes were out grazing. At last two came lounging in and were yoked, and I jumbled along, and joined my companions at Siem Riep. There I armed myself with my letter, and we all crossed over the water to call on the Governor. Besides my letter I took over also a one-dozen case of champagne as a lubricating present, the hotel-keeper having most disinterestedly advised me that the *demie* would not serve, and my grand letter demanding corresponding largess; but by the look of the man, I should doubt whether he had ever even heard of champagne! He had been out fishing, and was taking his tea in his ragged-looking costume and ragged dwelling, and the arrangement of the tea was curious. There was a tray with six small cups, full, and fixed in position; when he had sipped and finished one, he went to the other, and so on to the end, while we were being interpreted. He was very civil—Minister's letter and champagne combining—and arranged trotting bullocks and small carts and drivers for us, and away we went. The road was luckily a sandy woodland road. We were more or less under trees of one sort or another all the way, and there was no jerking. By-and-by we came in view of the great width of the vast and most elaborate temple crowned with its five elaborate towers. Turning sharply to the right, we stood in full front to it, still some distance away, and about half-way up the broad, flat-stoned approach to it we found a large bamboo building among trees, where visitors find lodging. Here we all assembled, and forthwith walked up to take a first survey of outside aspect, courts and corridors.

Stand and gaze for a time, and then walk in. This is the Temple of Nakhon Wat, or "the Temple of the City," and I really think that that must be about the beginning and the end of my description of it. You must consult Fergusson, and study his illustrations. One very striking feature of the mighty pile was presented to me at once—for I was there some short time before the others—namely, the unlimited amount of detail—details in ornament of every variety, and on every possible surface, as well as *bassi relievi* in the corridors; and my attention was particularly drawn to this at once by finding a M. Raffegeaud on the spot, busily engaged with workmen in taking large careful models of various devices. He told me he was resident there for a certain period, having been commissioned by some French architectural and antiquarian society to secure a handsome collection for Paris.

With all our delays we had arrived from Pnom Penh in plenty of time to give us a good afternoon at the temple; and on my own behalf I at once took a quiet walk completely round the colonnades. The general effect is perhaps scarcely so finished as is indicated by Fergusson's woodcuts, 373 and 374; but the *bassi relievi* on the inside walls all round are truly astonishing. Fergusson estimates the whole length of these to represent 2000 feet, and to contain from 18,000 to 20,000 figures of all sorts. I walked round the four colonnades more than once, and agree with Fergusson that they are probably the most remarkable features of this temple. But really all is remarkable, above as well as below. I do not quite gather whether Fergusson ever personally visited the temple, or whether his very minute description is collected from authorities whom he has consulted. A sentence or two leave this doubtful. But if he has been there, I am surprised he overlooked one remarkable feature in the sculptures, which very strongly supports his view that the temple belongs to the snake worship and has not a trace of Buddhism. No one going over the building could avoid becoming his disciple in this estimation. The serpent is everywhere, and what is called the "seven heads" looked to me like the "capello;" but in one of the long colonnades or corridors—the third, I think, beginning on the right as you enter—there is one long, huge serpent stretching from end to end, and being carried on the shoulders or under the arms of a whole army of hundreds of figures. What Buddha can have to do with this remains to be shown. The allusion to Ramisseram is just; its outside is entirely unshapely, while Nakhon Wat speaks loudly indeed for itself in this respect. But it remains to be said that, as regards the corridors of Ramisseram, there is nothing in those at Nakhon Wat that, for me, can compare with them in architectural effect. Fergusson's detailed description seems to bring the building vividly back to memory, and the whole tone of the structure dissociates itself entirely from my associations with Buddhist structures. I know that when on the next day we visited the forests, now growing where the city of Nakhon Thom, or Ankor Thom, once stood, and came upon a large statue of Buddha, the sight was totally incongruous with my then pervading impressions, and he seemed to be a vulgar intruder.

But in aid of all the impressions that a general survey of the whole gigantic structure and a close examination of its marvellous details may produce, comes the still dark question, Who were the people that dwelt and built? For none are near that can be even alluded to in discussing such a question. Therefore, throughout the whole scene there pervades a hallowing atmosphere of mystery, with which, in these now overgrown solitudes, imagination might be tempted to toy, for the luxury of indulging in the supernatural.

We dined off our provender and wine, and passed our night very fairly in the bamboo house, bamboo poles floor and all, and prepared ourselves for an early bullock trot to the site of the old city, Ongkor Thom, or Nakhon Thom. For this we made an early morning start between five and six. Our soft sandy road lay through a perpetual and luxuriant forest, with now and then an exhibition of gigantic trees, all strange—strange underwood, strange sounds of birds' notes. After about twenty minutes' drive, we came to doubtless the most majestic piece of overgrown ruin that I ever beheld. It was the high arched, massive south gate of the old city. It was very lofty, broken, but not fallen, and not truncated. On the contrary, it was heïghtened, and adorned from the top throughout by the beautiful and copious embraces of its luxuriant destroyers. If anyone desires to see a noble specimen of wild green nature adorning and triumphing over ruined art, here it is. Passing under it, we entered somewhat farther into the depths of the forest, and came to the vast ruins of Baion. What this was at one time, it is almost a pleasure to feel the impossibility of understanding. It is said to have been more magnificent than Nakhon Wat itself; but the same wild growth that I have already referred to prevails here, and it is most surprising to observe how branches and runners have gradually intruded between enormous blocks, pushing them out of place, and revelling in an adorning destruction. All seemed a confusion of the majesty of ruin, for all showed size and power; and for myself, I did my best to keep my mind in the intoxication of admiration. We returned by about eleven to breakfast, and had the whole of the rest of the day at our disposal under the brow of Nakhon Wat.

On Monday, the 1st of December, Mr. Raffegeaud breakfasted with us, and we left for Siem Riep in our charettes in the afternoon, and slept there. All was in order (in Siem Riep order) to receive us, and the Governor sent me an extensive present of live ducks and chickens, which I had no misgiving in accepting to be killed, seeing that I totally disbelieved in the temple we had visited being Buddhist. Our bullocks trotted us well down to the creek in the morning, starting before four, and after somewhat of an unpleasant water excursion, we joined (as bound to do) the *Phuoc Kien* again, which lay at anchor on its return from Battambong, and sailed for Pnom Penh. This was our only chance of return, and we had taken our tickets accordingly. The interval gave us two full days for all we came to see; nor must I omit to add that our two French guns were not wholly wanton, but more than once enriched our larder with some snipe. At Pnom Penh we were delayed a day, as in coming up, which I spent driving and dining with Mr. Meyer. On the 5th we changed our steamer for the *Battambong*, Captain Noury, and sailed at 8 a.m. for Saigon, arriving at about ten the next morning. Thus our excursion occupied from the night of the 25th of November to the morning of the 6th of December. At Saigon I had to wait for the French steamer from Europe, the *Sydney*, till the 15th, spending the time in drives and dinners with Mr. Detmering. On that day we left at 2 a.m., I being on board the night before, and early on the 18th I was again at Hongkong. My twelve-months' patience had been well rewarded.

On my arrival there I found the whole town in a state of excitement upon the subject of an audacious piracy on the Douglas Steamship Company's boat, the *Namoa*, on the high seas on the 10th, within a few hours' steaming of Hongkong, attended with murder of the captain and of a passenger who happened to be on deck when the entirely unexpected attack broke out; and on this same 18th of December there was published by the *Hongkong Daily Press* a full detailed account of all the circumstances, with the following *résumé* for the French mail:—"Great excitement has been caused during the past week by a case of piracy on one of the coast steamers. The Douglas steamer *Namoa* left on Wednesday, the 10th instant, for the coast ports. After she had gone about sixty miles, a gang of pirates who had shipped as passengers, and whose numbers are variously stated at from forty to sixty, rose during the tiffin hour and took possession of the ship. They were all armed with revolvers and cutlasses, and fired down into the saloon. Captain Pocock was induced to come on deck under promise of safety, but was immediately shot down, and died soon afterwards. Mr. Petersen, a passenger, who had remained on deck instead of going down to tiffin with the other passengers, was shot at the commencement of the outbreak, receiving four bullets in the head. A Malay quartermaster was shot and thrown overboard, and another was so severely wounded that he afterwards died in hospital. Two European officers, another Malay quartermaster, and a cook and a seaman were also wounded. The pirates then proceeded to rifle the baggage of the European and native passengers, and obtained booty to an amount variously stated at from $20,000 to $40,000, and subsequently left in junks which were in waiting for them. The officers and European passengers, who had in the meantime been confined in the captain's cabin, then came out, and the ship was brought back to Hongkong, where she arrived the next morning."

This alarming incident concerns everybody, the more so that the same journal refers to several other cases of a like nature, effected or frustrated, since so late a date as 1874; and at the end of its editorial article writes the following remarkable and rather startling paragraph :—" But whatever is done, it will still be advisable, if not absolutely necessary, for the masters of steamships to adopt every precaution which prudence can suggest to prevent similar outrages, for it must be remembered that this colony is an Alsatia for the criminals of Kwangtung, and is periodically flooded with them when the hunt for them grows hot on the mainland. According to a Chinese estimate

—we give it for what it is worth—there are at the present moment not less than two thousand pirates, or would-be pirates, in the colony, and they only wait the opportunity to declare their predatory and too often brutal instincts. The *Namoa* piracy furnishes an instructive example of the ability, forethought, daring, and resource of the desperadoes with whom we have to reckon, and whose rendition, when applied for by the Chinese Government, is made so difficult."

Though not personally concerned in this most daring and monstrous proceeding, yet it came near enough to my movements to make me feel that I might have suffered the like horrors had I happened, on the *Namoa*, or any other coasting steamer, to have travelled with a large number of steerage Chinese passengers (as was the case here) returning to their homes with all their savings from working in foreign countries. This was the evident temptation to the brutal crime, the fact having been disclosed by some accomplice, or perhaps being accidentally promulgated. I had always seen the stand of arms at the top of the companion—the *pro formâ* row of long guns and cutlasses—stacked all in order, and had silently smiled at their inutility, none of the guns probably being ever loaded. But what another instance of mocking incidents it is that a passenger should have made a remark upon them, and that Captain Pocock should have replied, "They are a relic of the past; years ago we used to want them, but we don't ever want them now;" he who an hour afterwards lay in dying agonies, and knowing that his steamer was in the plundering and murdering hands of those against whom every weapon and every nerve were requisite. At a later date, while I was in New Zealand, papers arrived with the satisfactory account that the ring-leader and several others had been caught, and had been tried, condemned, and decapitated within the twelve hours. That they would die with either bravado or indifference appeared to be expected by those who are best acquainted with the Chinese character, and it was thus, in verity, they met their death.

XXXIV.

THUS ended my whole Asiatic tour, which has suggested, or confirmed, or removed many floating reflections, for some present or future benefit, or for none at all. And it ended harmoniously, for I altogether escaped the unhappy scenes which have very lately taken place in relation to interference and invasion in matters of religion and faith, and which are very certain to break forth periodically unto the end. I suppose every one ought to admire perseverance in the face of difficulties, but surely difficulties should sometimes warn that the course pursued is wrong. There are millions who feel that Europe has no more right to intrude her religion upon Asia than Asia to intrude hers upon Europe; and this is a point that is entirely sponged out by those who presume to say, "We are the true, divinely appointed; you are the false; and we are ordered to redeem you." The assumption is tremendous. Europe has given, and is giving, all worldly improvements to Asia; Asia gave Europe her religion, which could never have been founded in Europe herself, but which Europe has nevertheless worked out and made her own, and which Asia will not have from Europe, refusing to make what to her would be the mere exchange of new mysteries for old. And this refusal is all the stronger, in that there are many important differences among the many teachers, who at the same time do not merely ask the giving up of the old but the acceptance and adoption of their own new instead. This, moreover, they preach in the case of a belief which, by a curious assertion, was originally "hidden from the wise and given unto babes," but has since shown a prolonged vein throughout history of arrogance and erudition. Again, the intruder is liable to be told that he comes without a book: for that his corner stone, the Bible, belongs to the Jews, who utterly deny those readings and interpretations by which he seeks to attach the New Testament to it, whose only real foundation is thus confessed to be the Old Testament (so called) as interpreted against those whose real book it is, and who must be supposed to know its purport. All these considerations are bound to be keenly regarded by propagandists, who intrude upon more ancient faiths, but they need not for one moment interfere with those who have accepted their belief from the beginning, and walk through life doing quiet good in virtue of it, undisturbed by the wranglings of controversy between those who, while striving to unsettle and proselytize others, are mutually striving among themselves to show that the one or the other of them believes and teaches either too little or too much.

The Buddhist tells the Christian that his new faith is a mere copy of his own old, and Dr. Marcus Dodds by inverting history writes (p. 138): "The voluntary incarnation of Buddha is a myth of later formation, and one of many in which there exists a very striking, and it must be owned perplexing, similarity to the most striking points in our Lord's career." The Buddhist naturally reverses this comparison by dates; while the follower of Confucius points to the great Christian Maxim as being only a later affirmative copy of the old negative which was centuries before propounded by his own philosopher, and which I have found frankly printed outside "Social Life of the Chinese," by missionary Justus Doolittle, "Do not unto others what you would not have them do unto you." This maxim, moreover, appears in the Talmud, and was taught by Rabbi Hillel.

Any amount of consideration for other peoples' and nations' articles of faith is quite consistent with, and indeed belongs to, the very firmest belief in a person's own, as imbibed at home and cherished through after life. This, mentally speaking, cannot be interfered with; nor ought to be so otherwise, so long as the golden rule is kept in view:—*Sic utere ut non alieno lædas*. Everyone has a right to propagate his own opinions; but they should be presented naturally—as his own; and not as being *à priori* imperative by special origin, and thus compulsory on all. Such a position is wholly opposed to common sense, and by common sense, for the due exercise of which we are profoundly responsible, cannot be accepted. It arises from the same self-confidence that imagined our own tiny, infinitesimal, dust-atom globe to be the primary of the Universe. Whoever assumes mysterious authority really does nothing more than minimize his own authority to speak at all, and opens the ground for a reciprocal intrusion.

I should fancy the missionary's self-imposed task in India is far less difficult and perilous than in China, though the Brahmins religiously resent any invasion of their Vedas, now some 3000 years old. In India, I am told, to the Roman Catholics is attributed (and I believe without contradiction) the widest success, and this seems very natural among Eastern people; for that communion exhibits all the mystery, music, poetry, and display that belong to the full-blown Christian Church, and without which mere unadorned and unrepresented dogmas appear dumb, frigid, and repellent. Besides, there is more familiarity and brotherhood between these teachers and their taught, and a less comfortable separate mode of living among the former than among those of the various sects. This may obviously be caused by matrimony, with its home, existing on the one side, and celibacy, without a home, existing on the other; the latter springing from an exaggerated importance being given to a mere crabbed suggestion that has served to strangle tens of thousands of choicest aspirations.

In a small and impressive volume well worthy of careful reading, written by Mr. Alexander Michie, of Tientsin, there occurs a note at page 52 with a small extract from the Reverend Dean Butcher:— "It is no sign of a true religion to affront a false." This is an excellent maxim, and I have never heard that it is to any extent contravened; but it has this main blot—that it speaks of a "false" religion.

But "false" is a word that can be readily thrown back where antagonism is brought into play: and it might well be asked, "Who is entitled to use it, where all preach mysteries, professedly insolvable?" There is a "true word spoken in jest" attributed to the late Archbishop of Dublin, Dr. Trench. He is credited with the witty saying that the proper way of spelling these two following words should be *auto*-doxy and hetero-doxy: mine and yours. The religious contender can never yield:

> "Quum solos credat habendos
> Esse Deos, quos ipse colit."

Every δόξα claims its own divine origin in one form or another. This should be always remembered: and the later born beliefs necessarily contain many modified features of the earlier, and are open to be thus crucially tested, when paraded.

Any particular cast of human mind or brain will follow others, or work out for itself its own beliefs and modes and objects of worship, and will fashion its own God, just as it will follow or work out its other subjects of thought. And on this part of the question I have long since copied out a written phrase of the late Cardinal Newman, written, I believe, when he was appealed to as to a passage in Shakespeare on Falstaff's death: that he was "bound to confess that there was no ultimate test of truth besides the testimony borne to truth by the mind itself."

XXXV.

"Cœlum, non animum, mutant, qui trans mare currunt."

They who o'er the ocean fly
Change not mind, but only sky.

BUT even without going any farther, I did not feel like this at all. Nor, indeed, was the line written by Horace as a general maxim, though he dreaded and abhorred ocean, even without having been sea-sick; but it was addressed to a friend who had gone to Asia to relieve his mind of a special cause of disquietude. The very essence and object of travelling is that it does change the mind, and is indeed the best mode of changing a mind that has been warped by too much sitting at home, and shutting itself out from the world to which it belongs, but which it has thus taught itself to treat censoriously, and to avoid like the outside of a self-conceived Garden of Eden of its own. No one with even the weakest of brains can come back with the same tone of thought as that which he went out with, and this result is just what those who have bricked themselves up in their own little existence at home call demoralization. They who experience the change think themselves the better for it; they who denounce travelling think they are all the worse. Nobody could mean, of course, that everybody is bound to go to Asia, but people can move about and get a great deal of experience of the world they belong to without doing that. Everyone, however, is sure to do as it best pleases him, but no one can pose as a sound preacher who would say, "Keep out of the world; thank God, I am content with my own garden." It is a real demoralization to sit at home till you think everybody outside your own gates is going wrong, and that all the stars were made for you. Nor, on the other hand, does much good arise from mere scampering for the mere sake of it. Of such it has been written in an odd (perhaps very exquisite) phrase that,—

> They never once possess their soul
> Before they die.

Yet, look again at the entangled and wrangling sort of literature that some people fruitlessly, or even mischievously, work out by travelling in their own mere brains at home; puzzling themselves and everybody else with spider's webs, and fancying all the while that it is thus they can assure themselves that they "possess their soul!"

Horace expresses himself much more tersely than above in another place,—

> Patriæ quis exul
> Se quoque fugit?

> Who that bids his land good-bye
> Also from himself can fly.

No, we never can get away from ourselves, though

it is a common saying that we may get "beyond ourselves." The

Post equitem sedet atra cura

points to a barbed arrow; yet even here diversion in travel may serve to allay, though, again, interruption and fatigue may serve to exacerbate.

Up to the exact moment of my own life, however, of which I am now speaking, I was not being driven about as an *exul* to avoid *cura*, and though I had steadfastly settled in my mind at starting that I would not mingle the ripe old associations of Asia with the brand-new energies and the no-ancient history of our Colonies, yet "when it came to the point" (as the phrase is) I felt quite ashamed of being so near those astonishing young giants of English life, Australia and New Zealand, without taking a look at them; so that I resolved to make bold and drop down to them instead of merely going home. Nor was it now quite, indeed, the chosen season for taking that homely step; although, by the way, our dear ill-behaved England is not unfrequently as bad in June as she is in December.

Therefore, once more, though now, alas! for the last time and ineffectually, I appealed to my hitherto constant friends, Butterfield and Swire, to see me safely to Sydney. "Oh, yes," said Mr. Mackintosh, with his ever-pleasant face of business, but he added, "I'm not quite sure you'd like it." Why, the vessel was to be full of tea, saloon included, with sleeping room only for one besides myself, and he (if I remember rightly) was going in charge of all the tea!

The offer was kind and well intended, and though it cut me sadly to the heart to feel forced to decline it, I felt confident that Mr. Mackintosh quite expected me to do so, which helped to relieve my anguish.

Accordingly, in mournful mood, I sought the office of Messrs. Russell & Cie., whose genial breezes blew away all my clouds by their according me a cabin in their Eastern and Australian S.S. *Menmuir*, Captain Craig, which was to sail on the 23rd for Sydney; and tea would here be confined to breakfast and afternoon, except on sea-sick occasions, for assistance; an exception, happily, not likely to arise with me, or I should never have been at Hong-kong. But what do you think of a merry lady I really met in these travels, who, while suffering that agony, alternated the exacerbations with real laughter at herself in the short remissions! As I have not the wit to invent such a picture, I need not most positively assure you, you may say

The story is true, for I saw it in print.

On the afternoon therefore of the 23rd I came on board the *Menmuir*, but not without a terrible scrimmage with my Indian servant, which it is as well to mention here for the sake of others. These servants, however honest (and I have no sort of complaint against mine in this regard), have a remarkable instinct of secrecy. Note its exhibition in him: he was afraid to come so far with me, and had made up his mind to stop and go home, but he kept this secret. I need not recount the small awful crisis that all this caused at the last moment. Suffice it to say that, by Captain Craig's kindness, I had just time to shake him off and leave him behind to get home with his money, although I had paid his passage; nor will I on any account omit to add that Messrs. Russell returned me the whole of this in Sydney. In truth, it turned out to be a happy incident, and I recount it here for the purpose of showing how necessary it is to make these people *speak out*. They manage English but badly, and to escape confusion get rid of the difficulty by saying "yes," and afterwards you pay the penalty. "'Yes,' 'yes,' you are always saying 'yes.' If I asked you if you had the devil inside of you, I believe you would say 'yes.' Now have you?" "Yes."

The passage from Hongkong to Sydney occupied twenty-nine days, from the 23rd of December, 1890, till the 18th of January, 1891, on which morning we passed through the Heads into the harbour. Thus I spent my Christmas and New Year's Day at sea. The voyage was without nautical incident, but we encountered the torrential rains of the season while steaming down the coast of Australia. The steamer was rather small, so that this circumstance proved more than usually inconvenient; but Captain Craig, the chief engineer, the chief officer, and our two or three passengers were all very pleasant, so that it was not difficult to make the best of things, which I found it possible to do with the exception of a sciatica. We passed my friend Luzon on our port, running down his coast on a very fine 25th, and on the 27th along the fine coast of Mindanao, regretting when darkness overtook us. Then we came upon the Dutch Celebes through the Molucca Pass, and sailed close under the coast of the island of Buru, which presented a rather remarkable aspect. It stood out as if entirely of a high-peaked mountain, to which the height of 9000 feet is given, and at the very top of it there is said to be a large lake. The vast foreground consisted of innumerable projections, including certain green serrated ridges, and the whole mountain was covered with dense forest. This was on the 31st of December, and with Buru I bid adieu to the year 1890.

The New Year's gift of 1891 was Delli, on the island of Timor, belonging to Portugal. Here we remained till 5 p.m. and went on shore. Here is to be recognized the vacuity of monotony in its true features. The few officials themselves complain of it, and no wonder. The whole island is far from belonging to Portugal. We landed on the north; then there is some fine mountainous country behind, which is inhabited by what are called savages, and on the south the Dutch are the possessors. As an evidence of the slovenly state into which the brain falls when it has not enough to do, the custom-house folks forgot we had one of their staff on board, and he himself did not jump off his chair till just after we had moved off, when he was despatched to land in one of the steamer's own boats. When one can get away from such places within a short and certain period it does some slight good to have seen them.

On the 3rd we rode into Port Darwin, and found England on the other side of the world. Here we remained under the jetty for the rest of that day and all the next, admiring (in a certain sense) the black, curiously-robed, and curiously-haired women, and the very ugly, but muscular, black men. Then we touched Thursday Island, very picturesque in appearance; came through Albany Pass, and were soused with the torrential rains. A new experience occurred to me on the 10th in the catching of a shark. If you suppose they wait till he is dead before they cut him up, *secundum artem*, you are mistaken. On the 13th we passed under the sun on his northern course, and after standing off Cook's Town and Brisbane, where my only impressions are of rain, we at last, as I have said, arrived off Sydney Heads a little before five o'clock on Sunday morning, the 18th of January. With all my fancy for morning views, perhaps this was a little too early. The Heads somewhat disappointed me. The North Head is bold and very curiously coloured, but the top is a dead flat. The South Head is not remarkable, and the entrance, being very wide, makes all the less show of itself. We turned to the left at once to the Health Station, and then to the right, crossing the entrance again to the Quarantine Station. We then steamed up the length of the harbour as far as Sydney, following it to the right to land at the quay. Long before we reached this spot the sun was shining brightly, and showed the various suburbs and the rising green and wooded hills surrounding the harbour. These are spangled all over with villas among their trees. The whole presented a sparkling picture, in the midst of which the Domain and the Botanical Gardens, where the Governor resides, formed a cardinal feature, with their green, well-timbered mounds of turf.

Sydney occupies a very undulating and, in parts, lofty position. I had to mount considerably before I gained my hotel, the Grosvenor, and in this respect there is a great advantage when you get there, for the general air of Sydney is decidedly heavy. Mr. Duncan, the manager, and all under him were very attentive, the only defect being one which appertains, I am told, to all Australian hotels, that the rooms are small.

And here I received the reward of an act of civility, for, knowing that Mr. Martin of Foochow, although stationed in Melbourne, was connected with the firm of Messrs. Lorimer, Rome & Cie, I called at once at their office, and found that Mr. Martin, though not in-doors at the moment, was nevertheless, by the merest chance, in Sydney. In this simple fact there was not much, but when he called on me it turned out to be everything; for on his inquiring what I was going to do, and finding nobody had given a hint to me about anything, he at once gave me the important news that I was just in time to catch the last trip to the Sounds in New Zealand. Dropping all Sydney thoughts, therefore, I made for this, and on Monday, the 26th, I was on board the P. & O. s.s. *Carthage*, for Melbourne. I was in Melbourne from the 28th of January until the 3rd of February, and visited Mr. Martin at Kew, commanding a fine open country, and in Melbourne itself I had the opportunity of witnessing a large city of active, moving people, and of large buildings, built in squares, with busy shops, and cable cars running to and fro and up and down the undulating streets, quite in the fashion of San Francisco. The whole speaks of enterprising and increasing life.

I also realized something of the hard blue Australian sky. But, like that of India, it is of too hard a blue. It is easy to say "Give me a fine day in England," but it is useless to say "Give me fine days." They are of the very best when they come, but they only peep in and laugh and run away. Nor is this all; for they are generally followed by some that frown darkly and coldly; reminding one of some of our companies, who pay us eight or ten per cent. one year, and nothing the next, with a call to make up losses into the bargain.

On Tuesday, the 3rd of February, I started in the *Wairarapa* about 3 p.m. for the Bluff in New Zealand, where I was to meet the *Tarawera* coming from Dunedin on this the last of the Sounds Excursions for the season. We touched at Hobart on our way, and came into the estuary of the Derwent at about ten on the morning of the 5th. We steamed up a wide stream with green hilly sides. After about an hour's winding through picturesque distant slopes, and turning to the right by the low rock lighthouse, and then to the left, we came in view of the scattered city on the hillsides. The moment was propitious, for in front lay seven vessels of the Royal Navy, the Admiral's (Sir G. Scott) flagship heading them. Mount Wellington, some 4000 feet high, formed a very prominent feature. The whole picture was very pleasing, partaking entirely of fine lake scenery.

From the 5th to the 9th we were on our passage from Hobart to the Bluff. The weather was fine, but somewhat breezy, and for one or two days we were constantly attended by albatross and mohawks. Although I had already steamed along the coast of South Africa, I had not yet become acquainted with this strange bird of the "Ancient Mariner." The savage monsters were even more attractive to behold, and much more gigantically so, than the kites in Jeypur. They curved, and swooped, and soared, and stooped, and brushed against the wind without one single apparent motion of their enormous wings, irresistibly reminding one, in this respect at all events, of Virgil's dove; but neither bird nor weather will bear the simile further. Nothing verily was there of the "*aere lapsa quieto*," for the full gale was blowing, and the wilder was the wind, the steadier were the outstretched seventeen-foot sails.

XXXVI.

ON Monday, the 9th, we arrived at the Bluff, and here I first put foot on a southern point of New Zealand, which we call the Antipodes of England. The *Tarawera* was not yet in, and was expected on the following morning. I therefore did not, as some did who had come on the same mission as myself, go up to Invercargill only to return, but contented myself with remaining at the local "Club House Hotel," where I was very comfortably lodged.

It was a day or two before arriving at the Bluff that I made up my mind, in convalescence from sciatica—take care of small steamers in the Australian wet season—that I must get some sort of young companion or helpmate to continue my journey with; and feeling now more among one's own people, a chance conversation with a young New Zealander on board decided me to enlist him to continue the rest of my journey with me. So that thenceforward I ceased to disregard your injunctions against travelling entirely without a companion, and Mr. John Cameron Morrison, of Wellington, was appointed to take care of me, it being a feature in the case also that he was young enough for me to take some sort of care of him.

On the 10th, being Shrove Tuesday, the *Tarawera*,

Captain Sinclair, came in very early, and we started for the West Coast Sounds at half-past eight. Of these excursions there are three, I believe, every season, arranged by the Union S.S. Co. of New Zealand, and the return tickets are taken at Dunedin, arrangements for the Bluff being included. The outing (to use that word) is a sort of a steamboat picnic, the Sounds being the leading object. The whole distance to and fro is stated to be 828 miles, and the whole time occupied up to the return to Dunedin (Port Chalmers) is ten days. This length of time is far more than is necessary for visiting the Sounds, but a whole day is spent in some of them for fishing and boating parties, or for simply walking on shore, so as to make a change from the steamer. Then at night there may be dances, or concerts, or recitals, or private theatricals; in short, all kinds of amusements. The vessel is fitted out expressly for the occasion, with all sorts of games on board, and so popular are these that even amidst some of the most beautiful of the scenery the players were the blindest and busiest. But people go on these excursions for the purpose of enjoying themselves, and are entitled to accomplish this not too often successful object in the manner most consonant with their dispositions.

The general character of all these Sounds, with the exception of Milford Sound, is a mixture of soft sloping forest down to the water's edge, with generally wooded islands in the middle, and rocks protruding through the trees. They are all beautiful.

Preservation Sound was the first we came to, between four and five of the afternoon of the first day. The gradually opening scenes as we sailed up were very sweet, until quite at the top distant serrated and barren peaks opened behind the green foreground buttresses in a striking picture. Here also are bossed islands which add greatly to the effect. As in picnic fashion, singing and dancing filled up the evening, and the whole of the next day was, or would have been but for the rain, spent in fishing or meandering, or hoping for fine weather.

On the 12th we visited what to my mind was the most exquisite in sweetness and variety of all our scenery. We started at five in the morning, and at about eight entered what is called "Dusky Sound." We of course steamed to the top of this, amidst a great variety of effects, produced by wooded islands as well as by hanging forests, the trees throughout all the Sounds being small, but very thick. In going up the "Dusky," however, we passed to our left a very beautiful, long, perspective opening, and to my great satisfaction, on our return, I found our course lay through it. It is called "The Acheron Pass," and leads into another Sound of truly exquisite softness and beauty, and this we traversed, to my infinite contentment and delight, even to the head, and anchored there for the night. This lovely retreat, unphotographed, bears a real sailor's name. It is called Wet Jacket Sound: inharmonious indeed with the fairy scenery it disclosed to us, but indicating, nevertheless, what too often happens here, that the weather can be fearfully wet. Not so, however, was it with us.

Here we did not remain a day, but steamed out to sea to get to George's Sound; and having to do so,

GEORGE SOUND : NEW ZEALAND

the wind took care to rise, which incommoded some for a while. This Sound did not so particularly strike me, coming after that of yesterday; but it is very pleasing notwithstanding; and anchoring about three in the afternoon, we remained all night and all next day, when there was a gay regatta, ladies and all contending, with a gay regatta ball at night. But on this day it must be confessed that the wind was strong and cold. Indeed, at one time the regatta seemed a doubtful ceremony.

Early on the morning of the 15th we sailed for Milford Sound, and here the scene completely changes. The coast increased in rocky character until we reached the entrance at 9.30. The character here is gigantic, the heights varying from five to seven thousand feet. The latter height is given to Mount Pembroke, on which there hangs a particularly fine white glacier. Here also is a real waterfall, not being one of those mere ribbons about which passengers would be continually calling out. These falls are called after the late Governor, Sir George Bowen; their great effect is produced by the second neck from above (there are two) falling into a confined pool, whence the waters rebound with height, force, and width—from perhaps 350 feet. The steamer anchored in front of them, and here begins what might almost be called the disappointment in this undoubtedly magnificent Sound. It stops quite short just beyond the falls, and subsides into comparative flats, whereas from the character of its scenery you would expect a prolonged perspective of a corresponding character. It is almost all entrance. But on your left as you look back to the actual entrance you should observe what is called Sinbad's Valley.

We stayed at anchor here all the Sunday and Monday, and until five o'clock on the Tuesday, for an excursion was to be made to what are called the Sutherland Falls. This is a hardish task, and the weather was very wet for the start on the Monday morning, but it was accomplished by some of the party, who gave no very pleasant account of their toil, though they highly appreciated the scene. The photographs did not greatly impress me. A yet harder excursion, without a return to the steamer, was undertaken by another party to walk to the Lake Te Anou, sail over it in a boat, and find their way gradually to Queenstown and Lake Wanaka. In this they also were successful and—fatigued.

Meanwhile we had made up our own party for a long walk to Lake Ida through the forest. It was scarcely worth the fatigue, and for myself I narrowly escaped a broken neck or limb by the breaking of a wooden bridge over a deep and very ugly chasm.

On the Tuesday morning the whole scene looked splendid under a peculiarly fine sunrise after the rain. which I found myself watching by the side of Mr. Peele, a New Zealand painter, well known and much appreciated. He had come with the rest of us to admire all these alluring scenes, and gather hints from Nature. And also came among the number three ecclesiastics of the Roman Church, whom it was quite refreshing to see joining in sympathy with all the amusements that took place. There was Archbishop Carr, of Melbourne, who indeed took the chair and gave out the list from time to time of the various performances; Bishop Moore, of Ballarat; Bishop Moran, of Dunedin, and one more whom I cannot find upon the list. What a difference there is among all the priests and preachers of the almost various Gospels! The educated Roman Catholic priest is always genial, and is not known among enjoying groups by his prohibitory and censorious separation: separation, which invariably breeds censoriousness: and whereof a sad example exists in the person of the pious Cowper; proving that piety of a certain class engenders the virtue of censoriousness.

There was unhappily a high wind and a rolling sea when we put our nose out for a direct run to the Bluff; but on the morning of Wednesday, the 18th, all we who were going to visit New Zealand were safely landed there, the boat going on to Dunedin. Before the passengers were parted, however, there was a general vote of thanks proposed for Captain Sinclair and his officers, and never was one better deserved; and a handsome subscription was made for the crew. Here also the Archbishop graced the ceremony by presiding.

Thus ended my excursion to the Western Sounds of New Zealand, and I shall always remember their great beauty, our most successful visit to them, and the happy chance that enabled me to catch the last excursion just in time; for had I lost the opportunity of adding all these pictures to the gallery of my memory, the loss would have been great indeed.

"And what do you think of them as compared with the fiords of Norway?" asked an acquaintance, who wanted to know something of what he hadn't seen. "How do you compare them?" "Well, I will tell you how: the Sounds are Fiords, and the Fiords are Sounds, and Norway is Norway, and New Zealand is New Zealand." How anyone who has seen both can pretend to put both into the same crucible and really compare them, I know not.

So soon as we were landed Jack and I made for the railway station, to go to the Albion at Invercargill that afternoon, and we left the troop to go on ahead next day. On the 20th we slept at Lumsden. From Lumsden we went to Kingston, at the bottom of Lake Wakatipu—called "Wakatip"—and thence we steamed up to Queenstown, lodging at the very comfortable hotel called Eichardt's. The day was cold and dull, and this no doubt contributed to my feeling what I had been warned of, that so far as Queenstown, at all events, Wakatip could not compete with the west. The scenery, however, at Queenstown is not to be despised by any means. The serrated ridge, called the "Remarkables," is indeed fine, and when sprinkled with snow must be more so. Mount Cecil also must be mentioned.

On the 22nd there was a drive with Mr. Johnson and Mrs. Moir, his married daughter, and on the 24th, the day being fine, I decided to go up to the head of the lake. The sides are barren, but the opening of the snow range, as it rides into view, is grand; Mount Earnshaw showing well, with a grand glacier. The head of the lake itself is flat and featureless, and the change in the apparent outline of Earnshaw, according as the light strikes him, is remarkable, a feature chiefly observable between the up and down passages of the lake.

Mr. and Mrs. Newell and their daughter, an American family resident in Melbourne, whom we had met on the Sounds excursion, being here, we made a day's drive to what is called "The Skippers," a very rough mountain road, and somewhat calculated to startle those who have not been habitual mountain travellers, the most notable point being "Siberia" (as it is called) and the rock castles. On the 28th we all started for Lake Wanaka, and in wet weather we went as far as a place called Arrowtown. Thence we toiled up and over what is called "Crown Range," whence there is a wide view, but not one the vaunted features of which greatly attracted me. The drive down was ugly, and the road was bad. Towards the close I just caught sight of Mount Aspiring and Black Rock to the left, Mount Ion lying to the right.

On the 2nd of March, Captain Hedditch took us up the lake, which I thought superior to that of Wakatipu. Note the Black Rock, so called because the top is black; Mounts Alva, Albert, and Alba; three A's. The snows and glaciers were frequent. The island Manuka also should be visited, with the strange lake, about 350 feet above Wanaka, always discharging but not showing any means of supply. If you like to clamber still higher there is a fine view to reward you. However much these two lakes may be appreciated by many, it seems quite clear that the two most beautiful in the island are those of Te Anau and Manipori. To neither of these, however, could I easily get, nor did I make any great endeavour to do so, for on the Te Anau the steamer had broken down, and on the Manipori there was no steamer at all. Moreover the road from Kingston, at the foot of Wakatipu, the proper point of departure, was bad, though fairly enough served with a now and then coach. It is to be hoped that the authorities have done something effectual in making this beautiful part of their country easy of access, and worth the journey on getting there. It must be well worth their while to do so; the scenery is obviously choice.

On the 3rd we were persuaded to go to Glendhu Bay for a sight of Mount Aspiring; but the journey was not successful in this, and particularly not so as regarded a high climb to see a large pond, represented below as being a lovely lake. No features of the day are worth recording. Hence our road lay to Dunedin, and the first night was spent at Cromwell. Thence crossing over the river in a cradle, we continued to Roxburgh, passing for some fifteen miles along the banks of the Molyneux, or Clutha River, and through some of the very roughest rocky country I have ever seen. From Roxburgh we drove to Lawrence with a coachman of pictureque memories, Mr. McIntosh by name; and there we found that vulgar but most welcome addition to the landscape, in the shape of a railway. To say that it took us "straight away" to Dunedin would not be precisely correct; for, as far as Milton Junction it wound about in a most remarkable, but no doubt necessary, manner. Finally, we reached Dunedin, the capital of the Otágo Province, the picturesque city of Dunedin, and "descended" at the Grand Hotel, belonging to Mr.

Watson, who also had been one of the visitors to the Sounds.

I remained in Dunedin till Monday, the 16th, Mr. and Mrs. Newell leaving on the 14th to meet again at Sydney; and in the interval I did my best to see the most of what I might almost call romantic Dunedin. The undulations of the country are striking, and the cable cars offer all facilities for moving up and down. I had the advantage of Mr. Martin's letter to Mr. G. L. Denniston, who received me at his house, put my name down at the Club (where I again met General Sir Allen Johnson), and gave me an introduction to the Hon. Mr. and Mrs. Reynolds, his father and mother-in-law, at Montecillo. What a fine air there is upon those hills; and in walking round the garden I could but exclaim, "What magnificent gooseberry bushes!" I was unfortunately out of season for the feast, but I was told that the produce of that common but most delicious fruit (I had rather be always among gooseberries than always among mangostines) is even inconvenient; friends and neighbours, with their children, being invited to thin them off. I hope you don't expect statistics of the city, for I do not intend to copy out tables which you would not read, and in which I should always have less interest than in the gooseberries.

My next city was to be Christchurch, the capital of the Provincial District of Canterbury; but on my way thither I had made up my mind to see Mount Cook, and this involved a rather serious and fatiguing diversion from the direct road. However, I undertook it, encouraged so to do by my young companion, and not less by my being able to take a passage everywhere, even to London, with Messrs. Cook and Son's active agent at the hotel.

Accordingly I took all necessary tickets, and we left by the eleven o'clock train through Timaru for Fairlie Creek, the latter being the branch railway station and starting point for the coach. We arrived there, to the Gladstone Hotel, at 8 p.m., in order to start away the next morning at 8 a.m. But I must not pass by this uneventful journey without recording my recollection of the remarkably pleasing scenery that I enjoyed in the train while running down from Dunedin towards Port Chalmers. Hills, vales, woods, and water all combined to charm in the sunshine. Afterwards, however, when we had turned well to the north, the country became flat, though no doubt fertile.

On the 17th, therefore, we started for Pukaki, having secured and paid an extra fee for the two box seats for myself and companion, this being an essential arrangement for anyone who values a real chance of seeing the country and getting information from the coachman as worth more than a few extra shillings. Our point for the day was Pukáki, the whole distance being fifty-six miles. The proprietor drove to Tekápo Lake and hotel, twenty-six miles, with the same horses, resting and watering on the road, which up to that point was not bad; certainly not worse than the hard food at the hotel; and Mount Cook continued to show himself as we came along.

Here we took a fresh coach as well as fresh horses,

and for the remaining thirty miles the road certainly became rougher, nor was there any farther change of horses. Henceforth the ranges of the mountains began to open impressively, and Mount Cook, with his 12,349 feet, stood forth very grandly. His form was remarkable, exhibiting a gigantic gable-ended roofing with a vast stack of antique chimneys at one end. Homely as this simile may appear, the effect was far from homely. At last we came to Lake Pukaki, where the accommodation at the hotel is as good as the small house could admit of; and if Mount Cook is ever to attract many visitors, more attention should be paid to this station. Our party, moreover, felt this inconvenience particularly; for a certain number had already arrived by the direct rough road from Lake Wanaka, and with now two roads leading to it the small accommodation is destructive of the Mount Cook excursion. The view is decidedly fine. Mount Cook appears to rise from the head of the lake, and all his surrounding companions show forth around him. To a remarkably fine craggy monster is given the not harmonious name of "Rotten Tommy," the allusion being to the brittle nature of the rock. Then there is the Seely Range, Mount Tasman, and others, all combining to attract attention and excite admiration.

But in truth Pukaki has no topographical right to lie upon the road to Mount Cook from Fairlie Creek, though apparently it must always continue to do so; and the reason is the utterly impracticable character of the Tasman River, with its quicksands and shifting channel. Otherwise this river might be crossed in a direct line westward before it enters the Pukaki lake;

that is, at the head of that lake, instead of at the foot to which the road to Mount Cook must thus be brought, at the expense of altogether a divergence costing thirty miles.

On the 18th we started early, and encountered forty miles of an almost always rough road. No change of horses took place, but they rested and baited while we lunched in the open, our view now including the huge Tasman glacier. But of this very little that is engaging can be said, for it is utterly covered with *débris*, while nothing can look much uglier than the Tasman river. While we were lunching a curious circumstance happened. A brown bird, very like a large partridge, and called by some fern-hen, came about us, in twos or threes. These, in order to pick up what they could, came boldly and slyly close up to us, and one of them indeed had its beak in my very pocket when the alarm was given. This habit of theirs is well known in New Zealand, and picnic parties are continually missing small things on this account. A great hunt after one in our case resulted in nothing; the manner in which the thief dodged in and out of the close bushes defied all efforts till it was time to move on. When we did so we still found the valley flat, barren, and ugly, and the Hermitage, as the name is, looked naked and dreary in the unfruitful space between the hills and mountains. But glaciers abound upon the latter, patched in various directions, and those on Mount Sefton, as you approach, are particularly fine. At the Hermitage we were welcomed by Mr. Huddleston, who, full of attention and interesting information, actively superintended and accompanied the chief excursions from the station.

I have said that the glaciers of Mount Sefton are particularly fine. They are not so extensive as some others, but they hang very precipitously, and thus naturally exhibit in a special manner all those deep fissures and ragged rocky surfaces that constitute the chief beauties of those marvellous accumulations of ice, now confined to mountain recesses, but claimed as having occupied, at some long past period, vast regions of now cultivated earth. For anyone who wishes to see glaciers with some of their most effective features, Mount Sefton should be well worth a visit; and another point is that, as a result of the almost vertical hanging of these glaciers, the avalanche is frequent. It was owing to my young companion's restless spirit in opening the door on the night of Saturday, the 21st of March, that Mr. Huddleston and I were called out by him to see as well as to hear by moonlight one that can compare with any I have ever witnessed, if not the largest of all.

Mount Cook, I may say, is of course closely visible (so to speak) from the Hermitage, but there is no such view of his general bulk as is obtainable along the road. Meanwhile there is a unique excursion of a day, by the Muir glacier with its astonishing cavity, over the mountains; and this, be it observed, includes what many a far longer one does not afford, the exciting novelty of a *glissade*. Other excursions there are, but to neither did I go, except to the Muir, for the weather was poor and in part bad, and this class of excursion has long ceased to be novel to me.

We were to close our pleasant visit on the morning of the 23rd, and at about two in the night we were waked by a downright furious mountain storm of lightning, thunder, and rain. At the hour of starting matters were calmer, but drizzling rain still continued for a space, hiding all views, though the weather gradually cleared up for outdoor luncheon, and a revisit of the fern-hens. Thus we came on to Pukaki, when, lo! a dilemma. In this out-of-the-way spot, immediately after our arrival, the driver—a very good one—came to inform us, to our horror, that the axle of the front wheels was broken, and that the coach could not farther proceed on its arduous duties. What was to be done? Most fortunately, some extra passengers had come up to us, and were returning with us in their extra buggy: Mr. and Mrs. Marsden, and two children; and this fact, with their very willing and friendly combination, served to help us out of what might have proved a very inconvenient state of affairs indeed. By riding nearly all night to and fro to a distant station, the coachman managed to borrow another small buggy and a saddle-horse; and with forces thus marshalled we covered our distance of thirty miles to Tekápo, where we took the other coach; Jack, to his great delight, riding the thirty miles. Yet were we not completely free from trouble, for before we arrived at Fairlie Creek, behold this second coach broke down, in the shape of the bursting of a strap. I wonder how the vehicles stand the journey at all. However, here we were not far from our destination, and rough efforts, employing rough means, and causing some little amusement, served to carry us through.

The evening of the 25th found us at Coker's Hotel in the flourishing city of Christchurch, the Cathedral city of New Zealand. But I must not omit to mention that in passing through Timaru, where we were detained for some hours, I availed myself of the opportunity of taking a very pretty drive, and visiting one of those large freezing-houses which serve to furnish us with so much excellent mutton in England. We were admitted to the real, dark Arctic regions of this most astonishing industry, and in the frozen passes we found ourselves surrounded by hard rocky carcasses, hanging dressed in winding sheets, destined to be thawed back, not indeed to life, but into a fitting state to be devoured and enjoyed by us men of prey.

I wonder whether in any other part of the globe any such marked difference can be found between two cities in the same island, and comparatively close to one another, as exists between Christchurch and Dunedin. In the former all is hill and dale ; in the latter all is flat. In the former prevails the atmosphere of the Kirk ; in the latter reigns the Church of England. I happened to be at Christchurch when the new bishop preached his inaugural evening sermon on Easter Sunday, and my young companion, who had early associations connected with the cathedral, urged me to attend. We went there, and the scene at the doors somewhat reminded me of the old scenes at theatres. Even standing room was scarcely to be had after the inward rush, and I left him there to find his fate, which he succeeded in doing successfully, and returned profoundly impressed with the ceremony throughout, choir and sermon and all; nor did I find this impression to be at all singular among many others.

I have said that Christchurch is flat. Nevertheless between the spreading city and its port, Port Lyttleton, about nine miles distant, there is an important range of hills, called the Port Hills; and in order to facilitate communication with the port the highly enterprising work was carried out of driving a tunnel through, more than a mile and a half, under the superintendence of Sefton Moorhouse. Port Lyttleton is very picturesque and full of life and shipping. As to the city, it will speak for itself. I am well old enough myself to remember the first movements and emigrations connected with the Canterbury Settlement, and I beheld it with wonder in 1891.

Declining the bore of attending the races on Easter Monday—what an incessant amount of racing there is in the Colonies, as also in Shanghai and Hongkong!—I started early on the 31st of March to Springfield by railway, on my way to Greymouth, for the express purpose of seeing the far-famed Otira Gorge, on the road. The drive to Bealey cost forty miles, with two changes of five horses each. I found the driving more remarkable than the country, particularly in the dark of the last few miles, and we came safely to supper and bed.

The next morning was the notorious 1st of April, and there was plenty of time to pass the jest of the day upon us, for we were waked at half-past four. Early dawn was fairly propitious, and in due time our coach started; but as we approached the great water-shed that frowns over the Gorge, and showed a height by my aneroid of 3300 feet, a low, dark brush of cloud swept up into our faces. Are we to be disappointed? "That's nothing," said the coachman; but it was something, for it soon enveloped us. Much of it, however, soon passed off, and when we began the real descent the mixture of sunshine and luminous mist aided the eye with imagination. It is a long way to come to see this gorge, which is scarcely five miles in length; but it is really a little gem. One most striking feature is its pitch, its rapid declivity. In the course of its four miles and a half you wind down fifteen hundred feet, and though you are all too soon through it, you may, if you choose, remain at the hotel at the foot, and wander up and down at your leisure. But the real way to see it is, after all, to come down it with the surprise of the descent, and with all before you and beneath you. There are some towering rocks at the head, but the winding slopes and lofty precipitous sides are perfectly mossed with foliage, among which I particularly noticed the Totára tree and the black birch. What we missed, being a little too late for it, was the flowering of the Rata tree. Two large scarlet blossoms in the green masses attracted my admiration, and the coachman gave them their name, but added the tantalizing information that a fortnight before the whole gorge was a-blush with them. So that if you go to see the Otira Gorge, go before the 1st of April. After passing the hotel you run through a long woodland drive, where the tree-fern abounds to an extent that reminded me of the virgin forests of Brazil; and the crossing of one or two stony dry beds of streams reminded me that I had a back. Thus we continued till we came to Taipó, which name belongs in native tongue to that continual black intruder into scenery, whose ugly name is introduced here because some old chief was lost in the dark river.

We now left the coach and came to Greymouth, passing over a wooden tramway running through a thick wood, and at Greymouth I resolved to take the steamer direct to Wellington. This I did by (I believe) the *Mawketra*, Captain Manning. The good captain could not, of course, do what was never yet done, not even by King Canute, command the winds and the waves, and they would indeed, in the opposite case, have required his very strongest command here; for if some of our coach passages had shown what wrenching and jarring were, so did Cook's Strait show us what rolling was until the last minute of the last of the many late hours which landed us safely in Port Nicholson and the Occidental Hotel at Wellington. And so, farewell to the South Island, or rather Middle Island, from which I part, but of which I bring along with me many additions to many pleasant memories heaped up elsewhere, and not forgotten. I have said Middle Island because the small Stewart Island is numbered as the South Island. My only regret at not having visited this spot of earth is that I missed seeing the almost fabulous crowds of the large penguin that in days gone by appeared in the old engravings.

In Wellington we have the seat of Government, and we have again a very undulating hillside city, for it is built upon the very shores of its land-locked port, Port Nicholson. Its importance in the colony speaks for itself; it can boast of many leading features, and among others—though I know not if this be actually a boast—of a prodigious quantity of high winds. The story goes that wheresoever you meet a Wellington man you may always know him by his instinctively holding his hat every time he turns a corner with you. After you have visited all the usual buildings of a city, take a drive, as I had the pleasure of doing with Mr. Parfitt, of the New Zealand Bank, and his niece, Miss Newell, of Sounds memory, round Evans' Bay, and visit the public park. Note also the very fine Club, and ask Mr. Parfitt to give you a lunch there. Here also I renewed my acquaintance and dined with Mr. and Mrs. Miles and Miss Rowlands.

On the 8th of April I went on to Palmerston and slept, and the question was, Should I go on to Auckland through the sulphur districts, or go to New Plymouth and take the steamer. I had already seen larger sulphur districts, for which I have no affection; and I fairly shrank from going to look on a chaos only to be told "Here the terraces once were." I therefore turned off to Wanganui, having, however, first made an excursion to Woodville and back, in order to see the well-worth-seeing Manawatú Gorge. At Wanganui the air seemed to me to be particularly fine during a two hours' drive along the banks of the river, which we had followed in the gorge. The country was undulating and pleasing, and though the gorse to a New Zealander's eye may not be pleasing, yet to my English eyes to see rich and abundant blossom all round was a delight. At New Plymouth we missed Mount Egmont, for the weather was very thick. Thence the *Takapuna* took us to Onehunga, and running across the eight miles by ten o'clock, we arrived at "Craig's Star Hotel," in Auckland, where I met my old "Sound" American friends of Melbourne, Mr. and Mrs. Newell. We were all bound for Sydney, and not only so, but when the steamer touched to take us there, we learned to our satisfaction that it was our "Sounds" boat, the *Tarawera*, with Captain Sinclair and his officers again on board.

Though Auckland has lost the seat of Government, it still claims to be the largest city in New Zealand; and certainly it has not lost the diversified beauties of its position. You must, of course, at least drive to Mount Eden and survey the scene. Its disadvantage is that the city cannot be reached by ships on the west coast; but if the day should come when a sufficiently large canal can be cut through to unite it nautically with Manukau Harbour, its importance would be vastly increased, and perhaps it might then call itself the principal port in New Zealand. What time may develop here and almost everywhere else in these islands remains to be known by those who will belong to coming generations. That the natural energies of the people may have led them to take too great early strides has its obvious inconveniences, but is no bad sign, for it betokens a desire to advance, which is always better than a lounging inactivity. We need not anticipate Lord Macaulay's figure, which he borrowed from Volney; but that New Zealand must necessarily grow into greatness is, we may fairly hope, a surer prophecy than that her sons may sit upon a broken bridge and stare at the ruins of London. God speed both Mother Country and Colony.

XXXVII.

We all felt ourselves quite at home on board the *Tarawera*, and there was no doubt we recalled the "Sounds" to Captain Sinclair. We embarked on the 14th of April, and we steamed in between the Heads of Sydney about five in the afternoon, all our party finding their way up the beautiful harbour to the quay, and thence to the well-known Grosvenor; one, at all events, among us, who was born in the Mother Country, reflecting much on the imposing fact of thus sailing, at the Antipodes, from one splendid colony to another, both belonging to the Crown at home.

From Sydney I was to sail for San Francisco, and as the *Alameda* was marked for the 20th, the very next day after our arrival, I could not leave before the 18th of May by the *Mariposa*, Captain Hayward, who had taken me out to Honolulu from 'Frisco in 1886. On the 20th, however, I went down to call on Captain Morse, who had taken me back from Honolulu; and then the next question was, how to fill up my time in the great city of Sydney. I made two excursions with Mr. and Mrs. Newell before they left for Melbourne, one to the Paramatta River, and the other to the Middle Harbour. Both were interesting; but there was another, to me, much more so. It was a drive with Mr. Fleming, a friend of theirs, who took us to Botany Bay, and there we lunched at the hotel which bears the name of Sir Edward Banks, and across the water we saw the obelisk which was erected on the spot where Captain Cook is said to have first set foot in 1770. This Botany Bay was always associated in our youthful minds with transportation and convict settlement. Little did I know at that time that its name was given,—not in connection with ruffians, but —because it exhibited such a wealth of plants and flowers. Indeed, it never was really a convict settlement, for it was soon found to be fit only for flowers, and the convict settlement was moved farther up to Sydney. The effect was curious on finding one's self upon this very spot, and locally associated with the names of Cook and Banks. What was going on there at the moment, however, awakened very different thoughts; these were races, and I believe that these were the moving cause of Mr. Fleming's most acceptable thought.

After my friends had left for Melbourne, Jack and I went up to see the Jenolan Caves—the usual limous stalactite caves—the name being, I believe, corrupted from that of the man who discovered them, James Nolan. Our first day was to Mount Victoria, and our second to the caves themselves, visiting the Imperial Cave in the afternoon of our arrival. As I had seen many others, including those very grand caves at Adelsberg, which I was the means of having properly lighted, as explained in the *Graphic* some years ago, I did not drain the cup by going into the others. This cave, however, is indeed well worth a visit. It exhibits remarkable features of both stalactite and stalagmite, and is exceedingly well lighted. It is the best of the group, but does not equal the great cave at Adelsberg; not only are its massive structures inferior, but the surfaces are dry and dull, whereas those at Adelsberg are in a perpetual state of glittering moisture. The approach to the station is very fine, and so are the extensive views you obtain on the road; but the general, almost exclusive, foliage is that of the blue gum tree.

In returning, we did not go direct to Sydney, but continued to Katoomba, diverging again in order to see Govett's Leap. Here the scene is very remarkable. You stand on an absolute precipice; far away in front of you are distant ridges, and the whole gigantic space between, lying some 800 to 1000 feet below, and rising up on the two sides, is a densely-wooded forest, adorned by a waterfall. The foliage here again is mainly of the blue gum tree; but poor as this tree is when close at hand, in the thick and distant forests its effects are remarkably soft. From the Leap we went on to Katoomba, and lodged at Mr. Goyder's spacious hotel, the "Carrington." Hence we went to see the Katoomba Falls, and afterwards the Leura Falls. You may fairly class all these three views together;

> "facies non omnibus una,
> Nec diversa tamen."

On the 11th of May we returned to Sydney; not to be idle, however, we arranged tickets for the Hawksbury River, but neither of us found himself able to rise to the level of the exaggerations.

We had now to think of leaving our pleasant quarters and to prepare for our passage to San Francisco. Sydney, like the rest of the world out there, is growing, and the old city is fast giving way to the new. Whether the huge new hotel I left in building and arranging will, for the present at all events, find the huge support that it must require to be successful, remains to be proved.

Meanwhile the Grosvenor will pursue the even tenor of its way, and life and movement will increase and multiply. What a mighty world has sprung up out in these regions since Captain Cook and Edward Banks first landed in the little *Endeavour*, of 370 tons burden, in 1770. But what of that? In 1992 men will say, "What a little place Sydney was in 1892!" Nevertheless, great as may be the after-growth, great is indeed he who plants the first foot.

So away we went for 'Frisco at four o'clock in the afternoon of Whit Monday, the 18th of May, and began with a very unpleasant rolling four days' passage to Auckland; and here we encountered that very inconvenience, already spoken of, of having to round the North Cape and come down to Auckland and return north again, which will one day be remedied by the grand canal that is to be cut to Manukau Harbour. Sailing again, at 2 p.m. on the next day, the 23rd, we steamed into fairer weather, and on the 24th, being the Queen's birthday, Captain Hayward ordered the *Mariposa* to be dressed throughout with the united flags of both nations. The scene was especially lively, and so were all the passengers at evening, songs, music, and recitals abounding—the Rev. Dr. Ellis, who was returning home with Mrs. Ellis after many years' absence, acting as the Corypheus. Then on the 30th it was Decoration Day in the States, and twin decorations and entertainments again adorned the occasion. In short, there was an abundant show of games and pleasant evenings all through the passage, without the necessity of solving the problem of the change of time when we passed out of eastern into western longitude across the meridian of 180°. We had a splendid plunge bath on deck while it was hot, and many lovely mornings, glittered with ten thousand sparkling stars upon the quiet purple ocean, as it threw forth in front its white fringes of foam, in seeming lazy protest against the rude disturbance of our prow.

But on one of these mornings there was a stoppage and a tremendous rush to the port bulwark. We had touched at one of the Samoan Islands, to drop a missionary, if I remember rightly, and to take some one up. Natives, male and female, were in the boats, and we gazed on them long enough to find they were fine-looking people; and with that we separated, our next incident being our arrival at Honolulu. This was on the 3rd of June. Many of us naturally disembarked until the following day at noon, and parties were made from the Royal Hawaiian Hotel to the Pali. The scene was not new to me; but I chartered an open carriage with Colonel Carr, and Jack came with us. Two large parties filled two other carriages, and the goddess was thus far honoured. How many changes have come about here since my already published visit in 1886!

We were now approaching San Francisco, for it was the 10th, and as we did so nearer and nearer, the fog, as usual, was there to wrap us in its cold, unwelcome covering. Heavily were we greeted on the morning of our arrival, on the 11th of June; and harshly were we waked at early morning by the hideous tolling of the fog bell. This is again a foggy entrance for me—the fourth — without the chance of seeing "The Golden Gate." We landed at noon, and having now seen so much of Chinamen in their own country, I declined the "Palace," which is full of them, and went with the captain and purser and several other passengers to the very comfortable Occidental Hotel at No. 240, Montgomery Street. So here I was again at San Francisco, and prepared to renew my journey through the States, and again to hail the Americans with their jugs of cream and rocking-chairs.

XXXVIII.

MY two leading objects at San Francisco were the excursion to Alaska, which I had missed, as in my former journey recounted, in 1886; and a visit to the renowned Lick Observatory on Mount Hamilton. As regards the first, I immediately put myself into communication with my friend of 1886, Mr. Hutchinson, and secured my two tickets for the 19th, and accepted his Saturday to Monday invitation to the Hotel San Rafael, which lies across the bay and at the end of a short railway. Thus, at last, I came to see this bay. The afternoon was perfectly fine, and we crossed the entrance, the *Oceanic* at the moment steaming proudly before us on her outward voyage. The general effect was well worth witnessing, but "The Golden Gates," as usual, did not quite come up to what I had been led to expect. At the same time, I have no doubt that from this point you lose a great deal of the impression which is produced by actually entering from the ocean.

The hotel of which I speak is really beautifully situated in very handsome grounds of its own, surrounded by undulating and wooded scenery, with a large mountain close in view, called Tamil Pais, and a ridged middle distance between; and if you will mount the water-tower you may thoroughly command all about you. The building is perfectly new and everything pleasant, except the perpetual music all dinner-time—when people who know what comfort is like to be quiet—in which someone was far too proud of his performances on "the ear-piercing fife." This retreat from 'Frisco was a discovery I had not looked for, and I recommend the trial of it to all. The air is perfect.

On the 19th, then, Jack and I started for Alaska. But when I say Alaska, as everyone else does, it will not be supposed that the real immense territory of that name, with its immense river, Yukon, is intended. The continually talked of and numerously attended excursion extends only up part of the narrow southern shred of it, as far as what is called Glacier Bay, and there it is that you behold the great culminating point, the Great Muir Glacier, that lies along the whole top of that bay. I had better say nothing about the (so called) descriptive guide-books, for I cannot approach them in their language of ecstatic imagination, and must therefore tread my humble path alone and speak accordingly.

We left at 9 a.m. by the *Walla Walla*, Captain Wallace, for Victoria, where we were to meet the Pacific Coast Steamship Company's *Queen*, Captain Carroll, coming from Puget's Sound, and we arrived there late at night, where I took up my old quarters of 1886 at Mr. Hardnagel's Driard House Hotel. The passage up was to me eventful, because I twice saw what I had for so many years longed to see, the thrasher-fish attacking the whale. Both these fish separately I had seen, the whale very often, and the thrasher once only in the Bay of Panama. In both these cases, as was confirmed on board, there appeared to be two thrashers to each whale. The style of attack, as you may know, is that the active thrasher raises himself high in the water and comes down with all his weight and hard under-substance, gradually beating the breath and life out of the whale. What the motive is, continues debatable among fish historians. Whether the motive is pure hatred, such as that which exists between races of men, or whether it is for devouring objects, such as that which also exists among lords of creation, I make no attempt to discuss here; but many assert that the object of prey is the whale's tongue. The first attack was near enough for us to hear the tremendous thuds with which the thrasher came down. Anything more like what might be a great black water devil—a highly heterodox one, I allow—I could not imagine, and when I caught first sight of the monster I almost thought it was one. Even if the whale dives he must come up again for breath; and the thrasher is there to receive him with all welcome. But what is as true as the rest of the story is, that almost always the thrasher is aided by a swordfish, who prods the whale underneath and prevents his even fruitless prolongation of suffering by diving. Thus it would appear that the object of both must be prey, and an easy instinct soon brings them together for the attack.

I hope you don't think this short description too long. I was glad of the diversion and of its memories, for (except for several of the passengers on board) I found a great deal of our Alaska passage very monotonous. We left our moorings at Victoria at 6 a.m. on Tuesday, the 23rd of June, and our weather was cold and windy, though somewhat sunny. The next day we reached Fort Wrangel, and stayed some hours in that uninteresting spot for the tide. Here we were in perpetual twilight. We passed the twenty-five miles of Wrangel's "Wrangel Narrows"—but not Miss Scidmore's "Wrangel Narrows," which I vainly strove to discern—and then we came upon the fine Patterson Glacier (*Americé* glazier) on our right, the grand feature of which is its great depth. Here in the pearly light of half-past eight or nine we anchored in a fine open bay, with a fair show of effective mountains at various points.

On the next day we came to the Taku Glacier at an early hour, and found ourselves surrounded with the arctic scene of water it had created by covering the surface far and wide with larger or smaller ice-floes. Nor was it by any means uninteresting to mark the fishing up into the steamer by iron grapnels of huge carcases of these floes, for ice supplies. We continued on to Juneau. The weather was not propitious. On the 27th we hailed a fine morning, which soon began to confess its falsehood by frowning into cloud and wind; and thus we passed to Chilcat. To-day the vast Davidson Glacier walled the waters in its cove; and there stands out another, much higher up, much whiter, and in some respects more impressive. Here the rugged mountain ranges became more striking than they had been heretofore, appearing above the continuous, unchanging, dead green of the unpicturesque pine, or spruce, or cypress. We left Chilcat about lunch-time, and now we were bound for our culminating limit, Glacier Bay, anchoring for the night in the arctic scene of Bartlett's Bay.

At 4 a.m. on the 28th we made the first turn of the screw, and about one minute more we made the first blow against a floe; and far indeed was it from the last. It was one continued course of blows against the floes till we came at length into full front view of the great Muir Glacier. We did not, however, anchor very near; near enough to give a fair perspective view. It rises a complete congeries of precipitous ice precipices and pinnacles above the surface of the water, and it should be at once remembered, so as to appreciate its volume, that it must lie deep and very deep below. The width of the face is called three miles, and the height is said to vary from 200 to 300 feet. That this height must, in the proportions that surround it, disappoint many at first sight, if they dared speak frankly, I know without asking. One passenger, indeed, at once said to me, ironically: "Don't say it's a humbug," to which I replied, "Wait awhile." People's eyes should be accustomed to these scenes. But disappointment is the fruit of so much out-of-breath nonsense that is written. The blight and the curse of all fine scenery is the commonplace exaggerator. We all, or nearly all, took boat and went on shore, many up the *débris* and on to the top; but with the Rev. Dr. Yarnell and two or three ladies I chose rather to walk along the shore up nearly to the foot; and this, for me, is the sight to see. On near approach you become aware of the craggy variety of the front surface; of the shadows, the ice shadows, and the ice lights of the innumerable recesses, spearings, and projections. All this was truly effective to behold, though the day was dull ; but presently, by great favour, I suppose, the sun shone forth, and lasted us for twenty minutes. His rays struck at a propitious angle ; and then came the colouring. From dark cobalt, through every stage of blue, through seeming golden blues, through and beyond all ultramarine blues, these colours varied. I have never seen anything approaching to this twenty minutes' scene of fairy colouring anywhere else, nor do I know any other spot that offers such a chance ; and if you really wish to appreciate this glacier, you must thus walk up to it—and take your hat off. Before we left, the steamer was brought up much closer to the full front, and there we stood ; but there was no more sun, and those who had walked over a small speck of the top saw no colour. Note also, when you are on the shore, where we were, you have the great advantage of a diagonal view. Mount "Fairweather" was indoors.

We sailed in the afternoon for Sitka, the curious capital of mighty Alaska ; and presently we were all thrown off our feet. We had struck a huge floe and bent a flange in course of extrication, giving us an infantine hint of what might be the sensation of a large ship striking against a large iceberg. Otherwise, we came safe to Sitka. Here, alas ! the morning of the 29th was wet, and prevented full appreciation of the scene, including the rather too distant Mount Edgecombe, seeing he is not 3000 feet high. The whole picture should be very pleasing, but why its would-be friends should insult the place by writing that it "surpasses the Bay of Naples in the grandeur and beauty of its surroundings"—grandeur, moreover, not being at all the leading feature of the Bay of Naples —I leave Sitka to inquire. The phrase is stark nonsense, and has no sort of application whatever. In the afternoon we left on our return, and I amused myself for some little time upon the high deck in watching the steamer through the vast quiet windings, and persuading myself into the harmless belief that we were wandering nowhere. But small red flags here and there kept renewing a sense of certainty through almost exciting bewilderment.

This for a time relieved the monotony I have hinted at; and that monotony chiefly arises from the dead, dark green, colourless colour of the continual and oppressive sameness of common outline, covered over with mere peaks of mountain firs and pines and cypress. The forests, instead of being a delight, are an oppression; and this is the case all through and through from Puget's Sound. Nor are there any really grand outside crags to relieve the eye sufficiently from the weight of this impression. But you may put up with it if you are very curious indeed to see the arctic floes and glaciers on the water. For my own part, I am very pleased to have made the excursion, and do not deny that I was fairly interested in so doing, though I must admit it did not occur to me to "sigh breathlessly in the ecstasy of joy," possessing, I suppose, only that somewhat curiously described phenomenon, "an earthly and material soul."

However, it is always pleasant to see people

pleased; and for the Americans I must say this, that when they are out on a holiday they are determined to be pleased. Moreover, if they can only get an Englishman among them they are set on drawing the badger; and if they can only urge him to make a speech and say something friendly and pleasant to them and of them, and join in their merry carouse, you are a mark at once. Your American is jolly independent, but he is jolly sensitive too, particularly as to what the Old Country thinks of him; and he cleaves to the meridian of Greenwich, for he knows it gives the giant offspring his pedigree among the nations. In the books of two ladies I was even summoned to write a distich, which will show the chaff and goodwill prevailing: and as the inspirers insisted they were without fail to see their lines in my book, each will recall her own. Both were, to a certain extent, tender. This was the first:

Alaska breathed a magic charm,
For midst her ice the heart grew warm.

And this being shown, behold, another pen was put into my hand, and I wrote the second:

Meeting was joy, and parting would be sorrow,
Did Hope not breathe—Believe in a to-morrow.

There was yet one more. The next was moved by a challenge that when everyone else is happy you yourself ought to be so, and would therefore never be sad:—

Thrice-happy heart, of feeling true,
Happy, when all are happy too;
Yet thou, in turn, must anguish find
When Fate to others proves unkind.

We touched at Nanaimo for coaling, and remained all day taking in their black and dirty wealth, and sailed at midnight. But until electricity be developed into a common moving power, what a real black diamond coal is ; and all praise indeed to those who carefully, most carefully, regard our precious "Coaling Stations" !

On arriving at Victoria at about six in the morning, by great good luck we found the *Umatella* there, which was to sail at eleven. It lay on the other side of the wharf, so that we had only to walk across after breakfast and get on board, when I had the pleasure of making the acquaintance of Captain Holmes, and was accompanied by Mr. Tedcastle, the Company's Treasurer, and Mr. and Mrs. Talbott, all of whom had been fellow-passengers to Alaska. We had a remarkably pleasant passage, with a remarkably good Captain's table, arriving at 'Frisco on Sunday night, the 5th of July, but too late to land ; thus making sixteen days for the excursion, by the Monday morning.

XXXIX.

MY visit to the Observatory on Mount Hamilton was now to be accomplished, in order to see that remarkable establishment, and to gaze upon the Moon through the largest telescope in the world. For this particular object the moment was most propitious, for it was now new moon, and in a few nights she would present the best aspect for the cross lights, just before the first quarter. Accordingly, by the help of my friends, I obtained an interview with one of the trustees, Mr. Phelps, of the Customs, who gave me a letter to Dr. Edward S. Holden, the Resident Director, which I immediately forwarded to him on the 6th, announcing my intended visit. The truth is, I was anxious for the night of Friday, the 10th, because the Saturdays are fixed public days, and I feared interruption if I took that chance only.

Therefore on Friday, the 9th, I and my young companion started by the afternoon fast train for San José, and dined and slept at the "Vendome," where I received my answer from the professor with instructions. Accordingly, at half-past seven on the 10th, we were on the early post-car to begin our journey, and a truly remarkable one it was; for the elevation at which the Observatory stands is no less than one of 4209 feet above the level of the sea;

and the winding road that mounts to it presents a most ingenious effort of engineering. Nor does the scenery fail to correspond. The large white dome that contains the monster telescope soon became apparent, and so continued showing itself, like a constant landmark of invitation, while we wound about among evergreen oaks covered with abundant mistletoe, with the beautiful Santa Clara Valley and Hall's Valley opening more and more upon us as we ascended. At this season of the year, unhappily, all was brown; but in spring the excursion must be nothing less than lovely, well worth the drive without the Observatory; only if there had been no Observatory there would have been no road. As it was, we gazed on vineyards, corn-fields (corn in our sense), and flowering shrubs, and arriving at the entrance, I was immediately met by Dr. Holden.

A walk all over the grounds and the establishment was the first order of the day, and I stood under the dome in wondering and respectful attitude. By-and-by we were hoping to wonder more. Outside we saw the Coast Range, the Diabolo Range, and the Sierra Nevada; and the head even of the bay of San Francisco was to be seen also. But, welcome as ye are, all ye views, "Watchman, what of the night?" "We are liable to hill fogs," said the Professor, "but I hope we shall be clear to-night, though there is an appearance I don't quite like." And when night came there really was an appearance that none of us liked at all; for there was a thick white fog over everything, intruding its own exclusive and unpropitious presence.

GENERAL VIEW OF MOUNT HAMILTON OBSERVATORY

When, however, the Saturday morning came with brilliant sky and some well-understood change of wind, the professor begged me to stay another night, a kind suggestion which you may quite understand I was nothing loth to fall in with; and well were we rewarded. Nor do I now regret the fact of its being a public night; for although there were some forty or fifty persons there, everything was conducted in the quietest and most orderly manner. Everybody saw, and nobody was hurried; and what we all saw was the Moon magnified 370 times, through the thirty-six-inch object-glass of this refracting telescope; the focal distance of the visual object-glass being 694 inches, or 57 feet 10 inches, and the tube a little shorter than the focus, as the true focal length is measured from a point in front of the object-glass, and in line with it.

When I say we saw the Moon so magnified, that is using the common expression. What we really saw was, of course, only a small section of it. For thus is our mortal capacity hemmed in; the larger the magnifying power the larger the field occupied by a comparatively small space. And observe the practical meaning of 370 times magnified. The full Moon is held to occupy one-half of a degree in the heavens; the whole arc, we know, contains 180°, or 360 halves. Therefore, the whole full Moon magnified 370 times would, if it could be seen in its totality, occupy rather more than the whole arc of our heaven; a tolerably startling calculation. Even now, a little mistrusting myself, though without reason, I insert a small extract from the professor's letter to me of

July 24th, 1891 :—"You are entirely right in your calculations on the Moon. The Moon is about ½ a degree in angular diameter, and 360 moons would just fill 180° from east to west, as you say."

We had three inspections; one before the public began, one in turn with the rest, and a third after they had gone; the whole dome and apparatus and especially the movable floor, being gradually and with perfect ease adjusted to suit the planet's own movement. The cross lights were vivid; Mount Theophilus was the grand object; his crater and the cone, like a double-blossomed white flower at the bottom, were so sharply and brightly discernible that you almost asked where they were when you took your eye away; they had seemed so real and near. They can measure these indeed; the crater is 18,000 feet in depth, and the interior cone is 6000 feet in height; and the Professor told me that they felt themselves able to say that the quality of the Moon's rocks closely resembled that of Table Mountain. Though I had seen Table Mountain, and indeed had now seen the Moon's rocks, I did not feel myself quite justified in offering any confirmation of this view. But is it not wonderful what calculations can be made? and in aid of this wonder it should be noted that, under the best conditions, the Professor can bring the Moon to about 150 miles' distance, from her 250,000, or thereabouts.

The mere inexperienced eye has to collect itself, or the brain for it, before it really knows what it is looking at. At first, all round Mount Theophilus looked like flat white plaster of Paris; afterwards it became ribbed, and then flat again. The eye was greatly astonished, as is always the case; but the change of light somewhat affects the question. Certain it is that the eye must be tutored to these sights. I was speaking to the Professor of an effect produced on my vision at the total eclipse of the sun which I witnessed from the top of the rock of Gibraltar in 1870, when through my glass I most distinctly saw the moon approach the sun like a great black globe; a globe. "That," said he, "is a well-known and explainable optical illusion." So much for the uneducated eye. But the repeated sight of the Moon through the Great Lick telescope left certainty upon the memory.

This establishing of observatories at great heights appears to be recommendable on account of the "steadiness of the atmosphere" that is thus secured, the drawback of occasional mountain fogs being considered of small comparative importance. I know not how our own on Ben Nevis satisfies our Professors. The height there is practically the same as at Mount Hamilton, the former being 4407 feet above the sea, and the latter (as I have stated) 4209. The two climates are, of course, wholly different, but of Mount Hamilton, at all events, it is considered that the position offers advantages superior to those found at any point where a permanent observatory has been established. And here I cannot but recall another high-pitched observatory on the Pic du Midi de Bigorre, which I saw in 1878. What its exact height was, or is, I did not record, but the mountain itself measures more than 9000 feet, and to the best of my remembrance the building stood in the top regions. Peculiar interest attached to it from the fact that it had been made his residence as well as studio by a retired French soldier—General Nansouty—who conducted it and kept up constant communications with the leading astronomers in Paris, devoting his life to astronomy in those solitudes. I was so impressed at the time by his strange resolution that I wrote and sent him a Sonnet, which he at once acknowledged, and as the book in which I published it is now out of print, I will here recall it in his honour, and in association with Mount Hamilton:—

> Mount, mount, and dare these rugged steeps on high,
>   Leave in the vale thy luxuries below!
> Where is thy merit here, thou butterfly,
>   That flutterest only in the summer's glow?
> But ye, whose hearts would aught of grandeur know,
>   Turn to these topmost crags your wondering eye;
> Behold a dweller here, who winds and snow,
>   Soldier of Science, bravely can defy!
> A white-haired warrior ye shall see revealed,
>   Who, working out his theme alone in age,
> And gathering glory in this other field,
>   Doth with the changing heaven and air engage:
> The sword of Science in his grasp ye find,
> Mars still at heart, Apollo tunes his mind.

Before leaving this subject, however, I must mention another very interesting circumstance. A few weeks after leaving the observatory my attention was called to a paragraph in one of the papers stating that Professor Holden had discovered something like snow in the moon. On this I wrote him, and now copy his reply:—

"*Parts* of the moon look as if snow were there, and *some* things can be, perhaps, best explained by supposing snow to be there. I am not, however, prepared to say that snow is certainly present. It may be—*voilà tout.*"

XL.

WHEN we left the Observatory on the afternoon of the 12th we returned to San José, but not yet to San Francisco, for I had a desire to see the establishment of Del Monte, at Monteréy; therefore, on the next day I took the train, called the Flyer, thither, and would recommend others to do so. The hotel is spacious indeed, raising in my thoughts the somewhat homely question, How many square acres of carpet are we walking over? The grounds are charming and extensive. Trees, lawns, and patterned flower-beds abound, and reading on seats under the branches is a popular pursuit. By the presence of Mr. and Mrs. Talbott, of Indiana, of the Alaska party, I was induced to join in the regulation drive of "The Seventeen Miles." So we all four went together, and greatly enjoyed its variety. Here also you may see the first beginnings of Monterey, and reflect upon the power and rapidity of development. We had seen our present dwelling, and we now saw the first wooden house, which, in fact, was brought out from England. Such things are not seen without producing an impression; and where can the end possibly be fixed to change and development, until there be nothing left to change or to develop? But why do people out here walk in the hot full sun with parasols of brilliant scarlet? Surely this is not a development of common sense, departing from the more sober and protecting colours of old? But it aids the complexion, throwing over it the bright vermilion of youth, either where it is not wanted, or where it is a useless fudge. The eye is so avaricious nowadays. Even to come down to the vulgar table, you will sacrifice the small delicious strawberry for the spongy pompous one; and you will fill your mouth with the grit of that nasty stuff, crystallized sugar, simply because it looks prettier than the old and much pleasanter "pounded."

On the 17th we were again at 'Frisco; and in moving about from friend to friend to accept of their hospitality, I became more impressed than ever with the enormous consequence to San Francisco of the cable car system of the tramways. How could I have dined with Mr. and Mrs. Dodge? or have enjoyed his introduction of me to Dr. Harkness and the Pacific Union Club? How could we have more than once climbed and descended and climbed again, wondering all the while, to Gough Street, to accept the hospitality of Mr. and Mrs. Mullins—Mrs. and Miss Mullins recalling Alaska memories—but for the cable cars? Contemplate the most aristocratic (Americans will forgive that insidiously creeping word) parts of the fast-extending city, and ask yourself, How came these dwellings here, but for the cable cars? And here I must call to mind a day we spent with Mr. Adolph Sutro on his vast property, "Sutro Heights," away on the hills. On our return in his carriage he stopped it in the middle of a wood, in order to say: "This is to be the centre of the city." It sounded strange, but I recalled the cable cars, and shrank from the responsibility of disbelief.

On the other side of San Francisco the roads are less adventurous, and the suburbs (so to call them) cheerful and happy-looking. Mr. Siegfried, a well-known and established merchant in 'Frisco, whose acquaintance I had made in the East, among other acts of hospitality, invited me to spend the day with him and wife and family at his house at Alameda. A prettier place for a quiet retreat from the irritations of business could not be well conceived than Alameda. It is called, indeed, "The City of Small Homes;" and that exactly represents its commodious but unpretending villas, with their square lawns and gardens, and front lawns trimmed in front down to the edge of the road. All suggests, as it were, a picture of pretty domesticity, as the name implies; but Mr. Siegfried has somewhat transgressed these bounds by the possession of a costly and surprising collection of rare orchids.

Then there is another twin spot, San Anselmo. Here also the American knows how to repose; and in particular, the district claims a position in the astonishing fruit production of California. Mr. Foss, whom I had met in the States in 1886, found me out at 'Frisco and entertained me at his newly-purchased fruit-garden, where produce seems inclined to crowd upon him. Certainly in these parts you find fruit abounding; but as a consequence there is much carelessness about it, and carriage of it to distances being an object, much is gathered before it is ripe, by which the tables of the city suffer.

My face was now set westward towards England, and the question arose, should I repeat my visit to the mighty ranges of the Canadian Pacific, or make a diversion to see the Shoshone Falls on the Snake River, and so pass through Salt Lake City and Manitou again? Curiosity as to the Falls prevailed. This made the round by Portland necessary, and we therefore left by the 9 p.m. train of the 31st of July. Mount Shasta is one great feature here, and we enjoyed a full view of him; but as a snow and glacier mountain I was not greatly impressed with him. Still, as so many know, there is striking scenery on this line. Witness that from Gazelle station, and the vast stretches and complicated varieties of what is called the Siskiyou Valley. Portland showed us Mount Hood looking very fine; and the 3rd of August took us up the banks of the Columbia River by train. I have already written that this is the proper way to see the river; but I will now add that it is best to come the way I came in 1886, down stream.

From the point of leaving the Columbia, near Walla Walla, we entered a dreary, and sandy, and sage-bush country till we came after the night's journey to the Shoshone station. We were then twenty-six miles from the Falls, and on the 4th took the usual carriage, to sleep upon the spot and return next day. Anything so dreary and therefore apparently endless as this drive I have never met with. Sage-bush country without intermission. Where is the river? where are the Falls? and when are we to get there? But time and distance were as they always were, and not subject to the measurement of content or discontent. Our driver did very fairly, and at last at a sudden turn and rapid descent through a most remarkable congeries of black precipitous precipices, we came upon the river and crossed it, after waiting and signing, to the Government Hotel. There they did the best for us. It is placed at the brow of the Falls, of which you obtain that class of view on the evening of arrival.

On the next morning you go with the guide down a very steep and trying path to the bed of the river below, and obtain your full view. The depth of the Falls is 210 feet; the shape is horseshoe, and thus measured in the arc give 700 feet; in straight line 600. There are these black precipices all round, and the general view is truly strange. The flow of water was good; and the water quite white and clear. Had it been at its full it would have lost this feature and been yellow. Were it not for Niagara, these Falls would probably be the finest in America; but the comparison must not be made, because the tremendous force and volume of Niagara is unapproachable, and therefore unapproached. Nevertheless, the whole scene is entirely different, and entirely original in its special features.

On our return we were persuaded to diverge through the Blue Lakes, stopping at a fruit farmer's for lunch; but we did not think this worth while, and resigned ourselves to the return sage-bush drive. Of this same country they say, as they say in Peru, that with rain it would burst into great fertility. I quite believe this of Peru, and have already written how I saw sudden flowers rise and perish under a dash of moisture.

The rise of the Andes, a late mountain development, according to geologists, seems to have stopped the rains from Peru, the whole undulating surface of which, running up to Arequipa from Mollendo, looks exactly like that of a rain-washed country. But these sage-bush wastes are comparatively flat, and it seems to be a forlorn hope that their latent fertility should be awakened by the rain. Ugly country still continued to Salt Lake City, to which we travelled through the night, and arrived at noon on the 6th.

What a change here since 1886! There are now two cities; the old one, with its separate dwellings and gardens and the water running down the sides of the streets, and the new one, very much like other new cities in the States. I had been introduced by Mr. Siegfried in 'Frisco to Mr. Sears, a polygamist, and a leading member of the Mormon Church, who had kindly bespoken my beds at the huge "Knutsford" in the new town, where we fared very comfortably; and he again introducing me to Mr. Grant and Mr. Cannon, both apostles of the Church, and both polygamists, we all five took a drive of inspection with Mr. Grant in his carriage. We visited the tabernacle and heard the pin dropped, but I fancy you must be on one particular spot to hear that minute sound through all the length of the building. We also visited the yet unfinished temple. Then there was Brigham Young's unpretending grave in the corner of a grass plat. It was a very pleasant drive, and we had abundant conversation, with arrangements for attending the service on Sunday. The full title of the church is "The Church of Jesus Christ of the Latter Day Saints and Polygamy." I am not quite sure that this word polygamy (a perfectly genuine Eastern institution) is now always added, because, in concession to the law of the land, polygamy is being gradually abandoned, though the High Church Party there rather appear to deem this step as somewhat partaking of a dereliction of principle.

On the Sunday we attended the service, when the whole building was closely crowded with a very attentive audience. Mr. Sears came with us; there was a special choir for the organ, and in the hymns all joined. Mr. Grant preached, as also two other leaders. On entering I had observed a number of high-standing silver flagons, and a vast number of chalices containing cut bread. These were the elements of the Communion. All cannot, of course, be communicants every Sunday, but a vast number were so on this day; and the elements were carried round by several, and partaken of by each in his place. But there was no wine; these silver reservoirs, continually appealed to, contained the pure water of the city, which is excellent. The two elements were bread and water, in which you are not bound (though possibly somewhat prone) to perceive some small protest against the form of the original institution.

We of course made a day to the Dead-Sea-looking Salt Lake, surrounded by its dry mountains. But the population do not leave it dead. It is alive with holiday-makers, rowing, swimming, eating and drinking, and enjoying the hot air, like other organized existences. Continual trains run to and fro, and many are the passengers. Here, also, in the new town I was surprised to see electrical tramcars, as I had seen them in other places; I believe at both San José and Monterey, and certainly in later-visited towns.

On the 10th we left by the Rio Grande and Denver Line for Manatou, in which beautiful spot I wasted a day or two, and drank the waters; Jack having set his full heart on riding up Pike's Peak on horseback. But, behold, since I so toiled up in 1886, there is a railway to the very top. I paid another visit also to the Garden of the Gods of the old Ute Tribe, insisting this time that I should enter by the grand vestibule or chief entrance, with Pyke's Peak full in front, instead of coming out that way. All, however, seemed accustomed to enter by what I call the back door, and to come out by the front.

Then we came on to my old acquaintance, Chicago, "The City of Lakes," where I sought the Grand Pacific Hotel, and where, in virtue of a letter from Mr. Hutchinson to Mr. Morse, I had the pleasure of visiting him and Mrs. Morse at their hospitable home. And here he took us one (among others) most interesting drive, viz. to the Jackson Park, the seat of the coming World's Fair. Under his guidance and protection he drove us into the territory set apart for this gigantic Exhibition, where we wandered about the one square mile allotted for its occupation, wondering and again wondering how out of such a mighty chaos beauty and order could be producible. They who see it in perfection will never see what we saw. Whether I shall go to see what they will see, is very doubtful.

Well indeed is Chicago called the City of Lakes, and well has she availed herself of the position which confers on her that title. What a gift of water; and what advantage taken of it! She probes the very fathoms of the inexhaustible resources. Go and wonder at the waterworks.

From Chicago to Niagara was inevitable, where that stupendous outpouring from the grand four freshwater lakes of the world, Superior, Michigan, Huron, and Erie, moans over the rocks towards Lake Ontario. The whole scene with the park has been considerably improved, but the Fall itself, though mighty, was not quite so voluminous as I had seen it in 1886. Very much depends upon the wind; the water is always there, but the Falls had been low all through the season; full enough, however, to carry one unfortunate man down in his boat while we were there. He was well known, and had been often cautioned, being much devoted to the opposing liquor, for which the water thus at last avenged itself.

From Niagara the next step was to Albany, with its enormous new capitol, and the Kenmure Hotel, *not* the Delaván House; and from Albany down the riverside, as of yore, to the Fifth Avenue Hotel, as of yore, New York. And really here the main question plainly was, after paying a visit to our good agent, Mr. McKeevan, of our London and Brazilian Bank, What is the next steamer to Liverpool? This was the White Star Line steamer, the *Majestic;* and a majestic passage we made of it, considering all things, though not of the very first rapidity. Liverpool and London now read almost the same; and on the 16th of September, 1891, I once more found myself, with a vastly increased gallery of mental pictures, in the same room and at the same table which I had left, then three years ago, and where I am now writing these last lines.

Shall I publish them? "We shall not be able to read them unless you do," you will say, "and to us you have promised their contents." "Then I am bound to do so." "Is there, then, any indisposition, implied by that last word? Should it not be a pleasure thus to record three years of your life well spent and in fulfilment of a promise made to friends? What do you fear—criticism?" "No!" "What, then?" "I will tell you. I fear the Thrasher, though I am not a Whale. I fear 'Thurkill's little account.' I fear the Publisher's bill. If either of you has ever published, you will know what these things always are. Did ever any other debtor side of an account, in the shape of charges, allowances, and deductions, exhibit such peculiar ingenuity? Trade feeds on brain. The only comparison that occurs to me to make is one with the barber surgeons in Naples. There the barbers bleed. Spirit of Dr. Dickson, hear! Hands, feet, and limbs are painted over their doors, and at every possible small point, especially between toes and fingers, "the life thereof" is shown to be spurting forth in sign of their ingenuity in bleeding. And such as are the Neapolitan bleeders, such are the Publishers!" *Que voulez vous? Il faut payer!*

These pages, then, I dedicate to you,
Feigning to deem their merits small and few :
But claiming that, at all events, they're true :
They're true.

My portrait you've requested me to show,
Before I older—or no older—grow ;
I'm old enough already, as you know :
As you know.

My three years' travel o'er, I'm here again,
Have all retravelled o'er with pen and brain,
And, for the present, shall at home remain :
At home remain.

Adding merely,
Yours sincerely,

J. J. AUBERTIN.